THE CULTURE OF UNBELIEF

STUDIES AND PROCEEDINGS FROM THE
FIRST INTERNATIONAL SYMPOSIUM ON BELIEF
ROME, MARCH 22–27, 1969

THE
CULTURE OF UNBELIEF

*Studies and Proceedings from the First International
Symposium on Belief Held at Rome,
March 22–27, 1969*

Symposium sponsors
THE AGNELLI FOUNDATION
THE UNIVERSITY OF CALIFORNIA AT BERKELEY
THE VATICAN SECRETARIAT FOR NON-BELIEVERS

EDITED BY

ROCCO CAPORALE

AND

ANTONIO GRUMELLI

THE UNIVERSITY OF CALIFORNIA PRESS
BERKELEY · LOS ANGELES · LONDON: 1971

University of California Press
Berkeley and Los Angeles, California

University of California Press, Ltd.
London, England

ISBN: 0-520-01856-7
Library of Congress Catalog Card No.: 75-138513
Printed in the United States of America

Acknowledgment is made to the Agnelli Foundation for permission to print the material
contained in chapters 1, 2, and 3, which were
originally copyrighted with the Foundation, and
for permission to use the transcripts of the discussion in the preparation of chapters 5, 6, 7,
8, 9, 10, and 11. Chapters 12 and 13 were prepared expressly for this volume under a grant
from the Agnelli Foundation.

To
GIOVANNI AGNELLI
Promoter of scholarship

FOREWORD

.

I was very much honored to serve as chairman of the Symposium on the Culture of Unbelief (part of the First International Symposium on Belief), which meant, of course, that I was mostly presiding over other people's intellectual productions and had little opportunity to exhibit my own. The editor's kindness notwithstanding, I shall resist the temptation of getting back at everybody here as I could not do in Rome. I have written extensively on the subject of the symposium elsewhere and I can see no point in prefacing its proceedings by reiterating my own frame of reference. In view of the scope and variety of material that follows I shall limit myself to some general observations.

The first observation, obvious and yet essential, is that the symposium had the character of an historic occasion. I think it is fair to say that this was felt by most of the participants. The feeling was reinforced by the rather amazing interest the symposium attracted, not only within the ecclesiastical and scholarly Roman ambience, but on the part of the mass media. The opening session in the tightly packed great hall of the Gregorian University was permeated by a sense of excitement that quickly communicated itself to the participants—also inducing in at least some of them a certain anxiety, since they felt that their contributions might not possibly meet such intense expectations. Throughout the symposium the participants were surrounded by the press, by observers from various ecclesiastical agencies, by television teams originating in places as far apart as Canada and Yugoslavia, and last but not least by the technological apparatus (simultaneous translation systems, visual and audial recording devices, and so on) that is an inevitable accompaniment of contemporary public attention. I do not say this in criticism—given the circumstances, there was probably no way of avoiding the commotion.

The symposium was a pioneering venture, in both the exciting and limiting sense of the term. It represents, above all, a first step in a *prise de conscience,* on the part of the relevant agencies of the Catholic Church as well as of social-scientific scholarship. On the part of the Church, of course, it belongs with that same *prise de conscience* of the modern world and its problems that has characterized its history since Vatican II and that gave birth to the Secretariat for Non-Believers which cosponsored the symposium. What especially impressed the non-Catholic participants was the atmosphere of complete freedom and openness that marked the symposium from beginning to end. There was nothing that could not be said, nothing that was not listened to by all concerned with courtesy and interest. Harvey Cox, in a subsequent article on the symposium, expresses this by saying that it has given him a new sense of what Rome might someday come to mean again—a place of openness and, indeed, catholicity in the literal sense of the word, a place in which all Christians and all men of good will could profoundly feel at home.

The *prise de conscience* on the part of social-scientific scholarship was of less dramatic significance, perhaps, but highly instructive all the same. To my knowledge, this was the first time that an international group of social scientists gathered to discuss this specific subject. This is significant, quite apart from the sponsoring agency. Most of the scholars participating in the symposium were sociologists. The symposium represents a ratification, as it were, of the new interest in the sociology of religion that has been slowly but surely mounting since World War II, and of the growing conviction among those engaged in this enterprise that a sociology of contemporary religion must of necessity broaden its scope to deal with the social dynamics of contemporary nonreligious culture.

The various contributions speak for themselves, most of them eloquently so, and the reader will have to integrate them in terms of his own particular system of relevancies. I should like, however, to point to five ambiguities evident in the symposium and the material issuing from it. I would like to say emphatically that this is not done in order to criticize the symposium or its organizers (since I was one of the latter, such criticism would be masochistic!). Rather, an understanding of these ambiguities will help clarify what took place in Rome intellectually and, even more important, will be helpful for planning future steps in this intellectual enterprise.

The Dialogue/Study Ambiguity

The Secretariat for Non-Believers, under the keen intellectual leadership of Cardinal Koenig, Archbishop of Vienna, is one of three recently formed agencies of the Vatican (the other two being concerned with non-Catholic Christians and with the non-Christian religions) whose purpose is to enter into dialogue with those outside the Catholic Church. The secretariat, unlike its two parallel agencies, has a peculiar problem in this regard: *its* partner in the projected dialogue is largely unorganized and even difficult to locate. Non-Catholic Christians and adherents of non-Christian religions are, at least in principle, available for dialogue in readily locatable communities. Nonbelievers, with the possible exception of Marxists (who, in any case, have their own problems both of nonbelievers and of separation between brethren), are not gathered in communities that are accessible for dialogue, even in principle. The secretariat's task, then, resolves itself first of all into a detective operation. Quite logically, social scientists, above all sociologists, may be called upon to play the role of auxiliary detectives. Within the secretariat's practical frame of reference, as naturally dictated by its ecclesiastical mission, the idea is *not* to engage in dialogue with the assembled sociologists, but to seek their assistance in pinpointing the putative partners for dialogue. In accordance with this logic, the sociologists at the symposium were invited with little if any regard for their religious *weltanschauliche* positions, but rather for their background in terms of their proper scientific work. There were Catholics and non-Catholics, and in a number of cases the organizers would have been hard put to identify a participant as either a "believer" or a "nonbeliever." Put simply, the logical goal of the symposium was study in preparation for dialogue, not, be it noted, dialogue itself.

It is correct to say that this logic was quite clear to the organizers of the symposium, both within and outside the secretariat. Probably it was also clear to the participant social scientists, whose professional ideology quite naturally inclined them to this definition of the situation. However, this was not so clear to some of the participant theologians, and certainly not to many of the outsiders who observed or covered the symposium. There was the widespread expectation that the symposium would constitute some sort of high level forum for the confrontation of faith and unbelief (the format of the opening session, with presentations by a prominent Catholic theologian, a prominent Protestant theologian, and a prominent Marxist philosopher, actually encouraged this notion). As the proceedings clearly show, very little of the kind took place—and, of course, in view of the logic of the event, it could not—take place. For the most part the symposium followed the logic of its organization. The lesson to be drawn from the aforementioned ambiguity is that dialogue and study represent two equally legitimate but logically distinct intellectual operations. To the extent that dialogue is a modern form of evangelism, the social sciences (and notably sociology) must be understood as *praeparatio evangelii*.

The Ambiguity of the Theologians' Expectations

My reference is to theologians' expectations of sociology. Conservative theologians, both Catholic and Protestant, tend to look at sociology with deep mistrust. They may have a point, by the way; such conservatism was not much represented among the vocal participants in the symposium. Liberal or progressive theologians (again, this is true in both confessions) tend rather to an exaggerated view of what sociology may be able to do for them. Such theologians tend to look toward sociology for authoritative insights into the reality of the modern world, if not indeed for authoritative programs on how to reform or revolutionize this world. What makes this worse is that "culture-prophets" and "critic-intellectuals" of every description have an inclination today to envelop their pronouncements in the jargon of sociology, thus obfuscating the line between ideology and science—with the result that the former is as often enhanced as the latter is discredited with different audiences.

Theologians vary, of course, in their ability to distinguish between these different intellectual operations going under the cover-all heading of "sociology." Whatever their adventures with ideology may have been, however, their encounter with serious sociology is very likely to be something of a let-down. Not only do the theologians discover that sociologists are in great disagreement among themselves, but that the disagreement extends to fundamental questions of method and of the validity of alleged empirical findings about contemporary society. This ambiguity in the expectations of theologians is clearly manifested in the work of the symposium. Most of the sociologists (including Oleg Mandic, who often speaks as a sort of Marxist ambassador in *partibus infidelium*) project, not authoritative insights (let alone programs), but rather prudent uncertainty not only about the phenomenon of "unbelief" but also about the mysteries of modern consciousness in general. Put crudely, it is occasionally difficult for the theologians to get their teeth into anything the sociologists are producing. This difficulty is most acute in the discussion that follows Charles Glock's presentation, which (inevitably, I daresay) eventuated in strict in-group squabbles among the sociologists present.

I should add, though, that I regard the frustrations brought about by this particular ambiguity in a rather positive way. If exaggerated fears concerning sociology on the part of theologians are misplaced, so are exaggerated hopes. In either case, I think, it is salutary for the theologian to catch a glimpse of sociologists with their sleeves rolled up (or, if you prefer, their pants sliding down). Nothing is more important for the relationship between sociology and its larger public than a more sober understanding of what sociology can and what it cannot do.

The Ambiguity of Discrepant Sociological Positions

This ambiguity is closely related to what has just been said about theologians' expectations of sociologists, although it transcends the relationship between the two particular disciplines. It is very much in the consciousness of the participant sociologists, who represented pretty much the whole spectrum of different positions in current sociology. Not only are there obvious differences in approach among sociologists from different countries (most clearly between the American and European representatives), but there is the recurrent dividing

line between "hard-nosed empiricists" (most plausibly incar-
nated in Charles Glock) and theoreticians of various denominations. The divisions among the latter are far-reaching indeed, not only in the abstract but in the manner whereby
they influence the approach to the subject.

Apart from the very visible peculiarity of the Marxist approach, one need only mention here the names of Talcott Parsons and his distinguished student Robert Bellah on the one
hand, and of Thomas Luckmann on the other. If the dialogue
between the Church and "the culture of unbelief" may be
difficult, so, heaven knows, is that between structural-function-
alism and phenomenology in current sociological theory. If
Catholic theologians have become sensitive to the offense
given by some of their terminology to outsiders, they may have
derived some comfort from the raised sociologists' eyebrows
that greeted, say, Glock's call for research instruments with
"cross-cultural and a-historical applicability" or such Luck-
mannian statements as "socially objectivated world views integrate transcendences that are subjectively experienced on
different levels." To be sure, different eyebrows were raised at
different times, but the sociologists had numerous occasion
during the symposium to practice the spirit of ecumenicity
within their own ranks. They did so with considerable success.

All the same, the ambiguity of discrepant sociological positions represented at the symposium indicates that, quite apart
from the relationship to theology, sociology must approach the
present subject under the handicap of severely divergent theoretical and methodological presuppositions among its own
practitioners. This realization is hardly new in the field, but
it is worthwhile recalling it in the present context.

The Ambiguity in the Definition of the Problem

The title of the symposium, "The Culture of Unbelief," was,
of course, derived from the name of the cosponsoring secretariat. Any likely alternate title (I, for example, should have pre-
ferred the term "secularization" in the wording) would have
generated other ambiguities. But it would have been too much
to expect that an international gathering of intellectuals, presented with this definition of their assigned problem, would

have refrained from spending a good deal of time in tearing it to pieces.

Inevitably, much discussion centers on the meanings and the possible empirical referents of the term "unbelief." Some of this discussion, in my opinion, is very useful, some less so. What is rather remarkable, though, is that the theoretical position papers, each in its own way, tend to deny the very existence of the phenomenon under scrutiny.

Thomas Luckmann, using the very broad concept of religion he derives from an intriguing marriage between Husserl and Durkheim, says, in effect, that religion is a universal attribute of the human condition, that unbelief in the sense of some sort of irreligion is anthropologically and sociologically impossible, and that consequently we must shift our attention from this unrewarding focus to an investigation of the new forms of "invisible religion" in the modern world.

Robert Bellah, on the other hand, suggests that the very notion of unbelief is a peculiar product of the Western religious tradition, with its strong (presumably Hellenic) stress on the cognitive aspects of religion; that unbelief along with the entire universe of discourse to which it belongs is increasingly irrelevant today; and that indeed we may be on the verge of a profoundly religious, new synthesis—one which he terms "a possible reunification of consciousness."

Talcott Parsons, in his interventions during the symposium and in his extended observations published in this volume, tends to strengthen doubt about the empirical reality of unbelief, which he sees in the context of a global institutional differentiation in modern society. Somewhat like Bellah, though (I think) with less enthusiasm, Parsons points to new religious formations in the making, specifically to a new "religion of love" that, in historical perspective may be seen as a "Christianization of the world."

I have elsewhere expressed my disagreement with Luckmann's concept of individualization, and I have grave doubts about Bellah's putative "reunification of consciousness" (possibly *not* living in California may be the *Sitz im Leben* of these doubts), as well as some doubts about the Parsonian paradigm of institutional differentiation as applied to contemporary religion. But I should like to point to the ambivalent impact these views, particularly Luckmann's and Bellah's, had on the participant theologians. The ambivalence was one of initial relief and subsequent new alarm—a little like the re-actions of a man told not to worry about his ulcer, since he does not have an ulcer, but rather has cancer.

The theologian worried about unbelief is concerned with the present and future fate of his religious tradition. It is reas-suring to hear that irreligion is something of an illusion, that there will always be and now is religion; but if the same theo-logian listens to what Luckmann has to say beyond this, espe-cially about the alleged religious forms of modern conscious-ness, he may remember his old worries about unbelief with some nostalgia. The same goes for Bellah's "reunification of consciousness" and Parson's "Christianization of the world." It goes without saying that social science does not need a terminological orthodoxy—there is room for different concep-tualizations of this as of any other problem. But it is important for all future work in this area that the different conceptual-izations be clearly understood, and that conceptual deline-ations not be confused with empirical statements.

The Ambiguity in Follow-Up Expectations

Finally, there was an ambiguity manifested, especially toward the end of the symposium, as to the best ways of following up the event. It is, of course, quite possible to view a symposium such as this as a unique occasion for discussion and contact, valuable in itself without any follow-up at all. The value of this symposium would allow such a position to be taken quite respectably.

Understandably, though, both the secretariat and at least some of the participants are interested in the question, "What next?" Two quite different notions come to the surface. The first notion, all the more attractive (certainly to myself) be-cause of the charming physical and social ambience of the occasion, is that this symposium should lead to others like it. The other notion, forcefully stated above all by Charles Glock, is that the most fruitful outcome of the event would be the launching of broad international research on the problem at hand.

The two notions are not mutually contradictory. The

sponsors, I believe, are now considering further international symposia, and this is something to be welcomed on scholarly, as well as ecclesiastical, grounds. Since I can hardly be classed as a "hard-nosed empiricist" in sociology, I should like to reiterate the support I gave to Glock's proposals in Rome. If nothing else, this symposium has shown how careful any responsible social scientist must be in his statements about the nature of modern religious consciousness. Empirical research in this area, especially research that has an international focus, is very badly needed. Such research, of course, is expensive and hard to organize. I cannot judge to what extent this symposium constitutes a likely launching platform for such research, but I hope indeed that the notion will not be lost in future planning.

The symposium was a significant event not only in ecclesiastical and (if I may use the expression) cultural-political terms, but also in terms of social-scientific scholarship. Conceptual and historical problems are lucidly brought into focus, as are problems of past and possible future empirical research. Whatever sequel the symposium may have, I feel certain that it will be remembered by all the participants as a noteworthy time in their intellectual biographies. If one must spend some days of a Roman spring in hotel rooms and around microphones— then by all means let it be in such pleasant company!

EDITORS' PREFACE

This volume presents to the general public the reflections of a group of social scientists and theologians who gathered in the spring of 1969 in Rome to explore "The Culture of Unbelief," and who have subsequently continued their interest in the subject. The book departs in places from the actual order of events of the symposium to accommodate papers prepared explicitly for publication after the symposium was over.

Following an introductory overview of the symposium and its significance, come the four position papers which formed the base of the symposium's discussion. Part Two contains the formal responses to the original papers. These responses were prepared prior to the symposium and functioned as priming devises for the general discussion. The most essential points of this discussion have been excerpted from hundreds of pages of transcripts and are documented in Part Three.

The papers that make up Part Four are a reflection on and a direct result of the symposium. We are most grateful to Professors Parsons, Wilson, and Bellah for their contribution to this section. We owe special thanks to Professor Peter Berger, the symposium chairman, for writing the foreword.

John Coleman, of the University of California, Berkeley, carefully reviewed the draft of the manuscript. His valuable suggestions and perceptive criticism have added considerably to the quality of this volume.

We have contracted a debt of gratitude to Robert Duvall, Assistant Professor of English at Pitzer College, for his tireless editorial help during precious summer months. As the author of essays on poetry and belief, he has a deep interest in the subject. Pitzer College provided a small grant to ready the manuscript.

But by far the greatest expression of gratitude goes to the Agnelli Foundation and particularly to its director, Dr. Ubaldo Scassellati, without whose encouragement and generosity neither the symposium nor this book would have been possible.

R.C.

Claremont, California   A.G.

CONTENTS

INTRODUCTION

·

ROCCO CAPORALE

All too frequently in the course of intellectual pursuit, vast configurations of man's behavioral landscape are seen at a quick glance, but explorations of these new scholarly frontiers later are abandoned. The sheer magnitude of the task of discovering what is relevant may keep the scholar from finding a key to a deeper understanding of human action.

The realm of human experience commonly known as belief has undergone this fate repeatedly. It has been relegated to theologians and religionists and only occasionally given a passing glance by social scientists. If belief has fared poorly, more so has its counterpart unbelief, which presents compounded problems of definition and analysis.

Consequently, in this collection of the proceedings of a symposium and related studies on "The Culture of Unbelief," the authors attempt an unprecedented reflection on a neglected phenomenon, the consequences of which pervade every aspect of social organization. Throughout the following pages there lurks a submerged consensus that something qualitatively new and unprecedented is happening to religion in contemporary society. Some theologians ponder apprehensively whether this is one more step down the ladder of man's progressive fall from grace, while other thinkers endeavor to redeem whatever can be saved of the ferment in today's religious domain. For their part, some social scientists view the present ferment as the rumblings indicative of the demise of conventional institutionalized religion, while others see in it the fruition of an age-old process of differentiation and upgrading, which has been thrusting the religious experience to the threshold of monumental new opportunities for relevance in the lives of men. Yet insufficient knowledge of what is happening to religion and belief in our times and the lack of refined conceptual schemes of analysis tend to preclude the hope of acquiring a broad consensus on the problem or of specifying clear projections of developments in the coming decades.

The description of these essays (and of the symposium that brought them about) as "reflections on the culture of unbelief" is not intended to create additional problems nor generate new levels of complexity. The authors are generally agreed that unbelief cannot be studied per se without prior analysis of belief and in intimate reference to it. But it is also clear that unbelief does not constitute merely a residual category of human behavior; the negative term may well point to a dramatic transformation in the groundwork of human religiosity.

Professor Bellah suggests that unbelief has become so generalized and diffused that it constitutes the indispensable stage for the transition to a new level of religious experience of worldwide dimension. By contrast, Professor Luckmann views the concept of unbelief as heuristically unproductive and devoid of analytical clout. These and other differing views on the subject highlight the need for more extensive analysis and justify the "objectification" and "magnification" which the concept of unbelief receives here. Unbelief, then, will be the primary object of this study, with related assumptions about belief implied in the mode of discourse.

1

What is the culture of unbelief? Who lives by it and in it? What does unbelief mean and to whom? How can it be scientifically studied and what is the value and purpose of this study?

In formulating answers to these and similar questions the scholars represented in this volume were confronted with some momentous realizations. The first was a humbling one: in spite of decades of sociological efforts, belief and unbelief are very much terra incognita. The desirability of a commonly agreed definition—and its impossibility—is taken for granted, and the futile search for a common ground of discourse is only perfunctorily gone through, considering the diverse frame of reference of the contributing scholars. Once again one could speak of the customary anomie that reigns among scholars when conceptions and definitions are in question. And yet, notwithstanding the realization that the subject of discourse is vague and imprecise, we come across what appear to be well-formulated and irreconcilable positions and pet theories, which render cooperative intellectual reflection unattainable.

The difficulty of coordination and consolidation of thinking among scholars is further compounded when representatives of more than one discipline are involved. Therefore, a second realization by the contributors to this volume reflects precisely the built-in difficulty of dialogue.

Beyond the ambiguities pointed out by Professor Berger in his foreword, there is the fact that a discussion on unbelief cannot be conducted with equal ease by the theologian and by the social scientist. As the limited presentations of the theologians in this volume illustrate (regrettably limited, but unavoidable), a theologian's position on unbelief—what can be said or how it can be said—is restricted. The social scientist, on the other hand, is permitted to move about more freely, may formulate alternative explanatory schemes, and, far from experiencing any threat to his discipline, may find in the study of unbelief a challenging area of investigation. A major difficulty arises, however, when the social scientist develops stronger than usual empathic capability and attempts to move his approach to profound human experience beyond the rational and objective canons normally demanded by science. The reaction to Professor Bellah's endeavor to *verstehen* the problem of unbelief indicates how compartmentalized the current approach still remains and how difficult it is to transcend the narrow boundaries of traditional disciplines, even against the evidence of their ineffectiveness when faced with problems of worldwide proportions.

Yet another realization is the appalling lack of empirical data on unbelief and the supreme ignorance of what really obtains in the world of the proverbial man in the street. So small is the patrimony of hard data available to us that, in the course of three-days' discussion and throughout the essays in this book it is nearly impossible to find substantive reference to systematic research which may be advanced as evidence for validated propositions.

In the light of this consideration, the essays having to do with problems of programs and research on unbelief are not academic exercises, but honest indicators of an awareness of some wide gaps in the field of sociology of religion as well as in theology. We must admit that we do not know enough about the phenomenon of unbelief to formulate even a minimum inventory of validated propositions that may constitute the basis of further analysis.

2

Having alerted the reader to some of the hardships of the task of exploration to which this book is committed, it is right to highlight substantive contributions that the following essays make to the field.

An expeditious route into the little known region of unbelief is, first, to retrace historically the phenomenon under discussion, locating it within the broad structural parameters of the societies for which evidence of its existence is strongest. This cross-cultural historical excursus permits us to identify some of the characteristics of the phenomenon, its variable location in the social structure, while also allowing the writers to outline several alternative schemes to interpret the sequence of events leading to present conditions (which schemes are, again, well-educated guesses, which of course need stronger validating proofs).

Concomitant with the historical perspective the theoretical essays strive to elucidate the notion of unbelief (and, thereby, belief) focusing specifically on its composite nature of cognitive and emotive orientation to a world view transmitted and sustained in the course of a person's belonging to institutionalized religious bodies. Going beyond merely terminological questions (distinctions among belief, faith, religious belonging, etc.), the writers formulate questions of nuclear importance in our society. Is an overarching system of reference still needed and viable in our pluralistic society? What happens when the agencies of socialization, which formerly inducted the masses into a specific mode of interpreting life meanings, are replaced by other agencies, which do not and cannot perform the same function? What are the consequences of the transition from institutional (official) to individual (privatized) systems of beliefs? And what of the Durkheimian notion of religion as integrator of society?

If we accept the hypothesis that belief is disappearing before a new mode of religious consciousness, diffused and deinstitutionalized, what continuities, if any, with conventional religion as we have known it can we identify? Where will be the religion's cultural location? Will the contemporary flare for emotiveness and expressiveness build new bias in place of the former credulity and propositional rationality that has perhaps bedeviled western religious experience?

Some aspects of the constitutive symbolism which may characterize upcoming religion are identified in the course of the essays, but there are few hints, if any, of how new religious trends may be institutionalized into enduring patterns and may be integrated into the unprescindable technological character of our society.

In another set of papers (some of which are intermixed with theoretical papers for the sake of internal coherence), the scholars endeavor to come to grips with the problem of researching the phenomenon of unbelief. Nothing short of the frank and exhaustive approach found in the presentation by Professor Glock and the discussion that followed could do justice to this area which has represented particularly irksome methodological difficulties. Given the undeveloped state of conceptualization on the topic of unbelief, how should a program of research be organized? With reference to specific research instruments, is survey research the best approach, or shall we think of the entire gamut of investigative devices available to the scholar, including, for instance, case studies, socio-psychological biographies, content analysis, and participant observation? Above all, does the novelty of the phenomenon call for new and innovative though untested methods of reflection and analysis?

It would be naïve to pretend that exhaustive answers to these questions are being offered in these essays; however, it can be fairly said that at various points in this collection of papers some of the crucial questions in the area of belief/unbelief are clearly and compellingly posed. This by itself is no mean achievement and constitutes a solid starting point for future research and reflection.

3

Having presented an introductory survey of the general problems suggested by the notion of a "culture of unbelief," it may be useful to outline briefly the connective tissue of this volume.

Luckmann's opening paper presents a global view of the history of unbelief, from its emergence during the time when society first became complex to its demise (presumably) in the not too distant future, when belief is projected to disappear entirely as a social fact. Belief (and correspondingly unbelief) does not here constitute a universally applicable notion but represents a highly restricted phenomenon, a specific vein in the development of society. As a "nonessential dimension of the human condition" belief represents the development of society from a primitive state of diffused and pervasive religiousness to advanced levels of institutional specialization and selective internalization of specific processes of socialization. In "primitive fusion" societies the notions of belief and unbelief are completely absent. As we move toward stages of institutional differentiation and independence within the social structure, religion assumes a specialized social role, develops its own organization, locates visibly and distinctly the "officially defined world view," and proclaims the monopoly of the system of meanings, departure from which constitutes unbelief.

The growing complexity of the social organization, however, generates several subsystems of world views, conflicting and not relating to the "official" model or belief. How does the individual handle these systemic discontinuities? In the modern industrial context he has a limited number of options, the most extreme of which is to relegate religious representations to the realm of rhetoric, to which he is subjectively indifferent, having moved beyond the point where systems of religious beliefs are subjectively relevant. The common denominator of postindustrial man's mode of belief appears to be a "neutralization" of official systems of belief and the emergence of "privatization" of views of the meaning of life.

The belief experience, therefore, which was but a part of the complex process of institutional differentiation of our society, must be understood as constituted by institutional definition and as reflective of conditions of social dynamics. In this sense it is on the wane and will eventually disappear completely.

However well defined and differentiated Luckmann's three

stages of development may be, the process he outlines falls into a familiar linear pattern that so frequently allures and mystifies historical analysts. From the additional papers, in fact, a plausible alternative scheme of interpretation seems to emerge which comes very close to a dialectical model wherein belief and unbelief are viewed as antithetic but continuous, the resolution to their opposing valence being reached by way of upgrading their respective social value into a qualitatively new phenomenon, which transcends their limitations but still retains religious significance. This position appears to underpin the contributions of Professors Bellah, Grumelli, and Parsons —with, of course, differing qualifications in each instance.

In his first essay (see chapter 2), Professor Bellah questions Luckmann's scheme and points out that the process of differentiation does not seem to have followed the trajectory outlined by Luckmann in any other part of society except the Western, Greek-influenced world. In oriental religions such as Zen Buddhism, Taoism, and Confucianism, a rational system of beliefs (in our sense) has failed to develop: Western biblical religions appear to be the only ones clearly based on cognitive belief. Non-Western religions are not about objective, cognitive assertions, and the differentiation process described by Luckmann seemingly cannot be clearly detected here.

Within the West itself, the decline of belief can be described better as a diminution of the overbelief of the masses, brought about by the expansion of the intellectual class with its skeptical challenge to orthodox beliefs and increasing leaning on the individual's religious experience. This trend has been growing since the emergence of the intellectual stratum in Plato's Greece. It is a change in scale, not in the substance of the event. The social scientist is less concerned with this collapse of traditional certainties than he is with religion's power of resiliency. All available evidence indicates the emergence of a new mode of religiousness, a nascent religion of mankind located in an unbounded community—a new religious consciousness which challenges all established groups and is not the product of any objective creed.

The objectivist fallacy, the identification of religion and belief which has characterized Western experience thus gives way to a generalized religiousness where conscious critical evaluation of religious conceptions by the masses has eroded conventional forms of belief and replaced them with a personal quest for meaning within a newly apprehended function of religion. In this sense nonbelief is generic to the contemporary religious consciousness as well as nonreligious consciousness, while at the same time the distinction between believers and unbelievers is obliterated by the fact that all believe something. Religion thus appears to be stronger than ever, if we view it as the diffused private quest for personal experience, individual authencity, and internalization of authority, in harmony with group purposes and values such as love, sacrifice, and communion. In this view, religion is not a cognitive experience: it does not stand or fall with the vagaries of what we have known as belief.

We may well be in a revolutionary situation with respect to science, religion, reason, and faith, at the verge of a possible reunification of consciousness wherein the unconscious dimension will become part of overarching schemes of interpretation. In this sense Bellah sees conventional religion as faltering but also classic forms of nonbelief as collapsing.

A similar view is expressed by Monsignor Grumelli in his essay which constituted one of the opening statements of the symposium. From an ecclesiologist's point of view he reaches conclusions substantially the same as those of Professor Bellah: the parameters of the religious phenomenon of our time are basically changing and a radical rethinking of some of our basic assumptions is needed. He focuses on atheism, as a subtype of unbelief, or, as Professor Parsons later puts it, as the classical (ecclesiastical) epithet for unbelief, and attempts to clarify some of the complex relationships that exist between atheism and secularization. Secularization offers a deep ambivalence with respect to belief/unbelief (atheism), thus illustrating how blurred the line between belief and unbelief is. It may even be said that secularization performs a conciliatory function between the two, as a halfway house. While secularization often leads to unbelief, it also precipitates states of religious awareness and fosters religious growth, away from cognitive and dogmatic beliefs and closer to appreciation and concern for a variety of expression of enduring human concerns.

When writing his essay, Professor Parsons had the advantage of having been a participant in the symposium and also of having access to the collection of papers delivered there and the transcripts of the discussions. In his customary penetrating way, he gives us not only a masterful view of the development of belief in Western society up to and including the contemporary crisis expressed in the religion of love movement, but he also offers a valuable synthesis of his most relevant thinking on religion, which up until now was found widely parceled out in his many writings. His reflections on the "culture of unbelief" go much beyond the frontiers that had been lightly explored during the symposium and in the other essays of this volume.

Side by side with its strong cognitive component (the cognitive *bias*) that expresses itself in propositional statements, belief in the West has also had a much neglected noncognitive component, which cannot be ignored if we want to account for the variations in the roles of belief.

Because they pointed out this feature of belief, Freud, Durkheim, and Weber can be seen as precursors of the contemporary scene and, in a way, as important intellectual mediators who emphasized the noncognitive component of religion. Durkheim made a greater contribution in this regard than the other two in that he alerted us to the constitutive quality of beliefs as symbolic expressions of the moral community.

In the differentiating process of evolution, the religious as well as the secular components undergo differentiation both within and between themselves. The first major crisis of constitutive symbolism (beliefs) in recent times occurred at the Reformation, when beliefs in church and priesthood as machinery of salvation were discarded in favor of an invisible church.

The interreligious hostilities that followed the Reformation disappeared out of sheer exhaustion and gave way to gradual emergence of the notion of legitimation of pluralistic religious constitutions within a political society. The attenuation of differences between denominations and the blunting of the notion of disbelief generated the climate within which the "moral community"—of which Bellah speaks—began to emerge. The turning point in the process is characterized by an unprecedented legitimation of "expressiveness" in human behavior and a new permissiveness.

The final stage of this process is embodied in the ecumenical movement, which indicates that belief is no longer assessed in terms of cognitive commitment to one religious group, but in terms of participation in the moral community and sharing of a common religious orientation, which again Bellah aptly defined as "civic religion." Thus ecumenism is grounded in essentially noncognitive components of religion. In the present contingency, therefore, disbelievers are those who basically challenge the moral legitimacy of the modern human community, while those alienated from this community or minimizing their participation in it are more accurately known as unbelievers.

The genuine outbreak of the nonrational in Western religious experience is viewed by Professor Parsons as the end of the line, a religious ferment which, however, has enormous creative possibilities. Again, while church religion is being privatized, religious significance is being generalized to an unprecedented range in the previous secular community. We could say that expressiveness is the charism of our times, epitomized in the proclamation of the new religion of love, which incidentally includes and legitimizes aspects of non-Western religions to an unprecedented degree. The master symbol of the new religion is "community" and its pedigree is a direct socio-cultural Christian heritage. But it has no major prophet as yet and it has attained only a limited degree of institutionalization. On the other hand, the new religion is heavily tainted with moral absolutism, which separates it from those unsympathetic to it, not necessarily in virtue of any transcendent mission it claims for itself: its eroticism and permissiveness leave open the possibility of its turning aggressive, which may represent a regressive trend. Yet it cannot be denied that this emergent religion of love, which is totally world oriented and in which the nonrational components are very salient, has an enormous social potential for altering the present pattern of apparent unbelief into a turning point toward a new major cycle of religious development.

In a response that followed Luckmann's presentation, Professor Mandic briefly introduces elements of a Marxist perspective on the problem of unbelief. Belief and unbelief must not be apprehended on the basis of preconceptions, however scientifically underpinned, but with an open mind, ready to verify even the most appealing theories. The real-life situation cannot be comprehended if we confine our notions of belief and unbelief to the religious experience. Belief and unbelief are not limited to the religious dimensions and do not relate exclusively to the realm of the sacred. They are essential dimensions of the human condition; their function is to permit class-bound men to overcome their alienation in various ways and contexts. Our attention ought to focus on the intimate antithetical relationship which for every belief brings about a mode of unbelief, while establishing a transition ground between the two and generating a variety of unbeliefs.

Professor Mandic highlights the marginal consideration given in these studies to the Marxist thinking on belief and unbelief. The magnitude of the problem clearly suggests that this whole area ought to be given distinct and undivided attention in a study all by itself.

In some sense one could detect a broad overlap between Professor Mandic's criticism and the theories expressed by Bellah, Grumelli, and Parsons, and at the same time a wide difference with the statement of Professor Luckmann.

Professor Marty's response latches on again to Bellah's theory while attempting to restate from a different angle the continuity-development theory of belief. Marty agrees with Bellah that the stress on belief is being attenuated; but he also points out that the end of belief and the alienation from religious symbolism and officialdom does not represent the end of religion and the complete displacement of the cognitive function that conventional belief systems performed. In fact, he detects the emergence of counter-belief systems which have manifest cognitive dimensions. Belief is not being left behind, but it is being transformed and adapted, attenuated and demythologized, while retaining much continuity with historical religion.

The reactions of Harvey Cox, Jean Danielou, and Milan Machovec to Grumelli's paper elicit special interest because of their style and because of the substantive thought they introduce. Cox makes a strong case for the need to move away from Western provincialism and the equally Western penchant for dichotomizing everything in artificial classification. He questions the legitimacy of the distinction between believers and unbelievers considering that, whatever the cognitive content of belief and unbelief, we all reach out for what constitutes the ground of our being (a statement indirectly challenged by Wilson and Luckmann). Rather than indulge in "incestuous conversations" between believers and unbelievers, Cox pleads for ways of stemming on the one hand the overcredulity which is a graver problem in several countries (particularly the United States), and on the other hand of making the "church" more believable.

With the aim of highlighting the bases of dialogue between Christians and Marxists, Machovec pursues further this trend of analysis and emphasizes the fact that unbelievers are only "other believers," if viewed within the concrete context of a different set of beliefs. Irrespective of the cognitive component of their beliefs, all who burn with desire for *metanoia,* for change (as for instance the early Christians and more recently the Marxists), are to be recognized as believers. In this sense, secularization represents an up-to-date way of believing, a modern expression of the most profound and enduring human questions. To this mode of unbelief Marxism is definitely open.

Cardinal Danielou appears in agreement with Cox and Machovec that the distinction between believer and unbeliever does not correspond to the real state of things. But he goes on to highlight the ambiguities that he sees creeping into this whole area of discourse, especially when sociological categories are used. In the specific case of "secularization" he feels that this notion is in urgent need of more precise definition. From a theological viewpoint, if secularization means the triumph of empiricism and the death of metaphysics, or the alibi of ultimacy (the earthly city as the final goal of life), or a condition of society wherein Christianity is no longer accessible to questing spirits, it does not represent an advance, as would be the case if secularization meant the disappearance of mythical conceptions of the universe and the destruction of idolatries.

The problem of a transitional, intervening phase in the assumed development from belief into the new cycle of religiousness crystallizes much of the content of the excerpts from the general discussions. The terminological difficulties which pop up again and again reflect much of the conceptual ambiguities built into the notion of belief/unbelief. The French-speaking theologians, for instance, insist on the necessity of distinguishing between belief and faith, while both theologians and social scientists would welcome a clearer differentiation between belief and religion. From a more analytical angle, Professor Bellah introduces the distinction between "belief in" and "belief that," which largely reflects the distinction between emotive and cognitive components of belief. A further specification points out that belief is a composite of affective and cognitive elements within the inclusive context of community, which entails participation in an institutionalized interpretation of the universe. This adds an isomorphic relationship between belief and belonging to institutionally recognized religious bodies, with its concomitant requirement of behavioral indicators of appurtenance: to be a believer means not only to believe in but also to be seen as a believer by others.

These and other refinements of the terminological question take second place, however, vis-à-vis the central issue concerning the dynamics of development from belief to unbelief and beyond. Under what conditions and in what culture is unbelief possible?

In the particular instance of Christianity, unbelief emerges from within religion itself, and the first stage of unbelief consists precisely in the attitude of tolerance that develops within an up-till-now intolerant religious body. In the earlier phases of religious institutions the functional equivalent of what we now call unbelief was heresy, the wrong belief rather than nonbelief. This was brought about by the fact that Christianity defined itself in highly intellectual terms, developed a controlling body which sees religion in terms of propositional systems of relevance, and has fully developed the Greco-Jewish inheritance of exclusiveness. These three elements are presently undergoing deep alterations, leading to a state of provisionality in the way people hold religious beliefs, if they find any need at all to hold any belief.

More and more today the prime locus of belief is the subjective system of relevance each individual manages to develop for himself. This new mode of belief, however, is basically different from the one we have been familiar with in the past and so is the context in which new beliefs such as childhood, social justice, peace, expressiveness are emerging. In this sense Professor Luckmann's thesis that invisible religion is becoming a substitute for visible religion is acceptable, but it leaves open the question as to how the functions performed by conventional religion are being replaced and by whom.

The discussion makes it plain that in pursuing the conditions that account for the present variation in the realm of belief, a purely cross section of the current situation without reference to its historical genesis cannot be very fruitful. It may be worth noting that while serious consideration is given to Professor Luckmann's projection of future developments in the "belief saga," Professor Bellah's vision elicits strong reservations on the part of many participants. His approach is seen as reflecting heavily the North American situation, while neglecting crucial phenomena of other areas such as the unbelief of the European working class. Some participants object to the existentialism and the stress on personal experience over dogmatic faith in his presentation. On the one hand, theologians observe that Bellah renders faith fluid and plastic; on the other, sociologists object to the rhetorical mixing of experience with scientific analysis, or to the choice of students as the key location of the emerging religiousness.

However syncopated the movement of the discussion condensed in these excerpts, they permit an instructive glimpse of scholars at work, struggling to lay down key reference points for the clarification of this unexplored area.

4

The difficulties that beset the problem of conceptualization overflow into the problem of a research program aimed at filling the lacunae in our knowledge of belief and unbelief.

Can a paradigm for research on unbelief be formulated? Given the confusion and ambiguity in the effort to conceptualize the phenomenon of unbelief, under what condition is it amenable to empirical research?

Professor Glock considers such research not only feasible but also necessary and extremely promising. With this goal in mind he formulates a provisional operationalization of the concept of belief, and on the basis of this he defines a basic typology of unbelief intimately related to the notion of the sacred and its apprehension.

Perhaps even more difficult than the problem of conceptualization of unbelief is the problem of its measurement, fraught as it is with the hard choice between low-level-abstraction–culture-bound measurements (of sufficiently high precision), and high-level-abstraction–culture-free (but also very imprecise) measurements. Assuming that the two problems of operational conceptualization and of measurement are solved, the research needs address itself to the three basic questions of what is the nature of unbelief, what are its causes and its effects, and what brings about changes in unbelief. Also keenly important are formulations of meaningful hypotheses such as the one having to do with assumed dysfunctionality of unbelief to the integration of a group. Professor Glock makes a strong case in his presentation that a longitudinal, team, collaborative research effort cannot be easily organized. He clearly spells out the significance of such an effort for traditional sociological research and what a breakthrough it would represent in the sociological study of religion.

A singular value of Professor Glock's paper is the step-by-step description of how a research project is put together. Relying on his unequaled experience, he brings into configuration all the various tools and skills of survey research and lays down a master plan for what could be a truly significant study in the field of sociology of religion.

Professor Wilson, however, does not see this as going far enough toward a specific scheme of research. Glock's effort to establish widely applicable concepts is viewed as ineffective considering the great variety of beliefs. Wilson suggests that we accept the broad cultural concept of belief as commonly known, in virtue of which some people are considered within a religious purview while others are seen as having contracted out of that system. What brings about and sustains the culture of unbelief? Professor Wilson emphasizes institutional analysis as the primary mode of research in this context. He points out that belief/unbelief does not inhere in individuals: cultures carry belief systems. Rather than a head count, research ought to focus on institutions, organizations, communities, and patterns of social relationships. Institutions are increasingly exempting themselves from any supranatural legitimation. What needs investigation is the way culture facilitates or hinders orientations of belief or unbelief, and fosters or hinders the possibility of interpreting the world in religious terms. To be in line with our concern with the "culture of unbelief" we need to look at context situations and at institutions.

Even so, the question of whether unbelief can be an object of research remains problematic. While it is true that we are very ignorant of the culture of unbelief, this culture cannot be extrapolated by attitude surveys. It is an illusion therefore to look for a wide consensus on an operational concept of unbelief; and we need not wait for a well-formulated and agreed-upon conceptual framework.

The culture of unbelief is a new phenomenon that exists because of the recession of agencies and institutions that supported established belief systems. To comprehend it we need previous knowledge of two phenomena, among others: one, the process of institutional and cultural change; two, the way in which the culture of unbelief is integrated and made coherent with the institutions that support it. We must first study the culture of belief to arrive at the culture of unbelief. How dependent is a society upon religious institutions for the performance of its functions? And by what processes are these functions transferred to functional alternatives? What is the siginficance, for instance, of the fundamental change in the pattern of communication from the personal spoken word to the impersonal word of mass media? What is the living language of religion today? How does the changed conception of time—past, present, future, eschatology, eternal life—affect the chronogrammatic component of religious beliefs? How incongruous are beliefs in a technological way of life? To what extent can religious groups understand and adopt rational procedures, when rational organization seems incongruous with religious belief systems? Professor Wilson suggests that we cannot survey without a culture-bound starting point: we need to attack such questions from our culture's understanding of belief and go on to study varieties of unbelief.

The fact is, however, that, as Professor Luckmann points out, we have no convenient starting point, no commonsense notion of unbelief. Preliminary studies may be needed before a large-scale, cross-cultural survey is conducted.

Professor Glock agrees that a pilot or preliminary study would be necessary in order to provide provisional conceptualizations, and that a preliminary phase of investigation during which various instruments will be employed ought to precede survey research. Yet some optional consensus on conceptualization of belief and unbelief is needed as a broad view of the whole before focusing on parts. But the quantification in aggregate form that Professor Glock advocates finds limited support in Professor Wilson, who quotes the democratic fallacy and would rather consider a number of alternatives and use a variety of forms of empirical inquiry.

Wilson's preoccupation is echoed in Professor Bellah's question: if we are in a new religious situation, are traditional ways of research acceptable? The proposed research scheme may not be adequate because it runs the risk of missing precisely the object it set about to investigate. A research program ought to include emerging group movements, strategic to the whole scene but, because of their present marginality, unlikely to be included in a random sample. Luckmann concurred: if there is a qualitative change in religion, survey research may never discover it, but a combined approach which uses all available methods, including socio-psychological ones, may be more successful.

The limited consensus arrived at in the course of the discussion seems to indicate that a program of research ought to pursue three broad goals:

1. To define the range of functional alternatives in the sphere of beliefs and trace their social location. These alternatives will have to include out-of-the-way instances of belief, such as scientific pragmatism, astrology, Zen, fundamentalist Christianity, and so forth.

2. To define continuities of belief systems within the most important historical institutions, looking for signs of change in these systems, against the paradigm of Luckmann's developmental phases.

3. To inquire into new bases of unification of structure in our society and social integration that bring about new common entities beneath the apparently divergent characteristics of each structure (i.e., mass media, industrialization, the peace movement) along the projection outlined in the contributions of Professors Bellah and Wilson.

Bellah's short essay, "Between Religion and Social Science" brings this volume to a fitting close. Moving beyond the specific context of belief, Bellah escalates the problems dealt with in these essays into the realm of one of the most enduring contests of the past few centuries, namely the alleged conflict between religion and science. Bellah argues that the religious implications of social science point to a nonantagonistic differentiation between science and religion which is rapidly moving ultimately to resolve itself into a genuine integration of the two. This new integration is based on the conscious rejection of univocal modes of understanding reality. In Bellah's view secularization and the disintegration of religion are far from increasing: on the contrary religion is moving under new garbs into the very center of our cultural preoccupations.

It is interesting to note that toward the end of his classical monograph, *The Elementary Forms of Religious Life,* Durkheim felt compelled to spin off in the same direction and briefly cope with this same problem, although reaching somewhat different conclusions. In the writings of sociologists of religion one notices how every one of them is confronted, sooner or later, with this ultimate problem, irrespective of his starting point or of the area of specialization in which he excels.

Bellah's statement, which was directly provoked by the interchange that took place during the Symposium on the Culture of Unbelief, is a clear advance over conventional and often trite ways of dealing with this issue. But, in a large sense, so was the process that characterized the symposium itself: as this book illustrates, in spite of the contrapuntal rhythm of the dialogue between the participants (and in spite of the differing academic backgrounds they represent) the outstanding fact is that not infrequently they succeed in speaking a common language and staying within a shared frame of reference. This is owing in large part to the constructive and realistic approach brought to the discussion by social scientists and theologians alike who managed to keep their minds open to reexamine issues only provisionally resolved in the past. Considering the development of sociological thought on religion during the past decade, it is fair to say that many of these essays contain some of the most exciting and seminally rich statements on the problem of belief in our generation.

PART ONE

.

THE NOTION OF UNBELIEF:
PROBLEMS OF CONCEPTUALIZATION
AND RESEARCH

1

BELIEF, UNBELIEF, AND RELIGION

.

THOMAS LUCKMANN

1

Belief—I am using the word in its older sense in which it was eventually superseded by "faith": *fides*—belief and unbelief may seem to be constitutive parts of religion. In these days of increased communication between theology, history, and the social sciences, however, no one will be surprised to hear that this venerable pair of concepts does not occupy an important place in the sociological study of religion. Many social scientists may, in fact, raise an eyebrow at the suggestion that these two concepts can serve any useful purpose. It is salutary to treat the naïve use of these concepts in some writings in the history and sociology of religion with profound skepticism. At the same time, belief and unbelief are phenomena that cannot be ignored. Under certain conditions, this pair of concepts may claim a modest yet not entirely negligible place in the study of religion.

It may be helpful first to call to mind what belief and un-belief are not. They are not concepts referring to universal aspects of the human condition nor do they specify elementary structures of human consciousness. They cannot be placed on a level with the formal classificatory notions of social theory like "social interaction," "institution," "social structure," and so forth. Nor do they belong to that group of concepts about whose universal applicability there may be serious and pro-ductive rather than merely terminological controversy. One may legitimately ask, for example, whether terms like "social role," "religion," or "social class" refer to universal aspects of social reality, or whether they are methodological constructs of the "middle-range" that have empirical referents in some but not all historical societies.[1] But a cursory glance at what

1. Obviously I am referring to the concept of "middle-range" in a slightly different sense than, e.g., Robert K. Merton, in *Social Theory and Social Structure* (New York: Free Press, 1957), p. 9.

are generally known as ethnographic and historical data in the field of religion will show convincingly that "belief" and "unbelief" are concepts with a highly restricted field of application.

In ordinary usage the terms refer to the subjective aspect of what is perceived as an objective social reality. To the sociologist, however, they stand for a configuration of social-psychological elements that emerged in a particular type of social structure under specific cultural conditions. Belief and unbelief are not to be taken as constant factors in the psychological constitution of man but as the subjective aspect of social facts of a specifically historical nature. In the terminology of Durkheim they could be defined as the typical reflection, in individual consciousness, of certain *représentations collectives*.[2]

It is generally the business of sociology to take up and sift through what are in effect common-sense notions of social facts. The raw data of sociology consist virtually always of subjective reflections of *représentations collectives*. They are, in fact, anything but "raw"; social facts are constituted as common perceptions and interpretations of reality. In consequence, social facts always carry historical subscripts. The social scientist must not, at the risk of total evaporation of his subject matter, try to break the historical concatenation of *Lebensform* and *Sprachspiel*, to borrow from Wittgenstein a pair of suggestively descriptive terms.[3]

On the other hand, common-sense notions of social facts are not ipso facto categories of sociological analysis. Their naïve use in the social sciences may be just as misleading as the unreflecting, metaphorical application of concepts imported from different (for example, physical or biological) levels of analysis. The "first-order constructs," as Alfred Schutz called them, must be transformed into "second-order constructs." This means that common-sense notions of social facts are to be defined more rigorously than is ever the case in ordinary everyday usage. It means that they are to be placed unequivocally in the semantic context of the general constructs of social

2. Emile Durkheim, *Les Formes Elementaires de la Vie Religieuse* (Paris: Presses Universitaires, 1960).

3. Ludwig Wittgenstein, *Philosophical Investigation* (Oxford: B. Blackwell, 1958).

theory and that they must be used in accordance with the syntactic rules of science. It means, furthermore, that the relevance of the concepts to an area of substantive problems within the discipline must be specified. And it means, finally, that an indication must be given of the usefulness of the concepts in the collection and classification of data. This implies a kind of transformation formula by which the "second-order constructs" are retranslated into the "first-order constructs" that are the primary yield of research operations.[4]

We take it, then, that an historical social fact or, more precisely, that a common understanding of this fact which is itself historical, is reflected in the concepts of belief and unbelief. Furthermore, while belief is not an essential dimension of the human condition, it represents an historical articulation of something that is a universal element of human existence in society: religion. It may be hoped, therefore, that a sociological redefinition [5] of this concept will throw light upon an important aspect of a particular historical form of the relation of the individual to the social order.

2

Belief and unbelief are historical phenomena, but they are not contingent. Their emergence as social facts depends on a particular constellation of conditions, some of which pertain to the social structure and some of which involve the conformation of the socially objectivated world view. The former may be subsumed under the heading of institutional specialization of religion; the latter consist in the segregation of symbolic representations in the form of a sacred cosmos.

In the analysis of religion in complex societies— especially in modern industrial societies—it may be permissible to treat institutional specialization of religion and the segregation of a sacred cosmos as interdependent. It should be noted, however, that the formation of specialized religious institutions always presupposes a fairly distinct articulation of a sacred

4. Alfred Schutz, "On the Methodology of the Social Sciences," in: *Collected Papers I* (The Hague: Nijhoff, 1962).

5. Cf. for a more extensive discussion: Thomas Luckmann, *The Invisible Religion* (New York: Macmillan Co., 1967); also Peter L. Berger, *The Sacred Canopy* (New York: Doubleday, 1967).

cosmos while, on the contrary, the segregation of religious representations in the world view does not necessarily require a specialized institutional basis in society.

Segregation of religious representations means that two major domains become polarized in the world view. A corresponding bipolarity marks the culturally determined patterns of subjective experience. The relation between everyday life and the sacred becomes indirect. Only the "ultimate" significance of ordinary, habitual experience and, of course, the "extraordinary" experiences that break the routines of everyday life are taken to refer to the sacred level of reality, a level that often receives the status of the supernatural. The ordinary meaning of conduct in everyday life, on the other hand, is less rigorously determined by the logic of the sacred cosmos. The world of everyday life thus gives rise to more immediately pragmatic systems of relevance. Although some representations are set apart in the world view as specifically religious, their significance—and the authority of the entire sacred cosmos—rests on what may be called the elementary religious function of the world view as a whole. This function consists in the socialization of human organisms into an order that transcends the individual. Socially objectivated world views integrate transcendences that are subjectively experienced on different levels: they connect the fleeting sensation of the organism to a past and future that are embedded in shared, social dimensions of time; they link the individual to a community of the living and the dead; they bridge the gap between the private world of dreams and the public world of everyday life.

It is questionable whether the world view as an undifferentiated whole in fact ever performed this elementary religious function. Perhaps such was the case in the earliest forms of human society. Data on archaic societies indicate that certain representations already tend to acquire a special status within the world view. Even before such representations coalesce into a segregated sacred cosmos, religious representations may visibly symbolize—and in part perform—the religious function of the world view as a whole. "Religious" is nonetheless still "diffused" throughout the world view. Only when the sacred cosmos is sharply segregated from other levels of reality is the elementary religious function of the world view taken over as the special and exclusive function of religious representations.

Neither the social objectivation nor the social maintenance and transmission of the sacred cosmos necessarily requires an institutional basis of its own. In archaic societies and (to a lesser extent) also in what, for lack of a better term, one may call traditional civilizations, religious representations pervade such institutions as kinship, the division of labor, and the regulation and exercise of power. In such societies the sacred cosmos legitimates conduct in the full range of social situations and bestows meaning on the entire course of an individual biography. There is, therefore, nothing—whether it be their ecology, economy, or systems of knowledge—that can be fully understood of such societies without reference to religion. Clearly it is otherwise in highly complex societies whose social structure consists of relatively independent subsystems.[6]

The very pervasiveness of religion has as its corollary that belief and unbelief are absent as social facts. There is no such thing as selective internalization—or refusal of internalization —of the sacred cosmos. For a number of reasons individual members of archaic societies may be socialized with different degrees of success into the social order but the notion of unbelief would be entirely misplaced in this connection. It would be equally beside the point to use the concept of belief to describe the subjective results of successful internalization of the world view.

Institutional specialization of religion radically altered the relation of the individual to the social order. It hardly needs to be stressed that institutional specialization of religion is merely one aspect of a global process of social change: the segmentation of the social structure in consequence of the differentiation and specialization of diverse institutional areas. Attempts to discern the essential features of archaic societies are well known.[7] The typical conformation of such societies was described in terms of the primitive level of the division of

6. Cf. J. Milton Yinger, *Religion, Society and the Individual: An Introduction to the Sociology of Religion* (New York: Macmillan Co., 1957).

7. Cf. Guy E. Swanson, *The Birth of the Gods: The Origin of Primitive Beliefs* (Ann Arbor, Mich.: University of Michigan Press, 1960).

labor and by reference to kinship as the guiding principle of social organization. The prevalence of restitutive law and the absence of central political organization was noted, as was the peculiar form of solidarity and the pervasiveness of face-to-face social relations.[8]

The most general structural trait of this type of society, however, is emphasized in Redfield's concept of "primitive fusion." [9] Its meaning is well illustrated by the description of a Maya Indian peasant and his son working in the maize field. Their performance is neither an instance of kinship behavior nor an economic action nor religious conduct, but all of this at once, in an indissoluble unity of meaning. The concept thus describes a form of social organization where "bundles" of specific institutions are not tied together, that is, where institutions do not form functionally specialized domains. It is the "logic" of the sacred universe rather than the pragmatic logic of functional subsystems that integrate various institutionalized actions into meaningful wholes in the life of the individual and the community.

Our knowledge of the reasons for the transformation of certain archaic societies into the great ancient civilizations surely is not satisfactory. For all that, it is not difficult to see the common element in the various explanations which have been advanced. Increasing complexity in the division of labor, resulting from domestication of plants and leading to the production of a surplus over the subsistence minimum, the emergence of supracommunal and supratribal political organization for the management of hydraulic works, the differentiation of occupational roles and emergence of distinct social classes and a sharp rise in the inequality of the social distribution of knowledge may be all seen as processes of differentiation and partial specialization of institutional areas. While a certain differentiation of religious institutions seems to have accompanied this process everywhere it did not result in full specialization of these institutions. They remained closely intertwined with the structure of kinship and political organization.

8. Emile Durkheim, *De la division du travail social* (Paris: Presses Universitaires, 1967).

9. Robert Redfield, *The Primitive World and its Transformations* (New York: Cornell University Press, 1957).

The processes that led to the emergence of modern industrial society are somewhat better known and understood. One may say summarily that they were marked by an irregular sequence of phases in which not only economic and political but also religious institutions were increasingly more specialized in their functions. The social structure was segmented to a much higher degree than before into institutional domains. With the exception of religion, the norms of the several domains tended toward functional "rationality." After a long period of what may be called jurisdictional disputes between the domains, institutional norms in different fields achieved a remarkable autonomy. In other words, they became partly, if not fully independent from the sacred cosmos. The hierarchical structure of the world view was seriously weakened. "Ultimate" significance was no longer effectively diffused from the sacred level of reality into all reaches of the world view. A plurality of systems of knowledge came into existence, each developing an internal logic of its own and each having an institutional basis of its own. Not only technology and science and not only political ideologies such as, for example, nationalism but also the traditional sacred cosmos found a distinct, rather clearly identifiable location in the social structure. Various forms of competition and adaptation marked the relations between the various semiautonomous systems of knowledge and determined the degree of success with which they penetrated the world of everyday dife.

This indicates the profound transformation that took place in the internal conformation of the social structure, in the basic relations of the social structure to the world view and in the relation of the individual member of society to the social order. In the case of religion it was this general change rather than an intrinsic trend toward functional "rationality" that led to the increasingly restricted jurisdiction of specifically religious norms.

Institutional specialization of religion exhibited, nevertheless, some typical parallels with the specialization of other institutional domains. Specifically religious social roles were soon defined as parts of an emergent occupational and status system. Their exclusive task was the administration of knowledge and regulation of performance expressly pertaining to the sacred universe. The interest of religious experts in control-

ling recruitment and training led to a development that con-
forms in general outline to the process that sociologists like to
call "professionalization." The corollary of this process, the establishment of some kind of ecclesiastic organization resulted
both in the growth of specific institutional traditions and,
eventually, in the emergence of ecclesiastic criteria of functional "rationality."

In consequence of a differentiated pattern of social stratification and an increasingly heterogeneous distribution of
knowledge, religious representations, too, were unequally distributed in society. To be sure, everybody continued to participate in the sacred cosmos in some fashion. The function of
the sacred cosmos was, of course, similar, *grosso modo,* for all
members of society. But the typical, structurally determined
differences in socialization that characterize complex societies
eventually led to the articulation of different versions of the
sacred cosmos among the social strata.

The simple and stable relationship between the world view
and social structure that characterized archaic societies was
thus radically changed. The sacred cosmos had been an in-
tregal part of a rather homogeneously distributed world view
that was internalized in general processes of socialization. The
reality and authority of the sacred cosmos was supported by
the entire social structure and remained unproblematic. Now
the sacred cosmos obtained a distinct and, in a manner of
speaking, visible location in a restricted segment of the social
structure. It was internalized in specific processes of socialization whose character varied in a manner that was determined
by a complex social structure and a differentiated system of
stratification. With some simplification one may say that the
social structure produced its own internal "cultural contacts"
and "culture conflicts." Here was a double task for the religious experts. The maintenance and transmission of the
sacred cosmos now required the explicit formulation of an
"official" model of religion. This involved standardization and
systematization of religious representations and led to the
emergence of "higher" forms of sacred knowledge, that is,
of various theological disciplines. It also involved the interpretation of sacred knowledge in different modes that were
adapted to the structurally determined needs of different
groups and strata. This had not only "pastoral" but also

serious political implications for the emergent forms of ecclesiastic organization. In this situation the identity of the
elementary religious function of the world view with the articulated sacred cosmos and with the actual performance and
the social effects of specialized religious institutions can no
longer be taken for granted. In other words, "religion"—defined by its elementary function—and visible religion as an
institutionally defined social fact are no longer necessarily the
same.

Religious institutions may achieve different degrees of specialization. The process is of course not restricted to the history
of Christendom in Western society. In various ancient civilizations the presence of a priesthood indicates that religious institutions were highly differentiated—but the various forms
of theocratic government, divine kingship, and the like, also
indicate that institutional specialization of religion, for various
reasons, did not proceed very far. More highly specialized religious institutions may be found in traditional Islamic societies. But only the development of the Christian churches
in Occidental history resulted in full specialization of religious
institutions. To be sure, no single factor can account for this
development. In the background there was the sharp segregation of a sacred cosmos in Israel. Then there were the conditions surrounding the emergence of the early Church such as
the pluralism of world views and the differentiation of specifically religious communities in an empire whose political
and economic institutions already had a relatively high degree
of autonomy. Then came the long history of jurisdictional disputes between Church and state throughout the Middle Ages.
With the Renaissance the rate of change in society accelerated:
the growth of cities, the "discovery" of disembodied "classical"
systems of values and of knowledge, the contact with alien
civilizations, the peculiarly Occidental combination of science
and technology and, finally, the rise of modern capitalism
ushered in a new world. Only this intricate and unique combination of factors may perhaps explain why religious institutions were specialized to a degree not paralleled elsewhere.

In the emergent industrial societies specifically religious
communities are linked to ecclesiastic organizations with a
long tradition and with their own criteria of functional ration-

ality. The traditional sacred cosmos is held in clear monopoly by religious experts. The sacred cosmos is highly systematized in the form of doctrine and there is a proliferation of "higher" forms of expert religious knowledge. The entire domain of specialized religion is both highly autonomous and clearly divorced from the other institutional components of the social structure.

An important consequence of institutional specialization in religion is that the population that is not expert in religious matters participates in the sacred cosmos in a somewhat indirect manner. Specialized institutions predefine for it the cognitive and behavioral norms of what is properly religious. These institutions control the expectations and sanction the performances in matters that are recognized by everybody as distinctly religious.

This is the decisive point at which one may begin to speak of belief and unbelief as social facts. It would have been entirely unprofitable to define belief in general terms as the subjective correlate of a system of knowledge considered to be hostile to "religion." In societies in which the sacred cosmos is internalized integrally in the overall process of socialization into a hierarchically structured world view there is no belief nor unbelief.

In this light, it may be helpful to present in a highly schematic manner three main ways in which the location of "religion" in society is objectively experienced:

1. All conduct is "religiously" relevant. All situations in everyday life as well as the entire biography are endowed with a significance that refers directly to sacred reality. There is no specifically religious socialization; socialization *tout court* is essentially religious. There are neither belief nor unbelief, neither believers nor unbelievers.

2. Some kinds of conduct are "religiously" more relevant than others. Some behavior is determined by specifically religious norms, and the sacred cosmos is set apart from everyday life. But all conduct still rests on internalized general norms that are infused with sacred significance and all conduct is subject to general social controls.

3. Some patterns of behavior are generally recognized as specifically religious while other forms of conduct are guided

by distinctly different normative expectations. Religious norms are internalized in specific processes of socialization that are directly and indirectly controlled by specialized institutions. Definition and interpretation of religious representations is held in monopoly by religious institutions which may also enforce "correct" religious performance. It is under such circumstances that belief and unbelief emerge as social facts.

3

In contemporary society, institutionally specialized religion is still commonly perceived as the one and only form of religion. This is not at all surprising. Religion is sharply circumscribed in this social form, as well as highly visible. Belief is a distinctive social fact. Despite occasional highly sophisticated controversies among experts, a common understanding of concepts such as religion, belief, and the like is taken for granted in traditional discourse on religion.

The sociologist is not much to be blamed for having restricted his attention, too, to the "visible" or institutionally specialized form of religion. This, after all, was the concrete embodiment of religion through much of the history of our society. It is in this social form that religion became part of the received culture of modern industrial societies. The sociologist is generally inclined to see the subject matter of his discipline in terms of institutional definitions. Even if it is true—as I would suggest—that we have entered an incipient phase of decline of this social form of religion, even if we should be now witnessing the emergence of a new, "invisible" social form of religion, it is still quite evident that specifically religious institutions are very much part of the contemporary scene. Our present concern with the nature of belief as a phenomenon that is closely bound up with institutional specialization of religion is therefore more than merely an exercise in retrospection.

It was, and still is, a largely but not fully justifiable practice of sociologists to collect data on religion by describing the social distribution of belief. In doing so we are merely translating what is an institutionally defined "official" model of religion into the operational terms of social research. Our

discussion of religion under the aspect of institutional specialization should help us to draw out the theoretical implications
of this practice.

We shall use three pairs of concepts, each pair consisting of
one term that refers to the objective social order and one that
refers to the individual. The terms on the structural level are
(A) the world view (more precisely, the hierarchy of meaning
in the world view), (B) the sacred cosmos that is, the system
of religious representations), and (C) the "official" model of
religion (that is, the constellation of doctrine and ritual that
functions, in the context of institutionally specialized religion,
as a set of normative expectations). The terms on the individual level are (A) the subjective system of relevance, (B) that
set of subjective notions and values to which the individual
attributes "ultimate" significance and by which he will justify
his actions to himself and others, and (C) the subjective system
of religious belief.

To simplify matters, we may begin by imagining a society
in which the sacred cosmos represents and symbolizes the
hierarchy of significance in the world view and in which an
"official" model merely specifies the institutional basis of the
world view. We may further imagine that the terms on the individual level are perfectly isomorphic with the terms on
the structural level: the subjective notions and values of "ultimate" significance express the subjective system of relevance
and are articulated in the system of religious beliefs. These
correspondences are convertible between the levels: the subjective system of relevance is the internalized hierarchy of
significance in the world view, the subjective notions and
values of "ultimate" significance are the internalized sacred
cosmos, and the subjective system of religious beliefs is the
internalized "official" model of religion.

Needless to say, we are imagining the impossible. First of
all, the isomorphic relationship between the structural and the
individual level presupposes uniform and perfect socialization.
In the second place, the identity between the terms on one
level presupposes a simplicity of the social structure and an
entirely frozen, undialectical relationship between social structure and world view that even the most determined builder
of abstract models will find unconvincing.

We may use this crude model, nonetheless, as a first approxi-

mation of an ideal, typical construct. It is obvious that archaic
societies are somewhat closer to, and modern industrial societies the farthest from, filling the specifications of this model.
In archaic societies the sacred cosmos closely expresses the
hierarchy of meaning in the world view and the subjective
system of relevance is articulated in the subjective set of notions and values of "ultimate" significance. Furthermore, the
terms on the structural level, while not perfectly reproduced
on the individual level, are indeed rather faithfully mirrored
there. The isomorphy between the two levels is relatively high;
while no society knows perfect and uniform socialization (a
horrible conception, indeed), archaic society comes closer to
it than any other type of society. But, as we must immediately
add, archaic society is of course characterized by the absence of
institutionally specialized religion and—as we noted earlier
—the concept of belief is utterly misapplied there. In other
words, the last pair of terms in our model has no empirical
referents in archaic society.

It is easy to see, however, that among all the societies in
which institutional specialization of religion had sufficiently
progressed to produce, among other things, the social fact of
belief, it will be a society that has an otherwise relatively simple social structure that will at least distantly approximate the
specifications of our model. Such a society is exemplified in the
social order of the Middle Ages. To be sure, the social structure was anything but archaic—yet its complexity was certainly not greater (in many respects it may be said to have
been lesser) than that of the later Roman Empire or even
of Hellenistic states. At the same time, in the social order of
the Middle Ages religious institutions had achieved a rather
impressive degree of specialization. In consequence, this social
order exhibits a relatively high degree of congruence between the world view, the sacred cosmos, and the "official"
model of religion, on the one hand, and the corresponding
terms on the subjective level, on the other. In the analysis of
religion in this kind of society, the sociologist could have
safely adopted the "official" model of religion. To put it
crudely, we could have "measured" belief in terms of conformity with and deviation from the "official" model, accepting, at the same time, an institutionally predefined cut-off
point between belief and unbelief.

The question is whether such a procedure is legitimate in the analysis of religion in modern industrial societies. It is, of course, precisely the procedure that we still follow today, in parish studies, in research on religious attitudes, and so forth. But is it still a good procedure for getting at the facts of religion?

Research along these lines indicates a marginality of specifically religious beliefs in the industrial societies of Europe; it also shows a certain inner secularization of the traditional religious cosmos, a penetration of it by what has been called "civic religion," especially in the United States.[10] The apparent decline of what is, after all, a universal anthropological phenomenon should alert us to the possibility that our methods fail to penetrate beneath the surface of things. And yet we are reluctant to examine the theoretical presuppositions of a sociology of religion that may be inspired, to put it bluntly, by a vanishing social order.

It is of course easier to criticize than to offer constructive suggestions. Expanding the crude model by which we tried to describe some elementary features of the location of religion in preindustrial societies may, however, help us to understand somewhat better what current practice in the sociology of religion can and what it cannot do.

It is evident that in modern industrial societies the world view has a complex social distribution and that the coexistence of several subsystems of knowledge and values has undermined the structural hierarchy of the world view. The sacred cosmos no longer symbolizes in an unequivocal manner the elementary religious function of the world view. In all modern industrial societies several versions of the traditional sacred cosmos are, in fact, socially available. In all of them, moreover, various themes originating in the subsystems of knowledge and value associated with various institutional areas, such as politics and economics, vie for acceptance in the sacred cosmos. There is no one "official" model of religion; several "ex-official" models compete with each other and with models of socialization that contain no specifically religious representations.

The situation on the individual level is consequently ex-

10. Gerhard Lenski, *The Religious Factor* (New York: Doubleday, 1961).

tremely complicated. Different subjective systems of relevance
are produced in structurally determined variants of socialization. The subjective systems of notions and values of "ultimate" significance are no longer transmitted in anything like
homogeneous processes of socialization that remain stable
over several generations. Instead, they are increasingly constructed on a subjective basis, in what are almost self-steered
processes of secondary socialization. One is tempted to over-
state the case by saying that the individual shops in a market
offering various brands of religious and quasi-religious representations. On the other hand, consumer preferences are of
course structurally determined, influenced by class position,
among other factors.

This means that subjective systems of religious belief may
not be adequately understood as approximations of or deviations from some putative "official" model of religion. Admit-
tedly some traditional model of religion may still have a quasi-
official status for specified groups or social strata. This model
may thus determine the specifically religious aspects of primary socialization. But the social relativity of the particular
version of the sacred cosmos that was originally transmitted
soon becomes subjectively evident because the reality of that
sacred cosmos is not massively and generally confirmed and
supported by the social order. It would be useful to develop
a typology for what happens next. I must restrict myself to
some tentative indications.

1. a. The internalized ex-official model of religion may be
       retained in what, without pejorative intent, we may
       call a naïve attitude. It should be obvious that in
       modern industrial societies this will tend to lead to
       "objective" difficulties in the performance of nonre-
       ligious roles. Unless:
   b. the claims of specifically religious representation are
      strictly segregated in consciousness and "lived" only in
      specifically religious contexts. The subjective system
      of religious belief thus becomes a subsystem within the
      overall individual system of relevance.
2. The internalized ex-official model is "neutralized" in
   processes of secondary socialization and ceases to function
   as a subjective system of religious belief. Specifically religious representations may still form a reservoir of

rhetoric but no longer serve to integrate the individual biography into a meaningful whole. Within the individual system of relevance they are *indifferent*.

3. a. After initial "neutralization" of the "official" model the individual reconstructs from divergent elements offered on the market of "ultimate" significance, a private system of religious beliefs that does not resemble an ex-official model of religion.

  b. This case resembles the preceding one. But there the individual reconstructs after "neutralization" or a phase of "doubt" an ex-official model of religion as his own, private system of religious belief.

Only the cases 1a (the "naïve" case) and 1b (the "segregated" case) show some resemblance to different degrees of "belief" in preindustrial societies. It is clear, however, that the total social context in which "solutions" are practiced is quite different. As for the case 3b (the subjective reconstitution of the ex-official model) it cannot be denied that it looks similar to a "leap of faith" taken by individuals in preindustrial society. Yet here again, the overall context is quite different: it is, in a sense, comparable to a consumer decision and structurally similar to 3a.

And what about unbelief? In a social order in which religion is embodied in the form of institutional specialization the "official" model of religion not only defines belief but also establishes a cut-off point beyond which starts unbelief. The social fact unbelief is, in effect, constituted by institutional definition. The sociologist may therefore adapt the definition of religious experts to his research procedures.

The situation is somewhat more complicated if there are two or more competing "official" models. Evidently unbelief will be then a socially differentiated and, literally, a heterogeneous social fact. It is very likely that it will, if I may use this expression, "get blurred at the edges." Nevertheless, the sociologist's difficulties will be merely technical—although at the level of research operations considerable. He defines unbelief in relation to several "official" models. But if these do not divide the "territory" among themselves in a clear-cut fashion, what is one man's belief is another's unbelief. Is the sociologist to decide which is which?

A quite different and basic problem is to be faced, however, if religion is no longer represented in society exclusively by specialized institutions. The sociologist cannot continue to use the various "ex-official" models as the basis of operational definitions of unbelief. He must include models of socialization that contain no specifically religious representations. There could be, apparently, as many operational definitions of unbelief as there are socially objectivated models of socialization, whether these are oriented to a sacred cosmos or derived from ideological systems. This difficulty is serious, but more serious is the fact that some of these models will not provide cut-off points for unbelief. Evidently, unbelief will become, for the sociologist, an extremely arbitrary methodological construct.

We live in a period of transition in which a particular social form of religion, institutional specialization, is on the wane. Belief—in the traditional sense in which the sociologist used the term—is undergoing a radical transformation. Unbelief, on the other hand, is about to disappear entirely as a social fact. If this hypothesis is correct the only way to study the socio-psychological phenomena that were traditionally designated by the concept of unbelief will be by a technically and theoretically very difficult analysis of various kinds of highly privatized subjective *belief* systems. The notion of unbelief may be heuristically unproductive even today.

2

THE HISTORICAL BACKGROUND
OF UNBELIEF

·

ROBERT N. BELLAH

> Some will ask if I believe all that this book
> contains, and I will not know how to answer.
> Does the word *belief*, used as they will use
> it, belong to our age; can I think of the
> world as there and I as judging it?
>
> WILLIAM BUTLER YEATS

Unbelief, like theology, is a product of the Greek mind, one
might almost say, of the mind of Plato. In Book X of the
Laws, Plato argues for necessary theological beliefs: the existence of God, the immortality of the soul, and the moral government of the world. Unbelief in these propositions is a
crime and punishable with five years of solitary confinement
for a first offense and death for a second. Such notions are on
the whole quite alien to the Bible. Where the word "belief"
is used to translate biblical Hebrew and Greek it means not
the "belief that" of Plato, but "belief in," a matter not of
cognitive assent but of faith, trust, and obedience.

The background for Plato's thinking is, of course, the intellectual revolution in Greece associated with the Sophists
and Socrates. This great change, so lamented by Nietzsche and
Heidegger, involved a shift from unself-conscious expression
through mythical forms, even of such sophisticated thinkers
as Heraclitus and Parmenides, to the highly self-conscious
concern with whether myths are "really true" of the Sophists,
and a search for more stable bases of orientation than myth
by Socrates and Plato (though the highly artful use of myth
by Socrates and Plato raises a number of questions which must
be left aside). The problem of unbelief arose with the first
stratum of free intellectuals to appear in human history, and
Plato was deeply concerned with coping with its corrosive effects. The Bible was not, on the whole, created by a similarly

self-conscious intellectual strata, but by religious and political enthusiasts much closer to the common religious conscience. Questions of where to put one's faith, in idols or in the one God, and questions as to what kind of obedience the one God demands are central to the Bible, but such issues of purely cognitive validity are of very minor import. In general we can say that, until the eighteenth century, or even perhaps until the nineteenth, the problem of nonbelief has been limited to relatively small groups of intellectuals, cultural elites. The masses have been afflicted not with nonbelief but with over-belief, at least from the point of religious orthodoxy, in a dismaying variety of magical notions, superstitions, and taboos.

It is important to realize that Plato's theology is not in fact an accurate apprehension of traditional religion. It is the self-conscious intellectual's translation of that religion into terms that he can understand. The intellectual in the West, including the Islamic world, from Plato to Rousseau, has been in a very difficult situation relative to whether or not he "believes" that theology. Almost inevitably he cannot believe the version of the religion which is current among the (largely illiterate) common people. He requires either a highly complex intellectual structure of "proof" to underpin religious belief (Thomas) or direct mystical illumination (Suhrawardi), or a combination of both (Augustine, Al-Ghazzali). But intellectuals have been highly conscious of the social utility of popular belief. Avicenna argued that the masses required vivid images, not philosophic demonstration, and only such a religion would be of any use in controlling them.[1] Spinoza's *Tractatus Theologico-Politicus* emphasize the moral-political control function of biblical religion. As late as Rousseau we find a reassertion of Plato's position in Book X of the *Laws*. Book IV, Chapter VIII of the *Social Contract* requires subscription to the "dogmas of civil religion" which include the existence of God, the life to come, the happiness of the just, and the punishment of the wicked. Failure to subscribe to these beliefs is to be punished by banishment; falsely subscribing to them by death.

There seems to be a deep conflict in the minds of philoso-

1. F. Rahman; *Prophecy in Islam: Philosophy and Orthodoxy* (London: Allen and Unwin, 1958), pp. 42–44.

phers in the Christian and Islamic worlds, at least through the eighteenth century, between the complexity of their own beliefs and doubts and their sense of the absolute necessity of clear and simple beliefs for the preservation of social order. This led to dissimulation of what the philosophers really believed and to severe accusations against those philosophers who were thought to have said too much publicly. Partly this was because of danger from the fanatical mob or overzealous autocrats. But mainly it was a matter of a responsible assessment of the possible consequences of general consumption of esoteric views.

Yet we may ask whether the extreme anxiety in the cultural and political elites of Christian and Muslim societies about the propagation of skeptical views was indeed justified. Certainly from the nineteenth century on it became possible to assert that there is no God, no afterlife, and no eternal reward and punishment without, as in previous centuries, going to jail or the stake, and social order has not collapsed. Even the very grave instabilities which have arisen in the last two centuries do not seem to be mainly attributable to the decline of orthodox belief, though some might argue the point. Why in recent times has orthodox belief come to be openly challenged by large numbers of people and why have the consequences of this challenge not been more disastrous?

The rise of what would classically have been considered nonbelief in the modern world has been correlated with the enormous expansion of just those classes among whom nonbelief always was a problem: the self-conscious intellectuals. The growth of an educated elite continued steadily from the seventeenth century. The nineteenth century saw an enormous reversal of centuries-old literacy statistics as many Western nations began to approach total literacy. Educational systems were expanded and continue to expand to the point where in some parts of the United States over 50 percent of the youth population goes to college. Necessarily, subjects which were formerly the property of tiny literate minorities are now open to the public. Traditional forms of thought control have become unworkable.

This vast increase in literacy and education in the past two centuries has been intimately related to the rise of antiauthoritarianism as a major cultural theme. The notion of the dignity of the individual and his inherent freedom from purely external authority has become widely accepted. Hierarchical modes of organization have been challenged, not only in politics, but in the family, education, and religion as well. In place of hierarchy the stress is on self-control, autonomous choice of values, and subsequent self-regulation. Obviously we are far from lacking external constraints in any modern society, but the trend is to leave more to the individual's discretion and control. Culture, from being conceived as an exoskeleton, is becoming an endoskeleton, something self-consciously chosen and internalized, not immutably given from without.

Both the increase of education and the rise of antiauthoritarianism are part of a vast social transformation and are closely linked to each other. Autonomous self-regulation requires a highly individuated, self-conscious, and educated person. On the other hand such an individual cannot easily accept the dictates of arbitrary external authority. Again, this linkage is not exactly new in human society, except in scale. Intellectuals have never felt easy with external systems of authority. Plato, unable to accept the traditional myths of his society, made up his own. Augustine, feeling acutely uncomfortable with the literal, fundamentalist beliefs of his mother, had to have Ambrose's intellectually convincing arguments before he could become a Christian. Pascal, losing confidence in purely intellectual statements of the faith, found meaning in it as a true apprehension of the greatness and misery of man.

The intellectual has always needed to find a religious form which genuinely expressed his own individuality. This was seldom the naïve faith which he learned at his mother's knee. Often only through the greatest suffering has a coherent and authentic position been reached. Conscious of the agony of the struggle and of the dangers of doubt, intellectuals before modern times—Plato, Augustine, Al-Ghazzali, even Rousseau—have been ready to impose on others what in themselves had been so personal an acquisition. But in modern times as the intellectual classes have expanded this has become less and less possible. Broader and broader strata of the population have demanded the freedom of conscience which the philosophers traditionally arrogated only for themselves.

This change has gone along with and has been deeply interrelated with a vast change in the fundamental presuppositions of Western thought. The ontological split between subject and object and the assumption that the most fundamental truths can be objectively demonstrated have been called into question. Convictions about the meaning and value of life have become regarded as inherently personal and acquired through personal experience rather than objective demonstration. This has not, in the main, been accomplished through accepting the other side of the old dichotomy and collapsing into subjectivism and relativity. Rather there has been, especially since Kant, the increasing realization that, as in the words of Yeats [2] at the head of this essay, the most fundamental cultural forms are neither objective nor subjective, but the very way in which the two are related. This also was by no means entirely new, but involved a rediscovery and generalization of elements deep within the mystical tradition of Western thought and religion. This way of thinking allowed the collapse of the traditional certainties without the loss of faith and commitment, an apprehension beautifully expressed by Wallace Stevens when he says, "We believe without belief, beyond belief." [3] This shivering of the objective notion of belief allows a reassessment of religion in general and provides a key to why the collapse of belief has not been followed by an end of religion.

It is my contention that what I would call "the objectivist fallacy," namely the confusion of belief and religion, which is found only in the religious traditions deeply influenced by Greek thought—Christianity and Islam—and is almost completely missing in China and India, involves a fundamental misapprehension of the nature of religion, both the religion of the masses and of the cultural elite. Not infrequently the educated have even admitted that such beliefs were only convenient fictions—"noble lies"—for the control of the masses, while their own religion was more a matter of personal illumination. But I would contend that this was a sophisticated error in understanding the religious life of the ordinary man, which has never been primarily a matter of objectivist belief.

It is true that the intellectuals of the Church accepted ob-

2. Quoted by Richard Ellmann in his *Yeats, The Man and the Masks* (New York: Dutton, 1948), p. 263.
3. *Collected Poems* (New York: Knopf, 1954), p. 336.

jectivist assumptions. In crowning Greek reason with biblical
revelation, they assimilated revelation to an objectivist cognitive framework as though what was revealed were "higher"
cognitive truths rather than the direct confrontation with the
Divine that the Bible is concerned with. But a more contemporary understanding of religious life would perhaps give us
a more accurate apprehension of the real vitality of the
Church down through the ages. As Yeats informs us, "Man can
embody truth but he cannot know it." [4] This would seem to
be the case at least with the most important truths. Religion
is embodied truth, not known truth, and it has in fact been
transmitted far more through narrative, image, and enactment
than through definitions and logical demonstrations. The
Church is above all the body of Christ, the embodiment of its
truth, and it cannot be discerned through counting those who
assent to certain dogmas. The life of the Church has been its
capacity to produce human beings who base their lives on the
paradigm of the Gospels, the saints and martyrs, even modest
and hidden ones, who have constantly renewed it and are re-
newing it today. If the vitality of the Church has rested in its
capacity to reproduce itself in the image of Christ it is understandable that it can survive the collapse of dogmatic orthodoxies.

Of course, the centuries-long concentration, at least in some
parts of the Church, on orthodox belief must have had some
social meaning, as any sociologist would know. "Mistakes," if
indeed this is one, do not perpetuate themselves for no reason.
The effort to maintain orthodox belief has primarily been an
effort to maintain authority rather than faith. It was part of
a whole hierarchical way of thinking about social control,
deeply embedded in traditional society. Functional equivalents
to Christian and Islamic orthodoxy can even be discerned in
the establishment of Chu Hsi Confucianism in post-Sung
China and Tokugawa Japan, though, since the Greek assumptions about belief were missing, these orthodoxies were but a
shadow compared to those of religions farther west, and
crumbled away in modern times with much less outcry. When
new, less authoritarian modes of social control become established, however, faith does not necessarily disappear. In its
genuine form faith is never a matter of external coercion, of

4. In Ellmann, *Yeats*, p. 285.

what Paul Tillich called "belief in the unbelievable." Its modes have changed along with the great shift in religious consciousness of modern times, but it has continued to live both within and without the Church. Indeed the apprehension that faith is deeply embedded in man's existential situation and a part of the very structure of his experience, first powerfully expressed in modern times by Pascal and strongly reiterated in the early nineteenth century by Kierkegaard, has become an insistent note in twentieth-century religion. This understanding of religion seems to provide a more phenomenologically accurate understanding of ordinary religious experience than the assumption that it is primarily a matter of cognitive belief.

The modern shift in the understanding of religion has been greatly strengthened by the cultural revolution brought on by modern scholarship. It is now possible to move out of the cultural frame dominated by the Greek cognitive bias in both time and space in a way that was scarcely dreamed of two hundred years ago. Already in the eighteenth century a few thinkers, such as Vico and Herder, were beginning to discover in the poetic sagas of early European peoples ways of thinking quite different from philosophic thought. Vico, for example, came to see the world of Homer as far more dominated by symbolic words and actions than by logical argumentation. He even had the genius to discover that the street culture of Naples was in some ways more "Homeric" than was the culture of the educated salons.

The nineteenth century discovered not only scores of preliterate societies that tended to confirm Vico's and Herder's intuitions, but also great literate civilizations based on cultural premises very different from those of the West. In these highly cultivated societies, the "rational beliefs" of "natural theology," those things which it was assumed would be obvious to all men in all times and places, failed to appear—such beliefs as the existence of God and the immortality of the soul, for instance, both vehemently denied by Buddhism. Here inner experience and expressive gesture were far more highly regarded than creeds and syllogistic arguments. A great and influential religion like Zen Buddhism, for example, denied the value of any beliefs at all and Taoism showed the same tendency. Even Confucianism refused to speculate on the "exis-

tence" of spirits and held that it was enough if one simply
paid them proper respect "as if" they existed. More significant, of course, than the lack of certain views the West had
virtually identified with religion, was the fact that a rich, complex, and compelling religious life seemed to be possible in
their absence. Further evidence that oriental religions are not
on the whole based on cognitive belief is the almost total failure of the conflict between religion and science to materialize
in the Eastern milieu, even though in the minds of some
Western scholars it "ought" to have.

This broadening of the cultural horizon has played into
and reinforced postdogmatic religiosity in the West. There
seems little doubt, for example, that the modern liturgical revival has been stimulated by the recognition of the centrality
of ritual and symbol in primitive and Eastern religions as well
as in earlier periods in the history of the church itself. The
failure of the predictions of nineteenth-century rationalists
and positivists as to the impending end of religion have not
only become evident in the increased vitality of many aspects of Judaism and Christianity, but also in the vast array
of new religious and semireligious movements which have
arisen. Few of these tendencies evince any concern with the
dread conflict between religion and science, mainly because it
is assumed that religion is not a matter of objective-cognitive
assertion which might conflict with science, but a symbolic
form within which one comes to terms with one's fate.

When to these examples is added the fact that those most
vociferous in their denunciation of "religion," the Marxists for
example, are discovered to live in the grip of a great arche-
typal myth, the whole idea that religion can be ended by cognitive argument or disproof becomes even less tenable. Instead, the conclusion grows ever stronger that religion is a part
of the species life of man, as central to his self-definition as
speech. But the very plethora of religious phenomena in the
contemporary scene, the lack of an apparent consensus, raises
another serious question. Has religion retreated from the public sphere? Has it become totally privatized? Is it a purely
personal escape from social and political urgencies which
serves only to divert and titillate while the world slips ever
more deeply into chaos?

One aspect of the great modern religious transformation involves the internalization of authority, and this has profound consequences for religion. Of course there have been major breakdowns and counter-tendencies. Politically, fascism represents a new quest for outer authority and communism an incomplete or arrested internalization. Religiously, new fundamentalisms of various sorts have emerged in recent times. But if internalization has been the main direction, as I think it has, this might argue in favor of the notion of increasing privatization.

The contemporary religious consciousness certainly has a strong note of innerness. There is an intense preoccupation with authentic personal experience. Anything which is merely given by authority, which is compelling only because of the source from which it comes and not because it rouses genuine personal response, is suspect. There is even an increasing turn to the exploration of "inner space" and a feeling that much of the givenness of everyday life is a sham, a put-on, something suffocatingly constricting. Perhaps the contemporary equivalent to traditional nonbelievers would be those who do not experience this dimension of innerness, who accept the literalness of everyday as the one and sole reality. This contemporary turn within is intensely preoccupied with the self, as mystical religion has always been. And yet this quest for personal experience, personal choice, and personal authenticity is only partly identical with what is usually meant by privatization. The crux of the issue, again as it has always been in mystical religion, is the relation of this self, myself, and other selves, the universe itself. Only when the definition of self remains constricted to the petty private self, to self-worship, does the concept of privatization become relevant. A religious impulse which identifies the self with others, with man, with the universe, may be inner and individual, but it is not private. Far from making a purely personal sense of well-being its only goal (though by no means necessarily rejecting it), it can motivate to sacrificial involvement with others and suffering unto death for their sakes.

Indeed the search for personal authenticity has been more often united with, rather than divorced from, group membership and social purpose. Nationalism, with its frequently religious overtones, is an obvious example. A specific example is black nationalism in the United States, where a "religion of black power" has been discerned. The literature of black power reveals [5] that it is not economic or political grievances, though they are acute, that propel the activists but rather a profound need for inner worth and authenticity, a feeling that through the movement one can overcome self-hatred and the unconscious rejection of one's own blackness. The movement is seen not only as personally redemptive but also redemptive for the black community and perhaps universally redemptive as well. The great themes are love, sacrifice, and communion. Any nationalism runs the risk of becoming socially "private," of refusing to identify with any outside one's own community. But the controlling universalistic imagery may keep alive the notion of an ultimate union of humanity.

As another example, what I have called elsewhere "civil religion in America" has continued to produce new ways in which personal [6] and social vision can be fused. I have in mind a rather extraordinary phenomenon, the Peace Corps. This movement, sometimes known symbolically as "the sons of Kennedy," [7] though ostensibly a government agency, is actually more like a secular monastic order whose members take a voluntary vow of poverty and go out to work for the alleviation of the sufferings of the world. From the beginning it has been recognized that its significance is more (not "merely") expressive and symbolic than practical. The Peace Corps has almost consciously capitalized on the quest for personal meaning and authenticity among American college youth in the 1960s. The mode of operation of the Peace Corps—the lack of bureaucracy, the autonomy of the volunteer, his poverty—has from the beginning been recognized as perhaps more important than its objective achievements. The Peace Corps has been an expressive statement of the volunteers to themselves, to their own society and to the world, of certain value com-

5. Vincent Harding, "The Religion of Black Power," in Donald R. Cutler, ed., *The Religious Situation: 1968* (New York: Beacon, 1968), pp. 3–38.

6. *Daedalus*, 1967; reprinted in *The Religious Situation: 1968*.

7. The analysis of the religious dimension of the Peace Corps has been developed by Ricardo B. Zuniga in his thesis, "The Peace Corps as a Value-Oriented Movement," presented to the department of Social Relations at Harvard, 1969.

mitments which are basic to the American civil religion, in whose context Kennedy first formulated it. But partly because of the Vietnam War and more basically because of the division of the world into affluent and poverty-stricken people, the Peace Corps has had to try to transcend the American civil religion. To the extent that it has been unable to do so, it has failed to achieve its full potential.

Among a large section of precisely the most affluent, best educated, white youth in the United States (and I suspect this is the case elsewhere as well), nationalism has lost all appeal, however much they may sympathize with the nationalism of others. Intensely suspicious of purely personal ambition, of merely "making it" in the affluent society, they pursue their quest for personal authenticity outside the claim of any purely communal loyalty. Many of them seem, somewhat inchoately, to have taken as their first tenet the identification with and responsibility for the sufferings of others everywhere in the world. They seem a sort of latter-day embodiment of Comte's "religion of humanity." The recent worldwide outburst of youth in search of social justice, but motivated more by personal values than class resentments, is a kind of vivid surfacing of a vast value consensus which has been growing in the modern world and whose actualization youth impatiently demands. This great international moral movement which already has its saints and martyrs, its Gandhis and its Martin Luther Kings, who entirely transcend national identification, may be, though only half conscious of itself, the most significant religious movement of our times.

It is clear that this nascent religion of humanity is not simply at odds with existing moral and religious communities. Its antecedents include the Western ideological movements of socialism and liberal humanism, Christianity, and in the East Buddhism and Hinduism. Its chief tenets, the sanctity and dignity of the individual and the full flowering of human personality, have their roots in many traditions. But precisely because it is so intensely individual at the same time that it is social and moral, it is not a new "ism," a new exclusive community either of church or state. Instead, all existing churches, parties, and states are vulnerable to its criticisms. All, whether the Communist party, the Catholic Church, or the government of the United States, are under intense pressure to realize human freedom and human fulfillment and all, of course, resist to some extent, however much they give lip service. But while the practical problems of the world seem more insoluble than ever and there is little objective ground for optimism, it should not be forgotten that this great international community—a community without boundaries—continues to grow and to call forth the self-sacrifice of many. It is worth noting that Comte's rather ghastly version, still caught in the Western overestimation of belief, with its syncretistic rituals and artificial calendar of saints, has not been realized. This international moral community, which I suggest is immediately tangible when any two people feel that their mutual humanity transcends their commitment to any particular group or groups to which either of them happens to belong, is not the product of any objective creed or enforced dogma. It is the supreme contemporary example of how a stress on inner authenticity and autonomy can yet have the most profound social and moral consequences.

By arguing that religion and belief are not the same, that their identification is found in one great but historically discrete cultural tradition and not outside it,[8] and that even in that tradition it is no longer possible to maintain, nonbelief becomes generic to contemporary consciousness, religious and nonreligious alike. What is generally called secularization and the decline of religion appear as the decline of the external control system of religion and the decline of traditional religious belief. But religion, as that symbolic form through which man comes to terms with the antinomies of his being has not declined, indeed cannot decline unless man's nature ceases to be problematic to him. The difference between the committed and the indifferent, those with vision and those without it, exists today as it always has, but it seems unlikely that the proportions of the two groups have changed appreciably. If anything, the twentieth century has probably produced more than its share of the committed and the visionary.

If a quantitative decline of religion must be rejected as a characteristic of modern society, it is clear that modern re-

8. This point and indeed much of this paper are indebted to Wilfred Smith's unpublished paper "Believing as a Religious Category with special reference to the Qur'an," and other of his writings.

ligious consciousness is different from that in previous epochs. For one thing, a great shift in the balance between elite and mass religiosity has taken place. The unexamined magical and religious conceptions of nonliterate or semiliterate strata, which used to make up the bulk of the religious life in any society, has come more and more under conscious inspection and critical evaluation, as levels of literacy and education reach unprecedented peaks. This has involved the erosion of numerous beliefs and practices, some formerly considered essential to orthodoxy, but many peripheral or of doubtful orthodoxy. The old elite notion that religion involves a personal quest for meaning, that it must express the deepest dimensions of the self and in no way violate individual conscience, has been generalized as the dominant conception of religion in modern society. Enormous expansion in our historical and comparative knowledge of religion and of its social and psychological dimensions has made a naïve literalism impossible among ever larger numbers of people.

Yet the ultimate questions about the meaning of life are asked as insistently, perhaps more insistently, than ever. In one sense, this process leaves the organized church in the same place that it has always been: it is as necessary as ever to take up the cross and follow the one who was crucified outside the gates of the city. In another sense it relieves the church of a great burden. It no longer has to provide the social cement for an imperfect social order; it no longer has to double as the Nocturnal Council of Plato's *Laws*.[9] In a nonauthoritarian world the church can only be, as it was originally, a voluntary society. It becomes possible to recognize the operation of the Holy Spirit, to use Christian symbolism, in groups and individuals who would not call themselves Christian and to recognize a biblical mold in movements which proclaim their vociferous anti-Christianity. Christians can join with non-Christians in discerning the emerging value concen-

9. I do not intend to make Plato a villain. His own views were very complex. Books I and II of the *Laws* present one of the profoundest analyses of ritual ever written and do not suffer from cognitive bias. In making the man Socrates the very heart of his teaching Plato seems to recognize the importance of embodied truth. And yet there is little doubt that Book X of the *Laws,* with its troublesome implications, has had enormous influence.

sus, in criticizing existing values in terms of the standard of common humanity and personal integrity, and in insisting that values to which societies are already committed be actualized for all social groups. Multiplicity does not mean chaos. This, however imperfectly, has already been shown in America. Effective moral and political action can be carried out by those with widely different religious motivations.

In a word, much has been taken away, but much has been given. The modern world is as alive with religious possibility as any epoch in human history. It is no longer possible to divide mankind into believers and nonbelievers. All believe something and the lukewarm and those of little faith are to be found inside as well as outside the churches. The spirit bloweth where it listeth, and men of passionate integrity are found in strange places. If we have outgrown the idea of mission, we have probably also to outgrow the idea of dialogue, as though separated human groups must talk across a chasm. Christians, along with other men, are called on to build the boundaryless community, the body of man identified with the body of Christ, though all men are free to symbolize it in their own way.

THE STUDY OF UNBELIEF:
PERSPECTIVES ON RESEARCH

.

CHARLES Y. GLOCK

In earlier chapters Thomas Luckmann and Robert Bellah have considered conceptual and historical questions in the study of unbelief. It is my assignment to consider research strategies for future study. What kind of research is called for if we are to advance effectively beyond present understanding of the phenomenon?

It is evident from work already done that rather different views obtain as to what is worth studying about unbelief. Indeed, the paucity of work suggests the existence of a widespread opinion that the topic does not warrant study at all.

The problem in part is that unbelief can be studied from such a great variety of vantage points that their sheer number makes it difficult to choose among them. The choice is made the more difficult by the absence of a research tradition to help decide what next and best to do.

Research traditions rarely if ever get started because they are planned for. For the most part someone who has an idea pursues it effectively, and others are thereby persuaded to build on his accomplishments. That matters usually take this course is no signal that the process is inevitable.

The position I shall adopt is that a paradigm may be a functional substitute for tradition in guiding research strategies. Setting forth the range of possibilities in a systematic fashion cannot establish what we ought to be doing and in what sequence. By making clear the alternatives, however, a paradigm can make the choice perhaps easier and perhaps more rational.

Research on unbelief must first confront the related problems of conceptualization and measurement, and it is at this point that the present chapter begins. Luckmann and Bellah have given us a good start on conceptualization, and I have sought to elaborate on and formalize their ideas to the end of producing a conceptualization which is at once abstract, ahistorical, and cross-culturally applicable. With a conceptualization and method of measurement in mind, I next consider the kinds of questions which may be asked about unbelief and the means appropriate for their investigation. The chapter ends with a recommendation for a collaborative research project on unbelief—a project intended to produce in consort rather than independently basic information and evidence which we shall all require if unbelief is to be investigated effectively.

A Conceptualization of Unbelief

The starting point for the study of any phenomenon is a way to conceptualize it so that it may be subjected to sustained inquiry. This task has not been accomplished for the study of unbelief. So far, at any rate, confusion and ambiguity rather than clarity and precision have characterized usage of the term.

Part of the difficulty has been to establish the boundaries for inquiry. Unbelief can characterize a wide spectrum of the human experience; there can be unbelief in God, in astrology, in free will, in birth control; indeed, in virtually anything. What boundaries, if any, ought to be imposed and how are they to be determined?

A second problem is one common to all attempts at conceptualization: arriving at a formula both culture-free and sensitive to variations within and among different cultures. It has yet to be settled whether this criterion can be met for unbelief or, if it can be met, by what means.

Ambiguity has also arisen out of the tendency to associate unbelief and belief with religion. There has been controversy about whether such an association is warranted as well as about how religious beliefs and unbeliefs are to be distinguished from nonreligious ones. What constitutes religious belief when there is no religious institution has also been a source of contention, and some have suggested that the concept of unbelief has meaning only where religion is institutionally separated.

It is probably not possible to remove all ambiguity centering on unbelief or to obtain agreement from everyone—social scientists, churchmen, theologians, philosophers, the man in the street—on any one definition. But unless a formalization of the concept can be produced about which some degree of consensus coalesces, it is doubtful that unbelief can be raised to the level of a scientific concept or become a subject of fruitful inquiry.

The starting place for conceptualization is with the boundary problem—with trying to pinpoint just what it is we mean to include as unbelief. The choices seem virtually infinite; yet it is evident from the way unbelief is used in both ordinary and scientific discourse that we do not think of the options as being so varied. Whether there is belief or unbelief in birth control or in free love or in evolution or in a myriad other things is not decisive in making the identification. Ordinarily, it is one connotation, rather than a variety, which comes to mind.

The connotation will be expressed in very different ways. The man in the street will probably verbalize it as unbelief in Christ or God or Allah or Krishna. For others, unbelief will be the absence of a belief in any higher power, whether conceived in deistic, theistic, or pantheistic forms. Robert Bellah talks about it as "the literateness of everyday as the one and only reality." Some others probably feel that the essence of unbelief is captured in the notion of anomie.

These ideas are at once very different and very alike. Their common theme is that unbelief is constituted by a failure to experience the "sacred" and to feel—indeed to be—subject to its authority. Where the ideas diverge is their vision of the "sacred"; but even here, the differences are apparent as well as real.

There is agreement, I would suggest, that the central problem to which the "sacred" is addressed is that of the meaning of being. The "sacred" provides a perspective on life which transforms it into something beyond "the literateness of everyday life." There is also agreement that whatever the nature of the "sacred," it is transcendent of self. Whether thought of as God, as Nirvana, as ultimate reality, as the divine essence in all of us, or as the experience of personal meaning and authenticity, the "sacred," when believed, is an authority beyond self with the power to constrain self.

There is a distinction to be made, however, between supernatural and simply transcendent or natural conceptions of the source of "sacred" authority. In supernatural conceptions, the "sacred" is ordained by an otherworldly power to which this world is subject. The power may be held to reside in an anthropomorphic God or gods. It may also be a law of creation without deity, such as the Hindu idea of Nirvana or the ancient Chinese notion of a natural harmony of order in the universe. Indeed, modern science offers its own version of a harmony of order to which we may be said to be subject. In natural conception, an atheistic or agnostic position is taken on the existence of the supernatural. In this the authority of the "sacred" is internal to the beliefs themselves; one is captured by them, beholden to them, but there is no God or law of creation to say that this is the way it must be.

Supernatural conceptions of the "sacred" may be, borrowing Bellah's terms, objectivist or subjectivist; so may natural conceptions. We may speak, then, of four types of belief: objectivist-supernatural, objectivist-natural, subjectivist-supernatural, and subjectivist-natural.

Objectivist-supernatural belief is constituted by literal acceptance and internalization of a supernatural interpretation of meaning set forth and objectified in doctrine, dogma, and creed by an institution (usually a church), by a person, or by tradition. The doctrines of the Roman Catholic Church, the claims of a Father Divine, the Hindu law of karma, primitive conceptions of mana, all qualify as referents for objectivist-supernatural belief. They all contain a supernatural vision of the "sacred" and are set forth objectively, so that they may be accepted or rejected by those exposed to them.

Objectivist-natural belief is essentially similar to objectivist-supernatural belief except that the source of the interpretation of meaning is not supernatural. An orthodox Marxist would be an objectivist-natural believer, as would a National Socialist in Nazi Germany. Existentialists would also be so classified, as would those who accept any naturalistic philosophy or religion set forth and objectified by an institution by a person, or by tradition.

Subjectivist belief, unlike objectivist belief, is arrived at by the individual's working out for himself a meaning for his life which transcends everyday experience. Such elements of objectivist belief as may be contained in subjectivist faith are privatized interpretations rather than literal acceptance of objectified doctrines or creeds. Subjectivist belief is, or is close to being, unique to the individual, whereas objectivist belief is generally common to some group. This does not necessarily mean that there will be as many subjectivist beliefs as there are subjectivist believers; working independently, it is quite possible that people may arrive at the same conclusions. This, however, is a matter for empirical resolution and we shall have to have data before we can decide whether subjectivist beliefs can be meaningfully ordered.

Subjectivist-supernatural belief includes a conception of a supernatural entity—not a conventional entity, but one worked out by the individual for himself. The supernatural may be conceived of in theistic, deistic, or pantheistic terms, but it is always some force beyond this worldly comprehension to which this world and specifically, the subjectivist, supernatural believer is subject. For the subjectivist believer the supernatural functions as warrant for what he holds to be "sacred." The *subjectivist-natural* believer needs no such warrant. It is enough for him to feel that what he believes is specifically unalterable for himself; he is incapable of brooking an alternative.

Logically the system allows for only one definition of unbelief—namely, the failure to score as a believer in any of the four belief categories. Unbelief may also be defined, however, from the perspective of each belief category; thus, one may speak of objectivist-supernatural believers and unbelievers, objectivist-natural believers and unbelievers, and so on. Additional definitions of unbelief may stem from narrower conceptions of objectivist belief. Thus, from the perspective of Christian belief, a non-Christian would be an unbeliever, as would a non-Communist from a Marxist perspective. Consensus around any one of these definitions of unbelief cannot be expected, of course; nor is it necessary for research. Given this range of definitions, it is possible through research to test all of them to determine which one or combination is the most fruitful in illuminating sociological inquiry. It may turn out that considerably greater significance attaches to whether a person is an objectivist-supernatural believer or not than whether he fits into any belief category or not. It is also pos-

sible and perhaps likely that we will find the determining
factor to be, not whether or not a person is a believer, but
what kind and how strong a believer he is.

But these are questions for empirical investigation; we shall
have more to say about them later. Returning to the proposed
conceptualization, it is clear that it only begins to order the
alternatives and that considerable refinement of categories and
the introduction of subcategories will be required to operationalize it and make it subject to measurement. But the more
immediate question we must ask is whether it clarifies the
conceptual confusion which has plagued us in the past. Is its
solution to the boundary problem a satisfactory one? Is it at
once both cross-cultural and sensitive to variations between
and within cultures? Does it make feasible the study of unbelief in settings other than those in which religion is institutionalized? And is its distinction between supernatural and
natural belief a reasonable way to separate religious from
nonreligious belief?

These are questions the reader may wish to address for himself. For present purposes, it will be assumed that answers will
be generally in the affirmative and that we may proceed with
the other issues to which the chapter is addressed.

From Conceptualization to Measurement

To study belief is to find a way to measure it; conceptualization is only the first step, of course, in a necessarily long and
arduous process which we most often tend to short circuit
because the time, energy, and resources needed are, or are
assumed to be, beyond our command. It seems wise for present
purposes to consider what is involved in pursuing the task of
measurement without compromise. For this exercise we shall
assume that the conceptualization to be operationalized is the
one we have just described.

Since that conceptualization is intended to be applicable
cross-culturally and ahistorically, one of the alternatives open
to us is to consider a means of measurement which is also
cross-cultural and ahistorical. Practically speaking, this aim
calls for an instrument which could be administered under any
and all social and cultural conditions and which would validly

and reliably distinguish among types of believers and unbelievers.

The conceptualization is designed to allow such flexibility
but in practice would demand operationalization at only the
highest level of abstraction. At best, a common measuring
instrument would probably allow no more than the classification of believers into the four types—supernatural-objectivists,
supernatural-subjectivists, and so on—with unbelievers con-
stituting a residual category.

It would seem offhand that measurement at so high a level
of abstraction would not be useful because of the tremendous
amount of residual variation within any one category. For
example, orthodox Roman Catholics, Hindus, Buddhists, and
Muslims would all be lumped together as supernatural-objectivist believers. To make finer distinctions, however, would
require the introduction of culture-bound indicators of belief
and unbelief, the adoption of different instruments for different cultures, and the effective abandonment of culture-free
measurement. It may be that residual variation makes culture-
free measurement untenable, but given the advantages of such
a measurement, some investment in exploring its feasibility
would seem desirable.

Culture-bound measurement allows for greater precision
than does culture-free measurement; but—except possibly in
highly homogeneous primitive cultures—a fairly high level of
abstraction would still be required for an instrument which
can be commonly administered throughout a given culture.
For there is likely to be a variety of referents rather than a
single one for objectivist belief and rather differential exposure to the alternatives on the part of subgroups.

Consider, for example, the prospect of developing a common
measuring instrument for administration in the West, or even
only in the nation-states of Western Europe. Among the referents for objectivist belief would be Roman Catholicism, several
varieties of Protestantism and Orthodoxy, Judaism, varieties
of Christian and non-Christian sects, existentialism in its
several forms, several varieties of Marxism and socialism, and
so on. But there would not have been equal exposure to all of
these forms of belief. Some, for example, will have been exposed to a form of existentialism and will have rejected it;

most would probably have never heard of existentialism. Jews will probably have been exposed to Roman Catholicism, in the sense that they know it to exist and have some understanding of the tenets the Church espouses. However, their unbelief in Roman Catholicism is of quite a different order than the unbelief of persons reared in Catholicism who have lost their faith along the way.

Even if it is possible to comprehend all of this variety in a single instrument, it would only be common in small part and that part would have to use indicators at a high level of abstraction—though not quite so high as for a culture-free instrument. Again, one would have to expect a considerable amount of residual variation within categories of classification.

Precision can be improved without sacrificing a common instrument by narrowing the conception of belief and unbelief and/or by limiting investigation to more homogeneous populations. For example, belief and unbelief studied only from the perspective of Christian doctrine among persons who had been reared in that faith could be accomplished with considerable precision using common measurement. Such a choice obviously introduces its own compromises, but it is an available option.

Ideally, we should probably aim for not one but a set of interrelated instruments, ranging from cruder, more abstract ones which would be culture-free to more highly refined and precise ones of more limited applicability. Thus, for any given inquiry, we could choose that instrument or combination of them which best suit the particular research purposes. To move in this direction, we must first arrive at a conceptualization which we consider to be worth trying to operationalize. If we are serious about making unbelief the subject of sustained inquiry, we should probably take this step collaboratively rather than independently and competitively. Once we have agreed that a conceptualization makes theoretical sense, we should then want to proceed to see if it has empirical validity; if it proves itself, we can begin the process of moving from concept to measurement.

There are various approaches we can take. My own predilection—thinking still in ideal typical terms—is to follow a course which will allow us to discover whether a conceptualization as broad as the one suggested earlier can be operationalized to produce both more abstract culture-free modes of measurement and less abstract culture-bound and group-bound ones. To this end we should have to choose rather contrasting settings in which to pursue exploratory work; and, of course, the more such settings, the better.

For each setting our first task will be to refine our conceptualization so as to establish, insofar as possible without empirical work, the referents for supernatural and natural objectivist beliefs which exist in that setting. Such a procedure involves identifying the alternative objectified belief systems to which those residing in the setting might be exposed and to which they may or may not give their allegiance. Belief systems fostered by tradition, by individuals, and by institutions would be counted as objectified belief systems. For each of these referents we will also want to tentatively establish possible criteria by which believers and unbelievers may be objectively distinguished. Presumably the same process of elaboration and refinement cannot be pursued beforehand to order varieties of subjectivist belief; by definition, this can only be done empirically.

The next step involves empirical tests of the conceptualization as elaborated for each setting. These tests would be constituted by interviews in dept with a sample of the population in the different settings, the sample could be relatively small, since no quantitative purpose is to be served by these tests. The depth interviews would be virtually open-ended at the beginning and would become more directed as the interview proceeds. The open-ended phase would be concerned with establishing the perspective from which respondents themselves view belief and unbelief. Do they consider themselves as believers or unbelievers, and by what criteria do they arrive at their judgments? As the respondent's self-definitions are exhausted, the interview can become more directed, respondents will be gradually introduced to the formal conceptualization and asked to locate themselves, if they can, within the categories of belief and unbelief which the concept provides. Throughout the interview attempts will be made to establish the saliency of the issues under discussion. It will undoubtedly be important that some measure of saliency be included in whatever instruments are finally developed.

Once collected, these interviews can be analyzed to assess

the adequacy of the conceptualization. The test would essentially comprise a comparison of the information collected from the nondirected and from the directed phases to establish goodness of fit. Do the open-ended data fit neatly into the preconceptualization?

This operation could result in the abandonment of the conceptualization and a new start, alternately, if the fit is good enough, the process of revision and refinement can begin. Refinement would involve continuation of the process of specifying the variation within the four basic categories of belief.

At this juncture, presuming the conceptualization has proved to be viable, the task of constructing instruments can begin. As suggested earlier, it would seem advisable to think in terms of a set of instruments rather than a single one. The final products might comprise: an instrument capable of being administered cross-culturally; a set of instruments each designed to be used across the board in particular cultures; and a still larger set of instruments, each designed for use among subgroups within cultures. A virtually infinite number of instruments of the last variety are possible, of course. The ones to be actually constructed would be decided by the research questions to be addressed.

The construction process would require at least one test, but more probably a series of empirical tests, of the evolving instruments. These would presumably include some effort to establish the reliability and validity of what we have been calling the culture-free instrument. To make this test we can administer the range of instruments to equivalent samples in a number of settings. The culture-free instrument would be administered uniformly in all settings. At the same time and with the same samples, the culture-bound and group-bound instruments would also be administered but, of course, only in the appropriate setting and group. This procedure would allow intrasetting comparisons, to establish consistency between the ordering produced by the culture-free and by the culture-bound data.

There is no precedent in the social sciences, so far as I know, for pursuing the task of measurement in so comprehensive and thorough a fashion. Generally, because of lack of resources, as indicated earlier, but also because we feel we have to publish quickly and without collaborators, we manage to find short-cuts to measurement if we try to operationalize our concepts at all. The old ways have not produced a set of measuring instruments on any topic which is widely accepted and cross-culturally applicable. We shall have to decide whether the phenomena of belief and unbelief are important enough to warrant trying to break with precedent.

The Purposes of Inquiry

So far, we have taken it for granted that unbelief is a subject warranting inquiry. Now, with a definition roughly in mind, we are ready to test that assumption. We shall try to catalog the questions which may be asked about unbelief and evaluate the theoretical and practical importance of finding answers. Viewed statically, three basic questions may effectively be asked about unbelief: What is its nature? What are its causes? What are its effects? The introduction of the factor of time and the possibility of change add three additional but parallel questions: What is the nature of the change? What produces it? What are or may be its effects?

The Nature of Unbelief

Whatever our theoretical interest in the study of unbelief, the initial questions we are virtually obliged to ask about it are essentially descriptive. How does it manifest itself? What are its varieties? How prevalent are the varieties? Are the varieties and their distribution always the same or are they changing? If changing, what is the nature and pace of the change? Where does it manifest itself?

These questions, like all questions about unbelief, may be asked about virtually any population configuration—about a person, a group, the members of an organization, the citizens of a nation-state, and the like. Such questions are always asked comparatively. We anticipate some variation between subjects or within a subject over time, and we should not really be interested in unbelief if no variation were to be found.

Having discovered variation, we are inexorably drawn to do more than describe it; our initial predilection is to explain it.

The Causes of Unbelief

The question of cause, like that of nature, can be formulated statically or dynamically. We can ask what causes unbelief or what produces a change in unbelief. And both questions can be posed for any population configuration(s) we choose.

The choice we make will largely be influenced by the theory we wish to test. The theory, in turn, will have been affected by the way unbelief has been initially conceptualized. A considerable amount of theory building must obviously be done if unbelief and belief are to be studied as comprehensively as is called for by the postulated conceptualization. Theories of deprivation and secularization may be fruitful, as they have been in the past, in studying supernatural-objectivist belief and unbelief; their relevance to other conceptions of belief and unbelief has still to be evaluated.

Inquiry into the causes of unbelief is likely to be of more interest to theologians and to churchmen who have a stake in belief, than to sociologists, who, as social scientists, are, or ought to be, impartial. Most sociologists, judging from past work and extant theory, would choose to study effect rather than cause. Yet it is crucial to an understanding of the nature of belief and unbelief to know as thoroughly as possible how they are produced. Indeed, without such knowledge the scientific study of effects is scarcely possible.

Realistically speaking, greater agreement on conceptualization is probably called for before we can expect or demand new theory building and research concerning the causes of unbelief. Yet these tasks must obviously remain on the agenda for future work.

The Effects of Unbelief

The broadest range of questions which may be asked about unbelief concerns its effects. Like the study of nature and cause, inquiry into effects can be pursued statically or dynamically and at different levels of analysis. In this instance, however, rather than dealing with one dependent variable, we are confronted with the prospect of a potentially rather large number of them.

Existing theory and most past empirical work on effects are

rooted in a largely culture-bound, supernatural-objectivist definition of unbelief. The main thrust of social theory is summarized in the proposition that belief is functional and unbelief dysfunctional to the integration of the personality, of the group, and of the society. This proposition has never been rigorously tested, and by now its truth has come to be rather widely debated as evidence mounts that social disintegration is not a necessary consequence of secularization.

The great bulk of empirical work on effects has been more in the area of social psychology than in sociology, and all in all, it is not grounded in a consistent and comprehensive theory. Functional-dysfunctional notions have been the inspiration for many investigations; but some research has proceeded on a quite different assumption. Whatever the theoretical posture, a great range of possible effects have been explored, but not to the extent of producing general propositions in which we can have confidence. It is still being debated, for example, what effect conventional belief and unbelief have on such various phenomena as conventional morality, mental health, political attitudes and behavior, prejudice, attitudes toward work, achievement, and the like.

As with the study of cause, new research on effects ought perhaps to wait until we have a better grasp of the conceptual problem. There is now some urgency about both tasks. The profound religious and social change in which the entire world is immersed offers an unprecedented opportunity to study the significance of belief and unbelief for social structures, social institutions, and individual behavior. And whether existing theory pertains or not, the inquiry promises to be of considerably more than theoretical interest.

Modes of Inquiry

The range of methods available for the study of unbelief probably differs little from that for any subject matter, and among those engaged in such study the same controversies are likely to apply concerning suitable methods. Of course, underlying most disagreement about method are differences of opinion about what the important questions are, and investigators of unbelief are not likely to be deviants in this respect either. It would be folly to aim for agreement about what to study and how to proceed. It might help, however, if there were more understanding and appreciation of the possible contributions of different methods and more collaboration in using them.

The Nature and Incidence of Unbelief

The nature of unbelief, as already suggested, can probably best be understood by methods that are more qualitative than quantitative. Interviews in depth and participant observation suggest themselves as particularly appropriate means for establishing the morphology of unbelief. Qualitative content analysis of contemporary writings, ranging from biographies to novels to newspapers, can also provide insights into the ways belief and unbelief can be felt and expressed.

Such methods cannot answer questions about incidence, of course; here more quantitative methods are called for. Of these, the sample survey is probably the most feasible, given the still-prevailing tendency of nation-states to limit censuses to the collection of a relatively narrow range of noncontroversial social data. In the absence of surveys or censuses, there is probably no way to produce accurate estimates of incidence unless belief and nonbelief are very narrowly conceptualized. But even then, there are few sources of existing data to which we may turn, and these—membership records, for example—provide at best only very indirect and incomplete indications of incidence.

Qualitative methods also lend themselves to studying changes in the nature of unbelief over time, but again, quantitative procedures are required to study changes in incidence. If change is to be studied prospectively, the same primary methods discussed above are applicable. Participant observation and depth interviews can produce data to assess the nature of change qualitatively. Repeated sample surveys probably offer the only opportunity for studying changes in incidence with any precision. Records of different kinds are likely to be as unsatisfactory in assessing incidence at different points in time as at one point in time.

If change is to be studied retrospectively, the methodological problems become even more difficult, the more so the longer one goes back in time. Here, content analysis of prevailing literature at different time periods can afford important clues to the nature of change. Organizational records also constitute crude data for establishing change. There is no way to identify changes in incidence accurately, and certainly not using a sophisticated conceptualization of unbelief. Inquiry limited to the more recent past has additional means of data collection: older people may be interviewed about changes they have experienced over their life times, and the responses of different age groups to contemporary cross-sectional studies can be analyzed, allowing at least some inferences about change. These methods are worth pursuing, but if we are serious about the study of unbelief, we should not rely on such techniques to study change in the future.

The Study of Causes

The framing of the causal question sets limits on the methodological possibilities, but there are some opportunities for using the same data to obtain answers to different questions. If the question is why, *here and now*, some people are believers and others unbelievers, on what accounts for varieties of belief and unbelief, there is no wholly satisfactory method of inquiry; the time order of variables cannot be firmly established if data are collected at only one point in time. Inferences can nevertheless be drawn about time order, and for exploratory purposes there is an advantage in conducting a time-bound inquiry before embarking on inordinately more expensive and time-consuming longitudinal study. Though such inquiry cannot establish, for example, that a factor X leads to unbelief, it can determine whether the two covary. If they do, further inquiry to establish time order is warranted. In the absence of such covariance, further inquiry could obviously be dispensed with.

But how should such time-bound inquiry into cause proceed? The method must depend on the hypothesis to be tested and probably on one's taste in these matters. My own bias, as will be evident from my past work, is to begin with depth interviews with small samples and to end with surveys of large samples. The depth interviews provide information important to sharpening theory and developing research instruments, but such interviews are not suited to testing causal propositions. Though cross-sectional surveys are not ideally suited to testing causal propositions either, because of the aforementioned time-order problem, they nevertheless allow the exploration and partial testing of causal propositions as more qualitative procedures do not. In the long run, longitudinal research will be required both to describe and to explain changes in the patterning of individual belief and unbelief over the life cycle. More than one life cycle—and consequently more than one sample—will have to be the subject study if generational change is also to be tapped. Longitudinal study means repeated observations, surveys, or other means of data collection with the same or equivalent samples, while more qualitative procedures intervene to help in explaining the significance of quantitative relationships. The prospect for long-term longitudinal study of unbelief may be remote, but from among the alternatives, it offers the most promise—assuming adequate theory—of getting at the causes of unbelief at the individual level.

If the causal question is to be pursued at a more macroscopic level (if, for example, we are seeking to establish why there is a societal trend toward or away from unbelief or a particular type of belief), our best methodological choice, I suggest, is again longitudinal study of individuals, preferably by census but, failing that, by the sample survey. There is a tendency to identify surveys of individuals as a tool for exclusively social psychological research in sociology. There is some warrant for this identification in cross-sectional surveys; it is considerably less applicable to longitudinal surveys. Propositions of the order that urbanization or industrialization or increasing levels of education are the cause of a decline in, let us say, supernatural-objectivist belief can only be tested with precision through longitudinal data collected from individuals.

Again, however, more qualitative study is necessary to help to account for relationships. Once it has been established, for example, that urbanization is associated with a loss of traditional faith, we have still to learn what aspect of urbanization produces this effect. In instances of this sort, quantitative methods are capable of testing explicitly formulated hypotheses. More qualitative procedures are necessary to ferret out the hypotheses for more quantitative study.

The traditional method for the study of cause is the experiment. It is only narrowly applicable to the study of unbelief, however. Experiments might be set up, for example,

to test whether one body of curriculum material is more effica-
cious than another in producing objectivist belief. But most
of the propositions about the causes of unbelief that interest
sociologists cannot be simulated in experimental settings.

The Study of Effects

The study of the effects of unbelief is methodologically
similar to the study of cause. Unbelief shifts from being the
dependent to being the independent variable, to be sure, but
in studying effects, we are still engaged in causal inquiry. Only
now, rather than asking what causes unbelief, we are asking,
in effect, what unbelief causes.

For the most part, therefore, modes of inquiry appropriate
to the study of the causes of unbelief are relevant to the study
of effects; in some instances, in fact, it is possible to pursue
both aims simultaneously. Longitudinal studies are the most
suitable means to this end, since, properly conducted, they
allow for establishing unbeliefs as either cause or effect. But in
exploratory way cross-sectional studies can also tackle both
tasks simultaneously and help to establish which possible effects
and which possible causes should be studied more intensively.

While there is overlap, some methodological options are
only usable—or, at least, more usable—in the study of effects.
In the study of effects of unbelief on individual attitudes and
behavior, for example, quasi-experiments are an option not as
readily applied to the study of cause. Believers and unbelievers
matched on other characteristics can be exposed to identical
stimuli, and their responses may then be compared to assess
the difference, if any, that that belief or nonbelief makes.
There is a wide variety of postulated effects which can be
studied through artificially created laboratory situations—
among them prejudice, civility, political behavior, and mental
stability. As a result of the weakness that subjects cannot be
assigned randomly to be believers and unbelievers, such experimental work would have to be considered exploratory; but
the same weakness applies more or less in all methods we are
capable of employing.

Another option for studying the effects of unbelief on individual and also on organizational behavior is to investigate
response to real life situations in which an event or another
natural stimulus forces action or reaction. Situations will have

to be chosen for their relevance to the proposition one is interested in testing, but given the range of possible effects which unbelief has been thought to have, such situations for many topics are not difficult to locate. Communities are constantly confronted with situations where prejudice or conventional morality or civility are at stake. Since individual and institutional behavior in such situations is more visible, of course, than beliefs, it would not be enough to simply observe behavior; some means—surveys or depth interviews—would have to be introduced to assess belief structures as well. But properly conducted studies of this kind are capable of producing considerable insight into the significance of belief.

At a more macroscopic level we have already suggested that periodic studies of population samples can provide important information about changes in the patterning of unbelief and belief and allow the testing of propositions about the causes of such change. Such studies can also tell us about the effects of change. For example, does change in the patterning of belief produce greater or lesser feelings of anomie, alienation, uncivility, and so forth, in a population? Such information would be highly valuable in itself; but as sociologists, we should also be interested in knowing the effects of changes on the institutions of society, and here, clearly, information collected only from a sample of the general population would not be enough. Organizational studies of one kind or another would also be required, but they would stand to benefit considerably from knowledge about the more general ongoing changes.

The Question of Priorities

There will be agreement, I suspect, that seeking solutions to problems of conceptualization and measurement ought to be given priority in the study of unbelief. But these are not ends in themselves, and unless we have the next steps clearly in mind, we are not likely to generate a commitment to accomplishing the tasks of conceptualization and measurement; nor, for that matter, are the tasks best undertaken in a vacuum.

Differences in sociological tastes and talents are likely to lead to rather different opinions about subsequent steps. Some will favor concentrating on the morphological questions, others on causal ones, and still others on effects. Some will want to deal with issues macroscopically, others microscopically. Cross-cultural study will appeal to some, while others will favor a narrower course. And inevitably there will be differences of opinion about methods.

Under the circumstances it would seem that we have no alternative but to let matters take their natural course. It would be impossible to reach agreement on any one topic, nor should we really want to try. There are simply too many important questions to be answered.

But allowing matters to run their natural course can have rather different consequences. It can mean, as it has tended to mean in the past, that everyone pursues his own research interests relatively independently of the interests of others. Or it can mean that, without compromising our own interests, we recognize that they cannot be pursued effectively in isolation; that there are some things that we are obliged to collaborate on or they will not get done at all.

With regard to unbelief, the need for collaboration is most evident in the tasks of conceptualization and measurement. These are beyond the capacity of any one of us, and unless we join in them, we shall be forever complaining that individual investigations are inadequate, unacceptable, and worse. But collaboration is called for in more than conceptualization and measurement; it is also needed in data collection. We are unlikely to get very far in the study of unbelief without data, but basic data of the kind from which we can all benefit is not now being gathered, and it is not likely to be unless we collectively will it.

Everyone interested in the study of unbelief is likely to have opinions about the kind of data we ought to collect, and no one is likely to have an answer which will satisfy everyone. Nothing of great consequence will be accomplished unless an answer is attempted, however, and I shall address myself to this attempt in this last section of the chapter. The section constitutes, in effect, a proposal for a continuing study of unbelief on which, it is hoped, students of religion of both macro and micro inclinations might collaborate.

Basic information—which I judge to be of value to all investigators of contemporary religion—includes the distribution of unbelief and varieties of belief among the populations of different countries of the world. How do people cope with the problem of meaning? What kinds of believers are there and what kinds of unbelievers? And within countries, how do the types vary by major demographic variables—age, sex, education, income, occupation, marital status, and the like?

Having such information concerning any given point in time would be a great boon to inquiry into unbelief, and having it over a span of time would multiply its value. To know what shifts are taking place in the form and intensity of belief and in the incidence and variety of unbelief, and to have such information for different countries and in a form suitable for each of us to subject it to our own analysis, would be useful whatever our interest in unbelief.

Speaking realistically, there is no chance that such information can be collected once, much less repeatedly, in all countries of the world or even in a large number of them. We cannot expect questions about belief and unbelief to be included in many, if any, national censuses, and we are highly unlikely ourselves to develop the resources to conduct sample censuses in many countries. But it may be possible to have sample censuses conducted in some countries. To do so would be eminently worth collective effort.

Corroborating investigators would have to decide what countries to start with. Hopefully, they might include more than Western nations, most particularly developing countries. But if at the outset it were necessary to limit investigation to Western countries, to proceed would still be justified. The profound religious and social change in which the West is presently embroiled makes it close to being an ideal laboratory for studying unbelief.

It would be unwise, probably, to settle for conducting the study in one country or in a set of them which offers no variations of theoretical interest. On the other hand, it may be necessary to demonstrate that the data collections planned will be widely useful, and rather than abandoning the project, research in a single country might be justified as a stimulus to future investigations in others. Collaborators would want to include among their number scholars with the qualifications and interests to guide the work in the countries in which work is to be done.

What is conceived of as the prime element in the collaborative effort is a core study to be conducted using roughly equivalent procedures in each country. (Provision could also be made for the conduct of satellite studies, which may be designed for particular settings, but these we shall reserve for later description.) The core study would comprise sample censuses conducted periodically, preferably every five years, with a cross section of the population. Successive censuses would be conducted with equivalent samples, rather than the same sample, though on some occasions, and for special purposes, repeated interviewing may be carried on as a satellite study. Samples would be drawn by probability methods, sample sizes being decided individually for each country. But all samples would be large enough to allow descriptive statistics by all major belief and unbelief categories with a less-than-one percent margin of error.

The instrument to be used in data collection would be in part variate and in part invariate from one sample census to another. Its fixed part would comprise the central questions about belief and unbelief. These will presumably have been decided on a basis akin to the work in conceptualization and measurement described earlier and will comprise both equivalent questions to be asked in every country and specialized questions tailored for particular countries. They would include measures to assess both what is believed and what is not believed and the intensity of each. Demographic questions would also be included in the fixed part of the instrument.

The instrument's nonfixed part would be devoted at successive censuses to questions intended to illuminate understanding of the causes and consequences of unbelief. For example, long-standing propositions that urbanization, industrialization, the rise of science, or growth in education are a source of a decline in objectivist-supernatural belief, and that such decline will produce a breakdown in the integration of the individual and the society, could be made subject to rather precise test. Topics such as the relation between unbelief and achievement, unbelief and economic development, unbelief and life styles, and the like, could also be explored. Presumably with newer and finer conceptualizations of unbelief at hand, and with information coming increasingly to replace speculation, the range of possible topics that can be investigated using the proposed apparatus will expand beyond anything we can now anticipate.

The formulation of nonfixed questions for successive censuses should be a collective task at the beginning. The collaborators would want to give priority to testing those propositions about which there is most common interest. Later on a procedure could be adopted to allow individual scholars to be competitively chosen to take charge of particular censuses. In this capacity, each investigator would have major control over the nonfixed part of the instrument to carry on a project of his own choosing.

The minimum products of each census in each country would be a report showing the breakdown of responses by major demographic variables and a book or monograph reporting the results of more theoretically oriented analyses of the data. Once data have been collected and processed, copies on magnetic tape and/or cards can be deposited in data archives throughout the world and made freely available for secondary analysis.

These sample censuses would tell us much about unbelief, the more so as successive censuses are accumulated. They would not, obviously, tell us all we want to know. To pursue other problems—for example, the impact of changes in belief on the institutional church, or changing patterns of unbelief and belief among elites, or the economic effects of changes in unbelief—data collection operations other than sample censuses would be called for. Sometimes these could be carried on as satellite studies to the core study.

Satellite studies are conceived as auxiliary studies using the data-collection machinery of the core study. On occasion auxiliary investigation can amplify the general population sample of the core study with additional elite or other samples designed to produce enough cases to warrant separate analysis. Or, as suggested earlier, reinterviews of respondents in a core study may enable the more precise study of change more than is possible when successive equivalent samples are interviewed.

Satellite studies could in some countries be made a regular part of the successive sample censuses. Thus, for example, in Western countries it may be highly desirable to supplement the general population sample with a sample of religious professionals. The instrument used in satellite studies may be the same or different from the one used in the core study.

To implement these proposals will require several breaks

with past tradition in the sociological study of religion. It will call first for a change in the current practice for investigation to be carried on by scholars working alone or at most, in pairs. Second, it will require more of us to be less parochial in our sociological perspective. And, to fulfill the promise, investigators of different persuasions will have to begin to learn to work together.

Such breaks with tradition would be beneficial obviously whether or not the collaborative project described becomes the grounds for doing so. The special advantage of the project is that it could afford a common experience for concretely making the breaks. Scholars devoted to the macroscopic study of religion, I suspect, are the least likely to be so persuaded. They are not equipped usually to do survey research nor on the average, do they have a high regard for it. Yet, they could make significant contributions to informing and reforming the character of survey research on religion if only they would put their mind to it along with others who know how to do it. In turn, they stand to reap rich benefits from such research. How else in the end is macroscopic theory about religious change to be tested without systematic and periodic evidence of the kind that the proposed project would collect.

The structure and quality of social life will be shaped in the future as it has in the past by the conclusions men draw about the meaning of life and about the forces beyond themselves to which they decide to give allegiance. We are in a period where old conclusions are eroding away but also in a period where it is still very murky as to what new conclusions will be drawn to replace them. The effect is a remarkable challenge to the sociology of religion. It is hoped that the present paper, if nothing else, may prove a stimulus to meeting it.

4

SECULARIZATION:

BETWEEN BELIEF AND UNBELIEF

.

ANTONIO GRUMELLI

Two basic characteristics stand out in the history of sociological thinking:

1. The study of the religious factor has traditionally been
of central interest to sociologists, especially during the classical
period of sociology.

2. The study of religion, by providing the ground for very
valuable theoretical and methodological advances to the
emerging science, has played a central role in the development of sociology itself.

In the development of the sociology of religion proper we
can distinguish three major historical phases during which
the above two characteristics can be easily identified. In a
first classical phase, the religious factor in its traditional, organized and established form was analyzed comparatively and
key developmental trends were identified. From this approach,
the interest in religious studies paid off, so to speak, on the
methodological and theoretical levels.

In a second phase, the religious factor took its place alongside several other components of society and was seen within
the functional framework of the entire social system. Sociologists recognized the empirical value of religion as a crucial
variable of social integration and value legitimation above
any polemics or apologetic claims of sectarian nature. It
was also at this time, whether in connection with, or independently of the above development, that sociology of religion
came into its own as a distinct subdiscipline and major
branch of sociology.

During the third and contemporary phase of development,
sociology of religion has suffered from profound geographical
differentiation and deep internal ambivalence as to goals and
focus of interest. We notice first of all an overarching preference for sociographic studies with diverse overtones in
Europe and in the United States. In Europe, the sociologists

of religion ("religious sociologists") show a marked preference for descriptive studies of limited sociological import, but which are expressive of their authors' pastoral concern. In the United States several outstanding projects unconstrained by pastoral preoccupation have bravely attempted to rise to the level of major theoretical studies, but can be said to have failed to make an impact which would reasonably compare with the contributions of Weber, Durkheim, Simmel, Tröltsch, or Pareto.[1]

The difference between sociologists on the two continents extends to the approaches that they have brought to bear on the problems of organized religion. In the United States, sociology of religion has turned toward vivisection of the religious factor and has aimed at a critical evaluation of established religion, either by debunking some of the trite popular notions, or by reducing the religious experience to socio-cultural components. In Europe, the interest in the sociological study of religion has been sustained mainly by confessional preoccupations, in an attempt to use sociology as a prop for the advancement of religious institutions.

In both continents, no major sociological theory has been formulated in connection with, or as a result of, studies in religious behavior. In the current frame of reference of sociology of religion, which shows a marked leaning toward "religious pathology," the theoretical implications jeopardize the autonomy and dignity of religious phenomena to a lesser extent than was the case in the functional approach.[2]

1. Thomas Luckmann has extensively analyzed the divorce of sociology of religion from theoretical issues as evidenced by the neglect of the location of the individual in society (which was one of the merits of Weber and Durkheim), and by the identification of religion with church, with consequent focus on applied sociography of institutional religion. However, Luckmann hypothesizes that the present marginality of religion cannot be attributed to the advances of secularist ideology, atheism, or neopaganism, and so forth; he speaks of "inner secularization" as one aspect of the long range process of institutional specialization and a symptom of an emerging new form of religion. See Thomas Luckmann, *The Invisible Religion* (New York: Macmillan, 1967), pp. 17–27.

2. A typical example of studies bearing on "religious pathology" and, at the same time, one of the most serious pieces of research in the last decade is *Christian Beliefs and Anti-Semitism,* by Charles Y. Glock and Rodney Stark (New York: Harper & Row, 1966). In spite

With this formulation in mind, we can understand the sociologists' unwillingness to address themselves to complex and long-range problems of the religious factor. It is even more distressing to note the sociologists' incapacity to develop what Merton calls "middle-range theories" that might prove relevant to the discipline as a whole.[3] A latent fear is clearly detectable among leading contemporary sociologists to confront directly and extensively this problem in our time.[4] One sociologist who has spent considerable time in this field com-

---

of its stringent methodology and serious scholarship, the study precipitated sharp controversies and rebuttals from those who read into it an implicit indictment of religion per se on the basis of one atypical case of disfunctionality. In the same line of orientation, though less controversial, is the previous publication by the same authors, *Religion and Society in Tension* (Chicago: Rand McNally, 1965). The last chapters of this volume reexamine empirically the age-old problem of the incompatibility of religion and science without giving serious considerations to momentous changes that have taken place in established religious groups in recent times and also ignoring the fact that, over half a century ago, Emile Durkheim, in *The Elementary Forms of Religious Life,* raised the same problem at a much higher theoretical level and came to different conclusions.

3. In a well-known pioneer study of the religious factor in the early fifties, Professor Lenski courageously ventured to predict major trends in the American religious scene. Although some of these empirically derived predictions have been born out in the course of recent years, other and substantive predictions have completely missed the mark. His attempt to test the Weberian hypothesis fell short of developing into an original and coherent theory of religious behavior in an industrial society of the American variety against the background of a world-wide religious revolution. See Gerard Lenski, *The Religious Factor, A Sociological Study of Religion's Impact on Politics, Economics, and Family Life* (New York: Doubleday, 1961), pp. 361–362.

4. Credit must be given to J. Milton Yinger for raising explicitly several years ago some of the problems that are central to sociology of religion today. In his provocative *Sociology Looks at Religion* (New York: Macmillan, 1961), he had courageously stated as a central theme that "the student of society must be a student of religion; and the student of religion must be a student of society" (p. 8). In the same volume, he extensively analyzes the rapport between urbanism, secularization, pluralism, and religious change. But his most valuable contribution was the specification of the problems of research in sociology of religion deserving of renewed attention even today (ibid., pp. 134–167).

ments, "Sociologists stay away from sociology of religion because it is intellectual dynamite. . . ." Perhaps the most in-
controvertible indication of this prevailing condition is evidenced by the extent of funds allocated to research in sociology
of religion. In the United States, these funds represent but an
insignificant fraction of the immense sums earmarked for pre-
ferred fields such as the sociology of organizations, mental
health, institutions, politics, international relations, minority
problems, and urban development.

To top this rather heavy-handed indictment of sociology
of religion as the land of missed opportunities, it may be good
to remember that one of the most intriguing events in the
history of religious development, the Second Vatican Council,
was virtually ignored by sociologists throughout the world.
The council, incidentally, proved critical in invalidating a
good deal of preconciliar projections about religious behavior
made by sociologists of religion.[5]

Nevertheless, some events appear to indicate that we may
be on the threshold of a revival of sociology of religion. In
the first place, there are the momentous alterations in the conditions of established religious bodies. The Catholic Church,
for instance, has made its entry into a new phase of *aggiornamento* and development; it has brought about a new format
in a religious organization's capability for change and adaptation to social conditions. Second, and at the same time, there is
noticeable a radical modification of the general cultural back-
drop against which the religious drama evolves. I allude to
the mass diffusion of the entire gamut of phenomena that
range from religious revivals to indifferentism, secularism, or
atheism. We can affirm that the religious problem is posed
today in a different modality and calls for a new sociological
perspective.

Under these conditions, sociology cannot avoid a fresh
confrontation with the religious factor, because of the overarching and differentiated import of the religious problems
in our society; and because of the anticipated rich benefits that

5. The only sociological analysis of the Council, as far as we are
aware, is found in three studies by Rocco Caporale: *Vatican II, Last
of the Councils* (Baltimore: Helicon, 1964); "The Dynamics of
Hierocracy," *Sociological Analysis*, 28 (Summer, 1967); and his Ph.D.
dissertation, Columbia University, May, 1965.

would accrue to the discipline from a new orientation toward religious phenomena.

While recent religious sociography has converged on religious micro-phenomenology (that is, religious practice, correlates of beliefs, etc.), an adequate approach to contemporary sociology of religion has to deal with macro-phenomenology and large-scale parameters of the collective religious experience of our time. Sociology of religion has reached a stage of maturity where it can turn in this direction. Having experienced the frustration that accompanies a narrow approach, we have reason to expect that, with the widening of the scale of analysis, favorable conditions may be created, conducive to theoretical productiveness.

An additional characteristic of the changed dimensions in the socio-religious configuration requiring a change in the scale of analysis is the reflection within religious systems of the pluralistic traits characterizing contemporary society. In this climate of tolerance and diversity, it is easier to understand how secularization and atheism have come into their own and have established themselves as diffused forms of pseudo-religious orientation, even falling little short of becoming fully institutionalized.

Even granting that there is not nor could be a church of secularism or atheism, we can rightly speak of secularization and atheism as pervasive cultural attitudes clearly prevailing in various sectors of our society. Sociologically, this is an entirely new phenomenon and a far cry from the object of study to which Weber, Durkheim, Simmel, or Pareto addressed themselves several decades ago.

In brief, the referent of sociology of religion has undergone basic transformations, thus demanding a painful reappraisal both of the identity of the phenomenon under study and of the method of analysis. It may not be too audacious to speak of a threshold leading to a potential breakthrough in the area of sociology of religion with profound implications for the entire discipline.

Consequently, when we speak of secularization and atheism as crucial religious phenomena of today, a whole array of problems appears. As a carryover of the conventional approach, we may feel that the study of religion is so vast and complex an enterprise that attention paid to secularization and atheism ought to follow after proper attention has been paid to more central phenomena. In other words, why focus on secularization and atheism when we still lack a satisfactory grasp of fundamental processes within established religious bodies?

A statement of priorities in a program of research in sociology might relegate to last place the negative aspects of the religious experience. This reasoning would have some merit were it not for the fact that both secularization and atheism are more pronounced today than at any other time in man's history. Moreover, there appears to be sufficient indication that religious indifference is also reaching wider proportions. What contribution can be expected, therefore, from a sociological approach to the problem of the interrelationship between secularization, and belief and unbelief?

In beginning to posit some answers to such questions, it is well to review the range of problems identifiable in this respect:

1. The problem of conceptualizing the nature and types of secularization and atheism in different social contexts and levels of analysis.

2. The processes that underpin the historical development of the two phenomena in contemporary society.

3. The methodology most appropriate for their comparative study.

4. The problem of possible linkages and connections between the phenomena of secularization and atheism.

5. The significance of secularism for established religion.

6. The problem of a possible alteration in the postures between belief and unbelief; whether a transition seems to take place from conflict to dialogue, dialectical articulation, and complementarity.

Because the first three areas (the ontological, phenomenological, and methodological problems) are considered elsewhere in this volume, my intention is to approach the last three areas.

It may be argued that the distinctive notions of secularization and atheism ought not to appear in an unwarranted union. The first question we have to answer is what intervenes between the two components and on what ground may they be treated as conceptually isometric and/or coextensive? [6] Bearing in mind all the controversies that have revolved around the concept of secularization, it may be defined operationally as the process of detachment of society and culture from the influence of religious institutions or, more generically speaking, from the influence of the sacred, whatever its concrete manifestations and embodiments.

This description connotes a somewhat different perspective from that implied by Harvey Cox when he speaks of secularization as "the historical process, almost certainly irreversible, in which society and culture are delivered from tutelage to religious and closed metaphysical world-views." [7] It takes into account two major aspects of secularization; the *subjective*, pertaining to the individual person and his development into an autonomous believer; and the *objective*, pertaining to social structures, in so far as they are disjuncted from the sacred into autonomous spheres. This distinction may prove helpful in locating more accurately the etiology of secularization.

In pursuing this etiology, three basic factors are identifiable:

1. Ideological pluralism, the deepest aspiration of which is no longer the achievement of total consensus on fundamental meanings, but tolerance of diversity and acceptance of competitive and socially sanctioned behavior and prevailing cultural values, however heterogenous their source.

2. The second factor in direct relationship to the emergence of secularization is the intensified exigency of rationality. This rationality is an outcome of technological advancement and the habit of resolving problems within a means-ends form of decision making; partly it is due to the changed mode of social interaction, which has shifted from a particularistic and primary basis to a universalistic and functional-instrumental one.

6. See Guy E. Swanson, "Modern Secularity: its Meaning, Sources, and Interpretation," in *The Religious Situation: 1968*, ed. Donald R. Cutler (Boston: Beacon Press, 1968), pp. 801–830. Swanson outlines a comparative analysis of secularization and atheism and advances the hypothesis that modern secularization represents a case of structural differentiation in the content of religious doctrine.

7. Harvey Cox, *The Secular City* (New York: Macmillan, 1965), p. 20.

3. The third major catalyst of secularization is observable in the process of industrialization and urbanization which has transformed man's tribal and local style of life into a complex, sophisticated, anonymous, and essentially political restlessness.[8]

From what has been said, it follows that secularization cannot be identifiable with atheism. Secularization represents a more complex and diffused phenomenon. At the same time, however, atheism has reached such extensive proportions in recent years that the problem of possible overlap between the two phenomena needs to be raised, if for no other reason than to explain what may at first sight appear to be concomitant variations between the two trends.

Historically, in fact, any radical solution to socio-cultural impasses has often been interpreted in religious categories as conducive to atheism, the denial, that is, of the prevailing religious tenets of a given culture. Thus, for instance, the first Christians were often considered atheists, as evidenced by Justin's preoccupation to refute this accusation. He also points out that a similar accusation had been leveled against Socrates by his fellow citizens for his attempt to stimulate critical attitudes in the minds of young Athenians of the time.[9]

While pointing out, however, that no strict identity exists between secularization and atheism, it cannot be experimentally and empirically denied that secularization can lead to atheism under certain conditions.[10] Secularization, in fact, does not necessarily imply rejection of *all* religiousness, if only because it is a disjunction from the sacred; it may, however, lead to the abandonment of a given religion to the extent to which

8. Peter L. Berger has paid considerable attention to the process of secularization, bringing to bear upon his brilliant presentation the combined experience of a sociologist and a theologian. See for instance, *The Sacred Canopy* (New York: Doubleday, 1967), pp. 105–171; also Peter L. Berger and Thomas Luckmann, "Secularization and Pluralism," *Internationales Jahrbuch für Religionsoziologie*, no. 2 (1966), 73–86; and "A Sociological View of the Secularization of Theology," *Journal for the Scientific Study of Religion*, vol. 1 (1967).

9. Justin, *Apologia*, I, P.G. VI, pp. 327–441.

10. See Joseph Campbell, "The Secularization of the Sacred," *The Religious Situation: 1968*, ed. Donald R. Cutler (Boston: Beacon Press, 1968), pp. 603–616, where Campbell speaks of secularization and atheism as related forms of "religion of identity" and "religion of relationship."

a religious outlook was embodied in the cultural components of a society undergoing, say, substantial change. In this paradigmatic case, the ideological configuration which is assumed by atheism will reflect the social values that have brought about the disjunction between sacred and secular society, even to the extent of negation of belief in or worship of God. Thus, we may speak of various stages in the transition from secularization to atheism. If secularization cannot be said to be a direct cause of atheism, it can contribute significantly to its diffusion.

Consequently, in order to specify this complex nexus of "continuity" it is necessary for us to make a clear distinction between various types of atheism. We can speak of *cultural* atheism and of *ideological* atheism; the first follows the abandonment of religion as concomitant with the leaving behind of a culture with which the religion was integrally interwoven; the second is the result of a choice and an achieved conviction. We can likewise speak of a *sociological* atheism and of interpretative, or *protest,* atheism. Sociological atheism is a function of the social environment, as is every degree of religious indifferentism; interpretative or protest atheism, on the other hand, is brought about by the expression of individual or social protest in atheistic postures.

Finally, we cannot ignore the possibility that, at least in some instances, secularization brings into the open and to a level of consciousness a latent, though very real form of atheism. The abundant evidence available for this hypothesis helps us understand the otherwise unexplainable rapid transition in some individuals from an apparently intense religiosity to an equally virulent atheism.

From what has been said, it is clear that the nexus between secularization and atheism is extremely complex and spreads over a gamut of relationships and apparently contradictory sequences. On the basis of this variety and complexity, we hypothesize that the relationship between secularization and atheism can be one of continuity, as well as one of discontinuity or opposition. Like the process of rationality, secularization can be fertile ground for atheism; but by the same token, it can bring about religious growth and maturity. Because of this latter potentiality, secularization is not only basically distinct from atheism, but also opposed to it. This holds even when secularization is the catalyst for a latent atheism; for in this case, secularization may lead dialectically to a deeper awareness of the religious, or the sacred. While on the one hand, secularization undermines those forms of atheism based on emotive reactions or resulting from social conditioning; on the other hand, secularization lays down the foundation of a responsible and conscious religious commitment. Secularization can be the precipitant of religious disintegration as it can also stimulate new religious concern, eliciting the reaction of deeper, autonomous, internalized, and mature religious adherence on the part of some individual members of society.

Thus, in terms of the possible relation between secularization and atheism and the complexity of the rapport between the two, it becomes clear that secularization presents a deep ambivalence with respect to belief and unbelief.[11] The opportunity is open, therefore, not only to highlight the positive quality of the process of secularization, but also, to identify this process as the meeting ground for a promising encounter between belief and unbelief. Secularization, in fact, can operate as a "double-edged sword," cutting into unbelief as much as belief, and establishing unanticipated commonalities between previously antithetic positions.

Historically, whenever the worlds of belief and unbelief have assumed sharply distinct identities, the tension between them has been radicalized to the extent that belief and unbelief were viewed exclusively in terms of contrast and irreducible opposition. Such a posture has brought about the most rigid retrenchment on both sides and has rendered any form of dialogue meaningless and nearly impossible.

Apart from the untenable nature of such a stance, no one can fail to notice that, with the advance of pluralism and its penetration into all forms of social life, any polarization and radical extremism can be sustained only at the risk of one's

11. The ambivalence of the secularization process and the "final opportunity" it offers to Christianity is underscored in Thomas O'Dea, *The Catholic Crisis* (Boston: Beacon Press, 1967). See also Thomas O'Dea, "The Crisis of the Contemporary Religious Consciousness," *Daedalus* (Winter, 1967), pp. 131–134, on the modes of adjustment to the religious crisis brought about by secular pluralism, and the more comprehensive treatment of the complex problem in *The Sociology of Religion* (Englewood Cliffs, N.J.: Prentice-Hall, 1966), where the dilemmatic and ambivalent quality of secularization is extensively dealt with.

becoming marginal to the social scene. The present social context, therefore, offers a valuable opportunity for initiating an honest and productive dialogue. Once the dialogue begins, however, a new definition of the situation rapidly emerges, accentuating common interests, values, and premises shared by adherents to beliefs as well as by professed unbelievers. Such reflection suggests that the meeting ground is essentially the same as that which constitutes the basis of the secularization process.[12] If we, therefore, free this notion of the pejorative connotations which "secularization" has acquired in the course of misguided controversies, it will be possible to establish secularization's conciliatory function at the same time as its dynamic value in the direction of new levels of human meanings. What are, therefore, the meeting grounds between belief and unbelief? What basic concerns are shared by the two and can form the common language and dialogue?[13] A prolegomena for a dialogue may be posited along five main lines:

12. One of the most articulate analyses of this common ground between belief and unbelief is the concluding essay in Martin E. Marty's *Varieties of Unbelief* (New York: Doubleday, 1964), pp. 204–213. After a penetrating analysis of the originality of modern unbelief and of the varieties of unbelief, Marty states in two fundamental propositions the relation between nonintegral belief and unbelief: "Belief and unbelief are much closer to one another than to pseudo-belief and pseudo-unbelief respectively. . . . One finds people both inside and outside the Church who share substantially the same humanitarian aims; and they are ranged against ominous forces of repression, hatred, and regimentation that are at work in both the Church and the world." Marty goes so far as to speak of a Christian ministry in the world of unbelief and spells out its tactics and approaches.
13. See Paul Van Buren, *The Secular Meaning of the Gospel* (New York: Macmillan, 1966). Like a host of volumes written by professional churchmen this book represents a believer's search for a logical equivalent to the concept of "divine" which contemporary man does no longer understand. See also: R. Adolfs, *La tombe de Dieu* (Paris: Tournai Editions, Salvator Costerman, 1967); C. Fabro, *Introduzione all' alteismo moderno* (Rome: Editrice Studium, 1964); Ignace Lepp, *Atheism in Our Time* (New York: Macmillan, 1964); Henri de Lubac, S.J., *The Drama of Atheistic Humanism* (New York: Harcourt, Brace & World, 1964); J. Maritain, *Il significato dell'ateismo contemporaneo* (Brescia: Ed. Morcilliana, 1967); E. L. Mascall, *The Secularization of Christianity* (London: Darton, Longman, and Todd, 1965); John Cortney Murray, S.J., *The Problem of God* (New Haven: Yale University Press, 1964).

1. Pluralism's capacity to blunt contrasts and blend radical polarities.

2. The maturation of the human person and the increasing load of responsible choices which are shifted from the institutional level to the individual actor.

3. The shared concern for "temporal realities" and basic exigencies of individuals and groups.

4. The need to use common symbols and language in order to communicate with the largest possible number in a world which has reached unprecedented stages of cultural homogeneity.

5. A recognition of the autonomy of functionally distinct spheres of human activity, seen in terms of their own merit and not for their instrumental value as means to ulterior goals.

It would be illusory to think of this outline as exhausting the range of relations between belief and unbelief. Undeniably, opposition and tension are not automatically eliminated by the discovery of common concerns and ideological affinities. What is changed is the shared willingness to take a second hard look at oneself and recognize that which, from a sociological viewpoint, believers and unbelievers have in common.

At this point, the pressing question is whether this position is tantamount to a selling-short or a hasty surrender of convictions on the part of either the religious establishment or of the atheistic position. Is this an uneasy accommodation to which fellow condoners arrive on the ground of expediency, or does this new stance indicate a genuine growth and development, the fruition of a process of maturity both in the ranks of organized religion and of militant atheism? [14]

Undoubtedly, the changed configuration of human society in past decades has had a sobering effect on all sorts of radicalized expression of human commitment. Organized religion has not been exempt from this global process of self-reappraisal, scrutiny, and mobilization in the direction of social change. As far as Christianity is concerned, the efforts at renewal, *ag-*

14. In a synthetic essay, "Religious Evolution," *American Sociological Review,* vol. 20 (June, 1964), Robert N. Bellah develops the idea of religious evolution along the line of monistic and dualistic conception projecting a religious system for the future grounded in the structure of human action itself and implying the acceptance of the world as religious entity.

giornamento, and revitalization are too well known to need further emphasis. Positive and unprecedented steps have been taken at all levels of the Christian institution to express the readiness of the believer to include those outside the Christian tradition in Christianity's quest for meaning and relevance in the present problematic social arena. The very existence of new agencies for dialogue and study, such as the various secretariats at the center of Catholicism, is a convincing indicator of the deep rethinking that has occurred.[15]

Established Christianity, therefore, can be said to have given substantial proof of its good faith and honest intentions on the strength granted it by the presence and action of the Spirit that guides it. This process could not have been possible apart from the inner vigor that periodically prompts Christianity to reach for higher levels of purification and deeper understanding of its potentialities. As a matter of fact, in the economy of Christian development, external social factors together with internal ontogenic forces constitute the sources, or precipitants, of transitions to higher levels of performance.

We have identified the global process of secularization as one of the crucial vectors presently moving Christianity in the direction of change. What is singular to this process is the recognition of its latent affinity with the Judeo-Christian tradition; both operate on basically identical patterns and are sustained by similar values. Historically, in fact, the work of "salvation" in the Judeo-Christian tradition has been progressively freeing man from constraining conditions of tribe, ethnic affiliation, particularistic privileges, and the mediation of religious organizations. Thus, the human consortium lifts itself up to new levels of implicit religiousness by the institutionalization and generalization of values that, in time past, were the exclusive patrimony of a religious minority.[16]

The primary goal of the Secretariat for Non-Believers is to

15. To gauge how extensive the rethinking of the "idea of God" has been in recent times and how far reaching, see John A. T. Robinson, *Honest to God* (London: S.C.M. Press, 1963). The book is a bishop's acknowledgment of his incapacity to find meaning in conventional Christian categories, especially in the notion of God as a separate being or person.

16. For a masterly historical synthesis of the dialectical development of Christianity vis-à-vis Western society and modern industrialization, see the epoch-making essay by Talcott Parsons on "Industrialization and Christianity" in *Sociological Theory, Values, and*

organize and promote serious and exhaustive studies of the phenomenon of unbelief as a condition towards meaningful dialogue and mutual understanding. In the performance of its task, however, the secretariat comes up against the fundamental obstacle of having to deal with a reality which is not amenable to institutionalization, and, which in its diffused form, is elusive to easy identification and confrontation. Even research sociologists, whose omnivorous curiosity no social phenomenon has escaped, have assiduously avoided the study of residual religious factors, such as atheism, being fully aware of their enormous complexity and of the extreme difficulties in attempting to reduce them to researchable proportions. We have very limited interlocutors in our dialogue, for the unbeliever is nowhere and everywhere. There exists no Church of Atheism or Community of Unbelievers with whom the Confessional Church may exchange ideas. Individual nonbelievers conceptualize almost exclusively in terms of their own personal experience and speak in the name of no collectivity; no group delegates them to express common views and tenets.

Nevertheless, in a world of widening political cleavages and radically diverging contrasts, a move to bring together into productive dialogue the most widely separated religious ideologies represents a valuable contribution to generating a climate of understanding, mutual respect, and a common pursuit of truth and social well-being.

According to the postulates of some schoolmen of old, atheism is a logical impossibility; in reality it is an extensively diffused fact, the postulates of the philosophers notwithstanding. It is a *sociological* fact with distinct characteristics, modes of operation, and profound social and religious consequences. Its nature, modality, and significance within the broad spectrum of religious behavior can be ascertained only through systematic empirical research for which the social sciences are eminently qualified. Only on the basis of their empirical findings can religious bodies begin to understand the meaning of unbelief and program their analyses and their actions accordingly.

Sociological Change: Essays in Honor of Pitirim A. Sorokin, ed. Edward A. Tiryakian (Glencoe, Ill.: The Free Press, 1963), pp. 33–70.

5

VARIATIONS IN PERSPECTIVE ON
SECULARIZATION AND UNBELIEF

·

Discussion by HARVEY COX, JEAN DANIELOU, *and*
MILAN MACHOVEC, *under the Chairmanship of*
PETER BERGER

The Viewpoint of a Secular Theologian

COX: Many of us believe that the time has passed when being a
Christian will somehow mean discovering a common *humanum*. We are here to begin probing that common *humanum*
already uniting us across the kinds of barriers which we once
saw as divisions.

I think it is also a healthy sign that the conversation between the Catholics and Christian non-Catholics has now
moved into the stage where we can recognize that simply talking among ourselves is a dead thing. Catholics and Protestants
can talk for decades and nothing will happen. No real ecumenical reality will emerge until that conversation extends
to those who are not in either one of the major Christian
families.

For too long, "ecumenical" has simply meant "Christian."
I think at this consultation we recognize that "ecumenical"
must now have its true biblical meaning, which has something
to do with the entire inhabited globe. However, I have some
question to put to myself as well as to the sociologists and
others with whom we will be consulting.

I wonder first of all whether we, as Christian theologians,
have placed too much emphasis on the idea of belief. Christianity is perhaps the only religion with the idea of belief; it
is perhaps the only religion in the world where one can equate
adherents or followers with believers. In most other religions,
the outsiders are not thought of as nonbelievers. It may very
well be the case that we are guilty of a certain amount of
Western provincialism, and that there is something far more
basic and essential to our faith than what we have called belief

and nonbelief. Perhaps we can learn from other sections of the world something about ourselves and escape some of this Western provincialism, discovering, at the same time something about the Gospel.

The second question that I will be asking myself is whether we have really forced our fellow human being into an artificial classification when we create a category called nonbelievers. Nonbelief, *non-credenti,* is really a Christian theological category, and it is not really the name by which our fellow human beings know themselves. They may think of themselves as Marxists or scientific humanists or behaviorists, or, perhaps, members of the Ku Klux Klan, maybe even sociologists; but for them, the category of nonbelievers is not really a category. They do not organize themselves as nonbelievers primarily, and this is certainly not the name by which they know themselves. Perhaps our challenge is to move immediately beyond this definition, dividing the world between believers and nonbelievers, to see the infinite variety of human beings that one can discover among the mass of nonbelievers.

Another question I will be asking myself is what do we really mean by nonbelief, or unbelief? It is a very confusing question. All over the world today young people are looking for something which goes beyond the definition of reality as that which they receive through the mass communication media, or that which they learn from their elders. Sometimes this search takes very bizarre forms, such as experimentation with astrological beliefs, or mixtures of Eastern beliefs, or it may take the form of an experimentation with certain kinds of drugs, or exploration with the forms of sexual behavior which are not acceptable according to esablished Christian ethics. Nonetheless, behind this search, there seems to be an authentic reaching-out for something which is real, for something which calls into question the mere empirical reality around us. Although most of these people are not willing to call their search or that for which they are searching by the name of God, nonetheless, it is really a search for the transcendent, for that which goes beyond the merely empirical and the natural, the socially and culturally defined. Are we to think of these people as nonbelievers? I think not.

Perhaps a greater problem is that many of the earnest seekers and pilgrims of our times do not believe that conventional

Christianity really lives up to its own pretensions. When I talked with a friend of mine a few weeks before coming to Rome, a fellow-Christian, a Catholic Christian, he told me that he thought the best secretariat that we could establish would be a secretariat on "hypocrisy," since hypocrisy is really the major religious problem of our times—not unbelief. The vast majority of the people who attend mass on Sunday, and may even give the correct answer to the sociologists when asked about their religious belief, nonetheless do not really have a living belief motivating their lives, giving them hope, and uniting them to the rest of mankind.

I will be asking myself questions of this kind and asking them of my fellow-participants: How can we use the label of unbelievers or nonbelievers for people whose search for the transcendent is somehow more serious and sometimes more ardent than the search of people who can be called traditionally religious? What do we do with the problem of hypocrisy which leads people into this other path? And is the category of nonbelievers really a useful one? A recent Gallup research poll indicated that 96 percent of the people in the United States say that they believe in God. In that poll, I think that the United States exceeded Italy, a nation almost entirely untroubled by what has generally been called unbelief. And yet, I cannot believe, myself. I am an unbeliever in that I cannot believe we can accept this claim to belief and faith on the part of these respondents to the Gallup poll. Perhaps our tools for distinguishing what we mean by real faith and unfaith are not sharp enough either sociologically or theologically to make this determination. It may very well be also that the major problem in my country is not what we normally call unbelief, but quite the opposite. The problem may be credulity or overcredulity. We are coming into a strange time in the American culture when people are buying books on astrology, are consulting seers, using cards; it is no longer the hobby of the few, but it has become a widespread movement. What is the significance of this return to a kind of astrological faith in the midst of our secular city?

Finally, I certainly hope that during this conference we do not make the mistake of equating belief with the church and equating unbelief with the world. Nor should we make the mistake of thinking that the sociologists among us are the

representatives of unbelief, while the theologians are the representatives of belief. I think these distinctions are useless and
misleading.

Certainly unbelief is present in the church and belief is present in the world, and we must honestly recognize that fact. All
of us sociologists and theologians alike are men who want to
have a faith, who are a mixture of belief and unbelief, and
who meet each other mainly as human beings and not as
members of a particular profession. We are all in the culture
of unbelief, and the culture of unbelief is in all of us.

My last point, my last question, is what should Christians
and others be talking about? What is the subject of our conversation? I certainly hope it will not simply be the problem
of atheism, of belief and unbelief. I hope that the Secretariat
for Non-Believers is a secretariat which will be able to bring
together Christians and others to talk about the crucially significant human issues of our time: war and hunger and racial
strife and poverty. I can see the danger of an incestuous conversation between believers and unbelievers, Christians and
others, just as we have the danger of an incestuous conversation between Catholic and non-Catholic Christians. It may be
that the main reason for unbelief, whatever it is in our time,
is not that people find the Gospel incredible but that they
find the Church incredible. A church which calls itself the
servant of the Prince of Peace but which is unable to take a
decisive action against war; a church which proclaims the ideal
of poverty but continues to accumulate property is not a
church which is worthy of belief. Perhaps the Secretariat for
Non-Believers can eventually help us as Christians ask ourselves how we can believe the Gospel; because only as we
believe it, and only as the life of our churches demonstrates
clearly that we believe it, will anyone else give it very much
credit.

The Viewpoint of a Church Theologian

DANIELOU: I find Monsignor Grumelli a little too optimistic
about the phenomenon of secularization. For my part, I feel
that this phenomenon is extremely ambiguous or, more exactly, the word itself can have completely different meanings
—some of which ought to be completely rejected while others

seem to be more acceptable. It is a serious matter when we present secularization as an already accepted fact, without having defined beforehand with precision what we have meant by it. It is precisely this ambivalence that has brought about the confusion that surrounds this particular phenomenon.

As for Professor Cox's remarks and questions, I must say that, at various points, I find myself feeling surprisingly fraternal because of the way he stressed the importance of this dialogue. I would also say fraternal because I found him to be much more "religious," in a sense, than I had thought he was. I am very much impressed by what Professor Cox says, and on one point I am in complete agreement with him—that the distinction between believers and nonbelievers does not correspond at all to the actual state of affairs, and that in fact it is very difficult to determine what could be called "the borderline" of faith, if we define belief precisely as signifying a search for the ultimate meaning of existence, which constitutes for me, essentially, the religious attitude.

This example shows to what an extent the vocabulary about this subject is unclear; today, all too often, the word "religion" is used in a pejorative sense. For example, this is what Bonhoeffer does when he speaks about a "nonreligious Christianity" or what we do when we speak of a "postreligious Christianity." But what does this mean? The minute we speak this way, we are giving to religion the meaning of a magic representation, a mythical, theocratic representation, that has nothing at all to do with what men have called authentic religion throughout the ages. Professor Cox talks about unbelievers who are nevertheless seeking the absolute. Some time ago, while in San Francisco, I visited the Haight-Ashbury district, where one meets the "hippies"; I felt very close to them because I felt that these young people represented a fundamental protest against secularization—that is to say, against a technocratic society which has no room any more for the religious dimension, the metaphysical dimension of man.

Dialogue will evidently have to continue in order to enlighten us on these questions, for we find ourselves strangely faced with positions that seem to have reversed themselves. I, for instance, had formed a false idea of Professor Cox; I thought he was the man of secularism; whereas for me, what he has expressed is something completely different from what

I would consider the danger of secularization, the sense in which it would constitute a menace for the religious life of mankind.

I could perhaps make this more precise by taking up three points. If secularization means first of all the disappearance of a more or less mythical conception of the universe, where science teaches us through its progress to distinguish between primary causes and secondary causes, secularization is an advance in modern culture. It is quite clear that we all recognize that, in this sense, secularization is an achievement. It would be ridiculous to want to oppose science because it supplants certain mythical representations or certain magical rites. But if we understand secularization to mean that from now on the scientific way of knowing will become the sole type of knowledge, thus signifying the end of metaphysics and the beginning of the dictatorship of limited human sciences for the future of mankind, this would be a frightening setback for human culture.

The universe can be simultaneously the object of scientific knowledge and remain at the same time the point of departure for metaphysical knowledge; that is to say, it can lead us to the knowledge of something other than merely the laws governing phenomena. The universe can also be the object of poetic knowledge; even when it is known scientifically, it can still be known poetically. It is quite possible to go around the moon and find out that it is, ultimately, just an aggregate of cells. Meanwhile the moon would still continue to occupy a place in human imagination and continue to be the object of authentic knowledge. When Astronaut Borman returned to the earth, he looked at the moon and saw that it was beautiful. It appeared to him at that moment as an object of beauty and not simply as an object of scientific knowledge.

And here I should like to clarify a point on which I might well find myself disagreeing with Professor Cox, and on which, at any rate, I find myself in complete agreement with certain American theologians. We are told by these theologians that desacralization, or secularization, is itself a biblical phenomenon, and that the Bible is, by its very nature, a secularizing force. The Bible destroys all idolatries, those of yesterday as well as those of today, and particularly the idolatry of science and the idolatry of man. The Bible denounces all idolatries;

this is the sense of the biblical message. When we denounce the various idolatries, are we also attacking religion? In my opinion, the entire Christian tradition has been right in affirming that there is a perfectly legitimate meeting ground between the knowledge of God which we might have attained through metaphysics or through the various religions and the biblical revelation. For there is no fundamental opposition between the God of Abraham and the God of the Philosophers.

One of the essential aspects of the present evolution of mankind, and one of those aspects to which the idea of secularism is most closely associated, is the awareness that modern man has of having reached adulthood. In other words, for the first time in human history, man is aware of the fact that he is no longer necessarily a victim of cosmic fate or of sociological necessity. This is a change in man's fundamental self-awareness. The man of today feels that he will be able to tame all the energies of the cosmos, and today's youth is impatient when confronting the absurdity of private interests preventing human society from being rationally organized. The youth of today are questioning Biafra and Vietnam. It is against these and other world situations that the youth are revolting, because these situations appear to them as expressions of the absurd in a world in which reason could rule the relationships among men. Here we have a prodigious experience, and if this is what is understood by secularism, of course we are secularists; for we belong to this humanity which is aware of its youthful strength and we are proud of it.

If, on the other hand, by secularism we mean that this adult man no longer needs God; that he is from now on master of his own destiny; that his existence and his destiny need no longer come from someone outside of himself; then I think that this autonomy of man could only lead to disaster. This touches upon something said a while ago by Monsignor Grumelli: namely, that modern man is rediscovering the necessity of an ultimate reference without which his freedom can only lead to self-destruction and to anarchy.

So I come to my last point. The basic temptation for modern man is what I would call the alibi of ultimacy; that is, making the construction of an earthly city the final end of human activity. This is the most serious of all alibis for it is evident that it is the most dangerous one. It is evident that being involved in the building of the human city can appear to many Christians, especially the young, as the essence of Christianity. I think that this is the gravest menace, at present, for Christianity; it is a very grave menace because it is a noble menace. I believe, in fact, that a secularized Christianity is one in which the Christian fulfills himself through activity that is social, familial, professional, and political. In other words, if there is a God, our response to that God must be exclusively profane and there can be no specifically religious dimension to existence. But if by this we should mean that the Christian of today does not need to be anything besides the man of social or communal action, and that the Christian does not need to be the man of adoration, I say that this secularism would mutilate not only Christianity, but also all of human culture, thus depriving man of half of what constitutes his greatness and his nobility. It is in this former sense, of course, that secularism can have a valid meaning; but it could slip into a path that would finally lead it to challenge not only the mythical or magical values which are bound to past civilizations, but also the very essence of the religious attitude, in so far as it is the expression of man's fundamental relation with God. This secularization appears to me, if we should consider it as already achieved, to be a tragic menace for the men of tomorrow.

Here I return to a remark made by Father Grumelli; I think that in a given secular context, certain outstanding individuals acquire the knowledge by which they could attain a certain human and even religious maturity. But I also think that it would be quite illusory to see in a society in which the religious dimension were no longer socially perceivable, or were no longer visibly expressed—an expression evidenced in the places of worship, in the rhythm of existence, in the calendar —a society where it would be possible to spread the Gospel to the poor, the immense mass of little people. It is not a question of a few members of the élite; they will always be able to take care of themselves. The problem today is that of the future of the poor. I think that in a completely secularized society, it would be impossible for Christianity to be accessible to the poor. And that is why I repeat the phrase of a great Italian Catholic: "The real city is the city in which men have their home and God has His home." If the secular city is the city in which God has no home, I refuse this city because it seems to me an inhuman city. I do not believe that this kind of society is inevitable. Such a society could survive but it would survive because of our remissness, and because we would not have known how to carry on the battle as of old. We would have allowed this admirable technical civilization which is now being built to grow up outside of the religious dimension; the dimension which for me is the very condition required for a great human civilization. That is why I believe, basing ourselves upon this meeting today and upon the discussion that will follow, precise definitions of what is meant by secularization are urgently called for, because of the danger of entering upon paths that, in my opinion, could be profoundly dangerous.

The Viewpoint of a Marxist Theologian

MACHOVEC: We have heard a discussion between representatives from two Christian standpoints; I attend your meeting, however, as a Marxist—and enjoy it. I feel that it is quite logical to have Christians attend Marxist meetings and to have Marxists attend Christian meetings.

Our 1968 Czechoslovakian Spring introduced among other things the Dubcek principles in Church policy, a radical renunciation of former principles. We made the decision to encounter Christians with methods worthy of human beings, to speak with Christians, and, to meet them in dialogue.

So we speak about the questions of belief, unbelief, and secularization. I am glad to know that a Secretariat for Nonbelievers has been established in Rome. I am not sure whether its name is appropriate, whether we, the so-called unbelievers, are not really "other" believers or believers in something different. If I should attempt to explain what it means to be an atheist, not to believe in anything, then I should ask first what it means to believe. I am sure that if we look to the Evangelists, "to believe" did not just mean "I think that something is true." Belief was no gnostic statement; but it meant, rather, that Christians converted with all their souls, with all their personalities, that they had turned towards something great, something to be expected. It was an ardent desire for *metanoia*. Belief was a desire for conversion, for turning towards the new world. From this point of view, Marx and his movement are not a movement of nonbelievers, but the movement of those who seek the new belief, the new conviction, the new *metanoia*, the new great conversion, the new and deeper humanity.

Yet if I say, "I do not believe," this statement does not make sense unless it is referred to something concrete, to a concrete answer, a concrete negation. It is possible only to deny a certain concrete theism and not belief as such. Therefore, if one asks whether Marxists are basically atheists, I should answer that it has become difficult to know any longer whether one is an atheist or not; but that is not our business; it may be the business of the theologians, who are struggling to define God.

Something very similar can also be said about secularization, which may be understood as temporalism, a radical worship of all that is of this world. As a process, secularization may be viewed as a certain historical development from medieval depths to modern mediocrity, to modern everyday life, to modern man's being lost among things. But I would disagree with this interpretation.

Originally secularization meant something different; a secular way of believing, an up-to-date way of believing, something very similar to *aggiornamento*. I prefer this definition, which suggests finding modern answers to old and profound questions; we are glad to know that Christians are more and more dealing with these questions.

As regards atheism, it does not make much sense simply to consider oneself as an atheist. One has to ask to which form of atheism one adheres. There are various forms which are much below the level of religion. If atheism means that man does not have any feeling for problems such as guilt, conscience, any search for the meaning of life, that is a nonthinking atheism; it is an atheism of ignorance, of hedonism, of "consumerism." In this case, religion is closer to humanity, to real human life, as religion is quite able to ask the deepest human questions.

As a second form of atheism I should like to consider the critical atheism which is historically linked to religion. It criticizes religion sometimes even in a useful way. As you know, not only Protestant but also Catholic theologians have begun to include, and probably not without reason, Nietzsche, or even Marx, as a theologian *honoris causa* in the history of theology. Critical atheism can mean much more for authentic Christendom than just the nonthinking form of belief or pseudobelief.

The danger of this second form of atheism, which we went through during Stalinism, is that it was and remains negative; it lives on the priests' sins. When socialism is established as a power it will also manifest certain weaknesses; we have nowadays also a Marxist inquisition, Marxist heretics, and Marxist schisms. We are witnessing different tragedies in the framework of Marxism. Even under Marxism we have now the doctrine that allows powerful people to intervene against poor people. All this goes under the name of Marxism.

Of course, when Marxists are involved with these tragedies, they will ask for another form. It is not enough to deny the Church.

It was Pope John XXIII who showed that Christendom can also be something else than the opium of the people; that is how thousands and thousands of Marxists, socialists, and communists gained a sense for dialogue and for collaboration with Christians.

Therefore, I am convinced that the only true form of atheism, the third form, is a self-critical, humanistic Marxism which is ready for dialogue. That is why there are so many questions, and Marxism tries to give different answers—but also listens and is open to Christian questions concerning *metanoia* and the Kingdom of God. Marxism is open to the problems concerning the individual, human personality, renunciation, guilt, grace, and humility.

Proud, uncritical Marxism is dead, but I am also convinced that, just as when the Church sinned in different crusades, we shall also experience a Reformation. I am convinced that true atheism will take shape and will become a methodological question; it will continue the contact with Christians, listen to Christian questions, and not oppose metaphysical counterdogmas to certain Christian dogmas.

As there is a Christian dogma—"credo in unum Deum," the belief in one God—so most people think that atheists must have a dogma of God's nonexistence. This is not true; we doubt all these dogmas. But we do not necessarily possess any cosmic experience; we therefore have to remain open also

toward the deepest secrets of the cosmos, the same experiences
that moved Teilhard de Chardin.

From this point of view, when secularization is made equivalent to questioning the old dogmas—the dogma of Christ,
the God-Man, of the Incarnation—and what these dogmas
signify for the socialist age, for the age of Communism, of the
second scientific-technical revolution, for the cosmic age; then
the Marxists will no longer just shout as they used to,
"Mythology, mythology! Opium, opium," but they will understand that in the Bible there may be found also very up-to-date
questions, and sometimes even the very tragic problems of the
Marxists.

Twenty years ago when a Marxist opened the Bible, he said,
"mythology, fairy-tales, mythological cosmology." When he
opens the Bible nowadays, he finds also the question: "Where
is your brother Abel?" After all, that is the only ethical
question of all times and all ages, and it is the question which
the Marxists are tragically experiencing right now.

These to me are the bases of dialogue between Christians
and Marxists, the two greatest and also converging movements
in history and in the world. I am convinced that in this dialogue we can and must find the authentic meaning of
secularization.

BERGER: Well, it would be very presumptuous of me to sum-
marize what has been said. There are a number of points in
the three presentations where there is a surprising degree of
agreement. Let me only mention one: Professor Cox and
Father Danielou and Professor Machovec in different ways
spoke of the relationship of secularization, at least one definition of secularization, to triviality, and that triviality could be
regarded as an enemy and perhaps as a potent force in the
world today. Before we rejoice too much in this agreement,
however, I think one point ought to be made sociologically.
We should be very much aware of the fact that what is occur-
ring here is a discussion among intellectuals. Intellectuals are
people who write books, who go to international symposia,
who occasionally even read each other's books, and who are
very easily seduced into the belief that what they define as
modern man is in fact what goes on outside the limited world
of the intellectual. If there is any moral virtue to sociology, it

is in the perspective of sociology, where the world view of an intellectual is worth no more and no less than that of a ditch digger or a cab driver.

What we are really interested in is not our mutual definition of the situation, but how the situation is defined by people who actually compose the population of the society we are presently discussing. I am curious to know how each of the participants feels about the relation of his definition of this problem to what the masses of people in his respective constituency feel about this problem.

cox: I am happy to discover why I was invited. I suspected that I was invited to come here because I am one of the few theologians who can make any sense of sociologists, but I did not believe that it was because of my constituency. I am rather puzzled about what my constituency is but I suspect it may be people who, although they are uncomfortable about the form in which we have received the Christianity of the past, are sufficiently persuaded that there is something to it that they do not want to sacrifice simply to live in what we call the modern world. They are people who are trying to be fully modern men and also Christians, and I hope that constituency reads my books. That is why I rather believe that what I have said here today would represent the opinion of my constituency.

If Father Danielou is surprised to find me as religious as I am, I am in the Eternal City and the atmosphere has a certain impact on one. Father Danielou recognizes the danger of the secularization process as I do. Both of us feel that secularization is an improvident process. I have tended to emphasize the possibilities and the hopes that the secularization process gives us; he has chosen today to point out some of the problems of that process; but I think we both are very close to Father Grumelli, who has reminded all of us that this is an evolving process.

DANIELOU: Professor Berger's concern about the situation of humanity as a whole, and not only the situation of intellectuals, is really very important. My concern is that the situation of humanity as a whole is generally examined by sociologists who are themselves intellectuals. That is why so often one feels uneasy when confronted by analyses of religious situations made by sociologists. I have the impression of their producing criteria which are, in fact, criteria which sociology may reach; I am not quite sure whether these really cover the effective religious situation of humanity.

According to sociologists, we seem to be moving toward a total abandonment of religion in nearly all the countries of the world. This does not really correspond to the actual situation, and it is difficult to apply sociological methods to religious phenomena. I would even say that human science is insufficient in a field where factors of a different nature will doubtlessly intervene. From this viewpoint, I take up once more Professor Cox's intervention: we have to consider once more our often artificial classifications. Professor Cox said that the classification of men into believers and nonbelievers is often artificial, since many so-called nonbelievers are in fact believers. I abhor still another classification: the distinction made between practicing Christians and activists. I abhor this classification as I think there is nothing less exact than this kind of purely exterior division. For me, many so-called practicing Christians can be much better Christians than the so-called activists. Thus I am afraid of certain opinions based upon sociological categories, though, of course, I understand their being useful. This is one of the problems of secularization—in its atmosphere, sociology makes progress, but on the condition that it be not too ambiguous.

MACHOVEC: I am convinced that, as a whole, the role of intellectuals has to be enhanced in the world, and that the role of the scholar has to be more important in fighting, on the one hand, fanaticism, and, on the other, a certain primitivism. I am convinced that it is very important to understand Karl Marx's original intentions. His intention was to create, via the radical element of society, humane conditions, and to overcome all that is half-human, where men are not only exploited as a mass but also work at a job which does not promote intellectual and moral growth.

Our ideal, therefore, goes beyond the necessity to overcome so-called exploitation; we also want to overcome all kinds of work which prevent a man from becoming a genuinely moral and intellectual personality. From this standpoint the road towards a future classless society would also be the way towards intellectualization of the world. One should more and more take care of the quality and quantity of the education and culture of men. On the other hand, not only this tradition weighs heavily on human history but also the Platonic tradition. This leads us to unilaterally overestimate that which may be called spiritual or intellectual.

After all, we find that, when we consider certain dogmas as Christian dogmas (as for instance the dogma of the Incarnation), perhaps we are attacking certain Platonic forms of interpretation of early Christian dogmas. From this viewpoint, of course, I do not mean that everybody should become an intellectual, but rather that intellectuals too have to be liberated from Faust's "gray chamber," freed from the pseudoway of ideas, from the pseudoway where an ersatz world is made out of books, ideals, esthetic experiences, theater and the arts. This world is very important: there cannot be any progress without intellectual, scientific, and artistic values. But to live only for and of ideas is rather Platonic, or Manichaeistic; it is not the best that the Western Judeo-Christian tradition has to offer. The intellectual of the future should fulfill his life as a happy person, not solely as a person living on ideas.

PART TWO

·

RESPONSES TO POSITION PAPERS

6

GENERAL RESPONSE IN A DIALECTICAL KEY

.

OLEG MANDIC

My intention is to wrestle further with the problem of whether the concepts of belief and unbelief, as used in the preceding papers, correspond to the social facts they are reflecting. Or to state the problem in another manner, do they resist a verification executed on the basis of the methods that are employed by the historico-realistic current of Marxism, one of the five main different conceptions in Marxist pluralism today? Therefore, I address myself to the theoretical and methodological dimensions of that which is historical and sociological, as well as to the human dimensions of the problem.

It is commonplace to state that there are two ways of studying social facts: the first is to explain them on the basis of preconceptions deduced from previous scientific experiences, but not verified in new social situations which may have developed in the meantime. The other makes use of theoretical acquisitions only in preparing a methodological approach to the facts to be studied, leaving these facts to speak for themselves, in order to open possibilities for adapting a theoretical background of methods and techniques to everchanging social situations, and to permit the verification of conclusions by concrete facts.

If there is a conflict between theoretical conclusions and social facts in their concreteness, we have to abandon our opinions in favor of the facts. To accept this ideological posture about social events means to assume an obligation to make the theoretical implications dependent on facts and to put aside absoluteness—that is, belief in absolute rightness, when such belief contradicts known facts.

The concepts of belief and unbelief do not exist as phenomena of the concrete world, but are separate and distinct from the men whose particular characteristics the scientists classify in different ways. As every individual man is a microcosm in which his different qualities are integrated, reciprocally interfering and interacting, it is necessary to establish, if possible, the usefulness of such an interaction in this particular domain. The result of this linking shows that the specific and real situation is much more complex and cannot be explained by the mere antithesis of belief and unbelief. That is to say, the concepts of belief and unbelief cannot have absolute credit or standing; they must be compared to other similar notions and related to the concrete facts from which they are derived. In this way it will be possible to eliminate some philosophical preconceptions. I do not explicitly say theological preconceptions, because it seems to me that theology is a branch of philosophy.

We seek a broader purpose than examining the philosophical implications of belief and unbelief, taken in the theological-religious sense. We presently need to provide some clarifications on belief and unbelief as concepts reflecting social phenomena, consisting of certain social activities and of individual human behavior in historically determined conditions of time and space.

If we accept this presupposition, it is not possible to view belief and unbelief from their philosophical side as absolute concepts, by the conventional mode of proceeding through Aristotelian logic according to which A is or is not B, and if A is equal to B it cannot be C. The meaningfulness of social life cannot be adequately encompassed by this unyielding scheme. We need, therefore, to move away from philosophy which deals with absolute concepts and categories deprived of a permanent verificatory contact with social reality, and to approach sociology, the object of which is to study men within their social institutions.

The historical and sociological dimensions of the problem of belief and unbelief may be linked together because it seems to me that history is the sociology of the past and sociology is the history of the present. When we have to deal with concepts of belief and unbelief in historical and sociological dimensions, it is necessary to ascertain what they mean when compared with social facts. But there is no uniformity in defining what is belief and unbelief. Professor Luckmann states that these concepts represent "subjective aspects of social facts of a specifically historical nature," and that "while 'belief' is not an essential dimension of the human condition, it represents a historical articulation of something that is a universal element of human existence in society: religion."

Professor Grumelli considers belief and unbelief in philosophical and religious dimension, identifying philosophy with atheism.

Professor Glock stays out of the philosophical and religious dimensions by specifying four types of belief: objective-natural, subjective-supernatural, subjective-natural, and objective-supernatural; but he returns to philosophical absolutism which defines unbelief as a failure to belong, as a believer, in any of the four belief categories.

Professor Bellah holds that religion and belief are not the same; that their identification is found in one (but historically discrete) cultural tradition and not outside; that unbelief is generic to contemporary consciousness, religious and nonreligious alike.

There are two main questions that need to be answered. Are the concepts of belief and unbelief confined to philosophical and religious dimensions? Do they as absolute concepts, related to the sacred, exclude one another?

If limited to the religious dimension, unbelief is identical to atheism; but an inflexible application of this identification on the basis of Aristotelian logic would lead to the paradox that a Protestant and an Orthodox believer are atheists for the sole reason of not believing in the dogmas of purgatory, of papal authority, of the Immaculate Conception, and of Mary's assumption into heaven.

The Catholic Church was aware of such a paradox and created a specific category of schismatic believers to encompass all Christians who are not believers in specific Catholic dogmas. This means that even in the Catholic philosophical dimension, it has been perceived to be necessary to establish a particular category related to specific combinations of belief and unbelief. But in so doing, such Catholic philosophy admits the possibility that in the same concrete social fact belief can be coupled with unbelief.

Professor Glock is right when he stresses the existence of various types of belief, different from the religious ones, that have reference to the concept of the sacred. There can be belief in eternal justice and righteousness, in the progress of humanity, in the efficacy of the law, in the eternity of the state, in scientific progress, and so on.

Nevertheless, sociological observation indicates that for every kind of belief there exists some kind of unbelief, and vice versa. The effect of one's Orthodox believing is to make of a Catholic a kind of unbeliever: one can be a religious unbeliever, but this does not mean that he does not have beliefs of other kinds. A Marxist is not an absolute unbeliever if he does not have any religious belief, because at the same time he is a believer in the progress of humanity realized by the conscious activity of all men. It is not legitimate to link the concept of belief and unbelief with that of the sacred, because unbelief does not mean a total absence of belief, but the existence of belief of other species that partially, or as a whole, is not compatible with a particular, determined belief.

Consequently, to use Professor Glock's terminology, a supernatural-objectivist believer is at the same time an objectivist-natural unbeliever; a subjectivist-supernatural believer is a subjectivist-natural unbeliever; and vice versa, a natural subjectivist is an unbeliever from the viewpoint of supernatural and natural objectivism, and also of supernatural subjectivism.

Such a linking of the above-mentioned categories gives a dialectical view of the interpenetration and the interaction of concrete variables expressed in the generic terms of belief and unbelief. The most important point is: if unbelief is but another kind of belief, not the total absence of it, these two, unbelief and belief, have some elements in common. Professor Bellah has made this very point by asserting that "Christians can join with non-Christians in discerning the emerging value consensus, in criticizing existing values in terms of the standards of common humanity and personal integrity, and in insisting that the values to which societies are already committed be actualized for all social groups."

It seems to me that among so-called believers and unbelievers it is necessary to find some common denominators that would make a basis for fruitful dialogue. And such was the intuitive anticipation of the late Pope John XXIII when he emphasized the need for finding out what the participants in the dialogue have in common and of setting aside the items that are irremediably dividing them.

Professor Glock points out that the great bulk of empirical work in effect has been more in the area of social psychology than sociology, and that all-in-all there are no consistent and comprehensive theories of belief. Therefore, our efforts represent but an exploration of some problems connected with belief and unbelief and do not represent a search for definitive answers.

It is not possible to agree with the assumption that belief and unbelief are "concepts with a highly restricted field of application," as Professor Luckmann suggests; or that "the very pervasiveness of religion has as its corollary that 'belief' and 'unbelief' are absent as social facts." He stresses subsequently that specialized institutions predefine the norms of what is properly religious; these institutions control expectations and sanction performance in matters that are recognized by everyone as distinctly religious.

This is the decisive point at which one may begin to speak of belief and unbelief as social facts.

If a social fact is understood as an event which, thanks to the activity of man, produces effects having social implications, then belief, as part of determinate models for ordering the manifold nature of social activity, has social implications too. To deprive man of belief, both religious and nonreligious, means to reduce him to being a passive, insensitive robot, needing someone else to do his thinking for him.

Every human being must believe in something that offers an explanation of the universe, that defines the place and functions belonging to him and others of his kind, and that projects the future toward which man is moving.

At the beginning of distinctly human activity, the opposition between incipient human reason and natural forces permitted man to gain independence from nature. Having no knowledge about the relation of cause to effect that accounts for natural phenomena, man had to create belief so that explanations could emerge of the origins of phenomena and the influences they exercise on social life. Thus, beliefs are an essential dimension of the human condition; they are determined by individuals belonging to certain classes and other kinds of social groups in concrete societies. Beliefs are components of models, on the basis of which men perform different kinds of social activities.

In a class-society both religious and nonreligious beliefs perform the important function of permitting men of different class conditions to overcome their alienation. By alienation I mean the reflection of social antagonism in group consciousness, inducing individuals to consider themselves as passive objects of the action of social forces—for example, as objects of state authority, of laws governing the economy of their country, and so forth—without having any possibility for influencing direction; in this way, they believe in their estrangement from the factors which determine the laws and the intensity of social activity.

Such alienation may be overcome in two different ways; in both cases the impulse comes from belief. In one direction religious belief induces the individual to accept the social situation in this world by promising a better condition in the other world. In the other, belief changes the passivity of the first and induces believers, religious or nonreligious, to take the initiative for social changes, by making them creators of their own social destiny. Thus, and most significantly, belief and unbelief, as essential, human conditions, guide men in their social efforts to attain a better future.

7

RESPONSE TO BELLAH

MARTIN MARTY

Growing out of Professor Bellah's historical paper are five questions I have on the culture of unbelief. All of them follow the paper's direction and tendencies, because I believe it will thus be easier for us to keep our discussion in focus.

First question: "What is original about the modern situation?" If anything, Bellah would say: "What is original about modernity and post-modernity is not its religiousness, for religion belongs to the structure of mind, it belongs to the way all men or virtually all men put together their consciousness, etc." What is original is the end of belief stage. We are moving into an era in which the old Platonic-Greek-Western-Christian-Islamic-cognitive-truth approach to religion no longer holds sway. This was brought about by the subject-object split, while the place of cognitive truth is being taken by some new, perhaps apocalyptic, immediate kinds of religious consciousness or religions. How is this occasion, this novelty, not the end of religion, but the end of belief? The expansion of elites, the fact that the intellectual, critical community grew so greatly in the late eighteenth and in the nineteenth century, made it possible for people to question beliefs. This questioning was coupled with religious anti-authoritarianism, an attack on the imposition of dogma on other people. One of the meanings of Bellah's paper is that this new consciousness moves our questioning beyond the Christian stage of inquisition, in which you are interested in unbelief, mainly because you want to know, in Luckmann's terms, the cutting-off point at which you cut off and cut up. From the non-Christian or anti-Christian side, the new consciousness ends the old Enlightenment game in which Christians were all too ready to play, in which you lined up your truths on various cafeteria lines, and let people pick and choose which truths they liked, which ones they could demonstrate, which ones they could not.

Bellah makes a very strong point in his paper. I would like

to see more examination, however, of other features of the modern situation which, in my analysis, do not necessarily prevail but certainly do coexist. These features seem to grow at the same time as the things that Bellah sees growing: operational man, man going about his business in the legislature or the laboratory finding God. Priests and religious symbols are extraneous, superfluous, beside the point, not verifiable. Man becomes so used to living this way that he is not able even to raise the other questions.

I think we also have to face the fact that, however easy it may be to say that classical Enlightenment and classical Christianity and classical Marxism are called into question, yet we do not see in the modern and postmodern period the growth of overwhelming counter-belief systems. They are not merely the immediate experience; they are new kinds of consciousness, but they also have cognitive dimensions. What is original about the modern situation is that we have to give much more attention to it and not simply look at it as an avant-garde. I cannot accept Bellah's statement that the avant-garde always wins. I know all kinds of avant-gardes that lose, but I have the same hunch Bellah has, that we are seeing an avant-garde today that has a lot going for it, but we have to know a good deal more about what is original about the modern situation. I find it terribly difficult to pin down historically what is novel about modern unbelief or disbelief, nonreligion or irreligion. What really separates it from the Greco-Roman version, from the lucidity of Seneca, from the thinkers of the Enlightenment? As these people made a contribution to the past, so in our future research, we ought to do more.

Second, what is the contemporary role of belief? Another way of putting this question is: Has Bellah done justice to the whole shape of belief by stressing "belief that" at the expense of "belief in"? Now and then Bellah will come back to "belief in," which is called faith, and speak well of it. But belief as such is perhaps in more trouble than it has to be because of its rather restrictive definition. Luckmann says nonbelief is about to disappear as a social fact. Bellah says nonbelief is generic to contemporary consciousness. So on one hand we see a funeral of unbelief, and on the other, we see the funeral of belief.

Nevertheless, Bellah does us justice by presenting some kind of counter-evidence. He says, "Of course, there have been major breakdowns in counter-tendencies. Political fascism represents a new quest for outer authority, and communism represents an incomplete or arrested internalization. Religiously, new fundamentalisms of every sort have emerged in recent times." Perhaps, if you fed the three billion people of the twentieth century through some sort of computer the vast majority of them would be on the side of these counter-tendencies and major breakdowns. I think we have, then, to raise the question, as social scientists, how much credibility can we give to the gifted minorities if most people of our time seem to be seeking a system which has heavy elements of belief? Bellah also recognizes something of the survival of belief in his phrase, "All believe something and the lukewarm and those of little faith are found inside as well as outside the churches." I wonder whether to believe something at that stage can be reduced again to "believe in" without "belief that."

The strength of Bellah's paper, I think, is to show that what we Western provincials have regarded as a permanent, durable, organic aspect of religion was indeed an episode.

As Bellah says, much can be given and much can be taken away. Belief was indeed a contribution, he might even say a blight, from Plato and from something of the Greco-West. This kind of thing can come and go; religion was here before it and may well outlive it. In effect, this paper does to belief, especially in a cumulative dimension, what most theologians have been doing, during the last twenty years, to the concept of religion. They spoke of a postreligious stage, the end of religion, the end of religious man; Bellah is also speaking of a postbelief stage. I wonder though whether people who set up Vatican commissions are themselves all that narrow about what belief has ever meant; or whether the *non-credenti* have been quite that concerned with a kind of latter day, however mild, inquisitorial or evangelistic interest in the cutoff point in which cognitive alternates begin to appear.

Bellah himself sees another side; he states the true quest of history: "Religion is embodied truth, not known truth, and it has in fact been transmitted far more through narrative, image, and enactment than definitions and logical demonstrations." Faith is problematical, for the secretariat, for the Vatican, for Christian and Western man in a pluralistic world. When, therefore, Bellah reminds us that the option is still present for the Christian to follow and take up the cross, he is pointing not only to a "belief in" commitment but also a "belief that." The cross will come to a late twentieth-century man, connected and schemed as he is into such complex systems, that it would never occur to him to explore the commitment called forth by that particular Jew, in that particular culture, that long ago. So, belief versus unbelief and faith versus unfaith and religion versus nonreligion have to be thrown into our hopper.

The third question: What is the future of belief in a pluralistic world? This question grows indeed out of the second question, but I think we have also to isolate it. Bellah points out the ways in which religion belongs to the structure of mind and belief to an historical accretion through accident or contribution. But historians also know that when something has been entered into history, it may be notoriously difficult to have it removed. Eschatology, whether Marxist or nationalist, is somehow derivative from the original historical contribution of the Judeo and Christian source. I think that Bellah would argue that today's upheaval is so profound, that today's change is so extensive that even the traditional and historical deposit can be overcome. And it is being overcome.

I do not wish to minimize the depth of the crisis and the changes; but I do question whether, as I look around me in the world, I can see the removal of all features of this deposit. For it is precisely in a pluralistic world that there is a greater pressure in the cognitive features of the choice one makes. Astrological science, various superstitions, Zen meditation, or whatever the young people turn to, operate out of the immediate experience; and on the other hand, when people become missionary about these things, they have to invite people out of other commitments, other apathies, or other religious fundamentalisms into some other kind of commitment involving an examination of something equivalent to the truth claims of various faiths.

Number four: Whatever happened to the secular? We had a strange counter-set of tendencies in the 1960s, when the social scientists of the West, the historians, and particularly, the sociologists, the social psychologists, the anthropologists were turning up a hundred new religions a day; and the theological community was virtually united in its proclamation of the end of religion. The only base for the future of theology would be the concept of the postsymbolic, postmythic secular world. Now, we either have to say they have no empirical basis for their strivings, or we must be overlooking something that has changed much since 1965. My guess is that they are both right; in Harvey Cox's phrase, "the stakes are being raised on both sides." On one level, operational man becomes more cool and pragmatic and nonreligious; and on the other hand, people, sometimes the same people, become more fervid and more intense about religion.

I was impressed recently by Kahn's book on the year 2000.[1] He describes how our culture will be and remain sensate— that is, empirical, humanistic, contractual, pragmatic, hedonistic, epicurean, and the like. Kahn then reports on his reading of the philosophers of history of the nineteenth and twentieth centuries. All of them, he says, agree that this late sensate culture cannot last, and that it will be followed, some day, by apocalyptic, neoreligious forms, and that between the two there might be a period of anarchy and chaos. I have difficulty in seeing the total disappearance of the sensate in a world which places a premium on medical research and other kinds of technology and with which we simply do not want to part. So, we can have this operational side of the cool, pragmatic, secular man coexisting with all the forces which Bellah sees.

Bellah allows for both religious and nonreligious consciousness; however, I think he does not do much with the nonreligious consciousness. He also says that "religion as that symbolic form through which man comes to terms with the antinomies of his being, has not declined, indeed cannot decline, unless man's nature ceases to be problematic to him." So, we have this question: Is religion so embedded in man's character that to speak of secular culture and secular man would be either so highly exceptional that it would be a waste of our time or even structurally impossible? Indeed, in that case, it would certainly be a waste of time. I would side with those who say we see the stakes raised on both sides.

1. Herman Khan and A. J. Weiner, *Year Two Thousand* (New York: Macmillan, 1967).

The theologians left to themselves in their enjoyment of the secular and the social scientists left to themselves in the enjoyment of the religious do need each other very much.

The final question verges a little into the theological communities, and it is the only one that strains at the edges of Bellah's concerns. How does one choose his religious symbols, for integration, without belief, or in the era of after-belief? This is no problem in a primitive world or a prepluralistic world when your primal apprehension of reality allows no more choices than one. The religion of your village, your valley, your ghetto, is the only option. But the strain and stress is psychologically terrifying on the person who wants to move from general religiousness of the symbolic formative character of his mind to a more specific commitment.

Certainly, few have ever made their faith commitments as Plato did, purely and merely cognitively, propositionally, by assent to truths. Again, I question whether, then or now, we are capable of making a commitment without some sort of cognition. If you are asked to follow a particular manifestation of the divine, a particular way of the cross to a particular garbage dump called Golgotha, you are indeed involved in a partly cognitive kind of commitment.

I would say, therefore, that belief is not left behind but is infinitely transformable and adaptable. Belief goes through a metamorphosis, so that its original cognitive import is often left behind or barely recognizable. Belief becomes attenuated, demythologized, remythologized, twisted—but somehow there is a thread of continuity. I think that Bellah has beautifully demonstrated that one tradition has so greatly overstressed belief that belief is in trouble today, and in trouble particularly among the most gifted and intuitive people on the scene. I think Bellah is correct when he points out that other more durable features of religious life have to be stressed in the world of the future. He underestimates the contribution of the role of novelty to the very survival of the concept of belief in history. He thereby underestimates the crisis brought about when belief confronts the secular world. I think that Bellah underestimates this crisis because of his partly empirical and rationally possible commitment to the proposition that all men are religious and that all cultures have a religious dimension.

8

RESPONSE TO GLOCK

.

BRYAN WILSON

During the last couple of days we have been concerned with the problem of belief and unbelief in very general terms. We have discussed both our concepts and a number of generalizations. We have pointed to changing conditions in the Western world and have tentatively elaborated some models that might be useful in middle range analytical processes for the study of unbelief. We could not, I think, claim that we have come remotely near to specifying a scheme of research, or even to formulating our problem in the way which suggests testable propositions and the means of testing them. In a sense, we have not yet brought ourselves to the point where we can take advantage of the technical facilities of social research.

That we have not come so far is related to the extent of the problem with which we are faced. It is true that the majority of sociologists do not see religion as a particularly important phenomenon in the Western world. It is evident both from the way in which sociology departments are broken down into the various specializations, and from the attitude of most sociologists that religion is a peripheral and marginal item of sociological study. Certainly in Britain most people feel that if you are interested in the sociology of religion you have somehow contracted out of the really important hard problems of economics, international relations, and politics. In fact what one sees is that, knowingly or unknowingly, the Secretariat for Non-Believers has raised questions which are not only profoundly important for religion but also for modern man and modern society. And it is because these questions are so important for the whole of modern society that we experience such difficulty in specifying appropriate schemes of research.

We should not expect to translate the problems we have been discussing into terms appropriate for operational research in the short time we have had available. In this sense, it seems to me that Professor Glock's paper opens up important prospects not for what can be done immediately, but rather of what might be done in the future.

Glock understandably seeks some kind of boundaries for research projects; it seems to me that he pays far too much attention, in the early part of his paper, to establishing concepts which might claim some sort of universal validity. His sociological instincts lead him to seek concepts of a high order of generality and to formulate research proposals in a way that, without conceding much to particular cultural patterns, seeks to penetrate the sociological structures that underlie specific cultural contexts. I have some considerable sympathy with this wish to establish concepts of very wide, if not universal, applicability. But I should like to suggest that we might proceed initially in rather a different way. Let us concede the immense diversity of the belief systems in the modern world and of cultures, and abandon for the present the attempt to develop a conceptual framework that encompasses this diversity. In investigating crime, which is a much more elaborately investigated subject by sociologists than is religion, we accept at least provisionally the specifications of the law without anyone thereby suggesting that the law is immutable and should not be changed. In investigating non-conformity, even within our own field, we accept orthodoxy as an appropriate base line from which to look at nonconformist belief. In inquiring into nonbelief, we might accept the broad cultural concept of belief as we know it in our culture.

We need not be too concerned about differences in our abstract conceptions of belief and faith. We might recognize what is generally and socially recognized as the framework of belief and take this as our departure point. I do not wish to suggest that sociology should become captive to particular theological prescriptions. But let us take society as we have it and the religious belief systems as we know them and proceed from there. I do not think that this will preclude the possibility of dealing with pluralist traditions in Western society. We can accept belief systems with internal variations. The phenomenon in which we are interested as a base line is the stable commitment to articulated beliefs and prescribed practices, and the allocation of time, energy, and material resources to them on the part of particular people and in the arrangement of particular social institutions.

Our problem, however, is not to distinguish the staunch from the lax within belief systems; it is rather to recognize those who have contracted out of the belief systems of their society and those who have never effectively been brought into them and then to analyze their social composition, distribution, and influence, and the institutional and cultural agencies which cater to their needs, which reflect their unbelief, and which facilitate—and perhaps disseminate—unbelief as a way of life. (We recognize immediately a distinction between those who reject and, perhaps, consciously and actively oppose the belief systems which are available in their society and those who are simply indifferent towards them. These two groups sometimes stand in some particular relation to each other; we may expect to find different significance attached to these groups at different periods in a historical process of secularization.) This approach may offer a more immediate point of departure for research and a more definite basis of operation than we shall ever achieve by attempting to establish a conceptual framework of universal validity.

Looking at the framework which Professor Glock provides in his paper, I take his distinction between objectivist and subjectivist beliefs as my point of special reference. This distinction is fraught with great difficulties because precisely in this tension of the objective and subjective are many of the nodal points of religious belief. It is in the paradoxes and the tensions of the subjective apprehension of objectively stated propositions that many of the most interesting religious phenomena are to be discerned. If we were to look at conversionist religion, that is religion which is concerned with conversion by some sort of "heart experience" or emotional upsurge; if we were to look at pietism, which posits the intensification of moral commitment as a religious obligation; if we were to look at mysticism or even if we were to look at some of the gnostic creeds of Christendom—then I think that we should see that all of these play on the tension and with the paradoxes of subjective apprehension and objectivised statements of belief. In some sects—those minority phenomena in which, nonetheless, one may sometimes see important problems worked out in microcosm—there is indeed a conception of subjective salvation and objective salvation about which the sectarians themselves are more than half-conscious. These sects recognize that objective salvation can be stated in terms of faith, in terms of the prospects available to them through the general tradition of salvation by Christ (in the Christian tradition); but they also recognize a subjective salvation in coming into the heart of the small community. Some of them are quite aware of the significance of this subjective apprehension of what is an objectively stated possibility.

After introducing his conceptual scheme, Professor Glock says something to this effect, and I quote: "For each setting, our first task will be to refine our conceptualization so as to establish insofar as possible without empirical work, the referents to supernatural and natural-objectivist beliefs, which exist in that setting." Now, I should not wish to be called an arch-empiricist, or to out-Glock Glock in his empirical qualifications and ability; but I really do not see why we should be so concerned about doing anything "insofar as possible without empirical work" when we have a problem of this kind which exists before us in the real world. Can we not conveniently, and quite pragmatically, accept the historico-cultural situation in which we live as a convenient point of departure?

I do not think that to take up this position commits us directly to any normative or theological positions, and I do not see why it should preclude the possibility of working in what Professor Berger has called "methodologically agnostic procedures" in sociology. If we accept the fact that Western societies have a pluralistic tradition of belief we avoid embarrassment to which highly generalized abstract conceptualization exposes us, and which I detect in Glock's paper where he finds it necessary to explain that the nonbelief of Jews in Roman Catholicism is of a different order from the nonbelief of persons reared into Catholicism. I would rather recognize this directly as a matter of fact that we can all comprehend than come to it through the elaboration of a conceptual framework of a high order of generality, proposed simply to encompass in one formal scheme the unbelief in Buddhism, Hinduism, science, Marxism, religion, or any other type of ideological formulation.

This approach also avoids the temptation—to which highly abstract sociological theoretical schemes are vulnerable—of claiming universality for formulations that are in fact quite specific to the Western tradition. I do not wish to suggest that it is inappropriate to apply the concepts of Western rationality to other cultures; we are necessarily engaged in interpreting other cultures in those terms that are inherent in our own tradition. However, in so doing, we must not impose the imperatives of Western logic on to the first-order categories of other cultures. I think Glock comes close to doing just this when he proceeds on the convenient and, it may be, methodologically justified, assumption that commitment to one belief system precludes the commitment to another. I think that that particular circumstance can by no means be assumed of other cultures; it is a cultural emphasis of the highest intellectual tradition within the Judeo-Christian-Islamic complex of traditions, but it is found to a very much less marked degree in other world religious systems. Indeed, we are aware that at the level of folk religion this type of exclusivity is not always found even in Christianity. If I feel unwilling to accept Glock's conceptual framework and prefer a much more empirically historical-cultural approach—based on the acceptance of religion and society at an emergent level from which we can begin our work; nevertheless, I am perfectly prepared to endorse, as far as they go, his research proposals for unbelief. I should like to see the type of inquiry that he proposes in his paper as one among several possibilities of research, but I should like to see it augmented by an approach of quite a different kind.

Glock's paper proceeds rather strongly on the assumption that belief inheres in individuals. I want to suggest that belief systems do not in fact inhere only in individuals but that cultures carry belief systems and unbelief systems. It may be that, in the modern world with its highly integrated role performances at high levels of specialization, what individuals actually believe as private persons becomes scarcely relevant to many of the social involvements in which they find themselves. The fact that freedom of choice is emphasized especially in America, but increasingly throughout the Western world, suggests to me that freedom is in fact of very little importance for the vital and continuing processes of society.

The choices men make do not in the main affect the social performances in which they find themselves involved. Except for extremists, the differences of belief and unbelief become relatively trivial and relatively inconsequential for the on-going social process. This of course is an oblique comment on the process of privatization of religion.

I feel, then, that the principal thrust of research into un-belief ought not to be a head count of individual dispositions but an analysis of social institutions, of organization and of communities, and of patterns of social relationships within them in order to discover to what extent these communities, organizations and structures are informed by supernational conceptions of the world and are characterized by the be-havioral correlates of such beliefs. If we were to mount a research program of this kind, we might discover structures which appear to men as "natural" in the sense that men have not organized them consciously, and that such received struc-tures are explained, informed, and characterized by super-natural beliefs. We might also discover that men legitimate their received traditions, the traditions which they have not themselves consciously created, by reference to supernatural charters and manifestos, very largely to prevent undue dis-turbance of those structures.

If we look at the structures more typical of the modern world, we find consciously constituted organizations which in most instances have very much less need for legitimation of any supernatural kind but need only a certain pragmatic sanction. There is, of course, one particular sort of institution which cuts across the distinction that I am trying to make, and this is the type of institution which is itself concerned with the promotion of an ideology. The church—which we may take as an example—is in large part concerned with promulgating a particular teaching, a particular set of be-liefs. But it is interesting to note that the church should con-tinue to use models—perhaps must continue to use models— which are in the background. Some of its structures come increasingly to resemble those of the consciously organized bureaucracy. In this context—of life increasingly governed by machines—individual beliefs would become almost idio-syncratic if it were not for the persisting structures which give beliefs some objective specification, and which carry them on from one level of cultural development to another.

In such a technocratic society belief becomes something of a private luxury for which there are certain persisting social institutions. But these institutions become increasingly vestigial and persist at the fringes of contemporary society; and it is this, of course, which justifies one's sociological colleagues in saying that the sociology of religion is a peripheral discipline, unimportant in the modern world. It is clear that these institutions are mostly now concerned with those free areas of men's time, their leisure, in which they might conceivably escape the technocratic impress of modern culture. We should not, however, overlook the fact that increasingly leisure itself is also invaded by the technological, that it is machine-transmitted, and consists in very large part in the use of machines for one purpose or another. (I use the word "machines" in the wide sense, to describe a range of technical apparatus.)

There are certain consequences of the abandonment of supernatural belief systems which put into jeopardy the individual's capacity to deal with the world in which he finds himself, but which also put into jeopardy civic order in the world. I believe that there are things which the machine culture cannot achieve. I believe that the search for community, which in various ways we have talked about for the last couple of days, the search for stable enduring relationships, the search for affectivity in the modern world—now occur in an environment in which the machine culture dominates and in which man ceases in some way to have "authentic experience"—by which we usually mean personal experience at an intimate level. This is the alternative to the machine culture that we have evolved. (I put this in as an aside, so that no one should think that I am holding up a banner in favor of the highly rational machine-oriented world which I think is coming into being.)

In these machine-transmitted cultures, we may find unbelief as the easiest line of resistance for many people who are prepared to "go along with" the circumstances in which they find themselves, and to block out, in one way or another, processes of reflection and circumstances of personal anguish.

The character of role performances in the machine-dominated contexts of the modern world have implications for what men believe about the supernatural and the moral imperatives they derive from it. Yesterday we talked at some length of childhood experience and primary socialization in the modern world. Let me say something about the extension of this into processes of secondary socialization. Among office workers in the United Kingdom, to give an example, it used to be that a particular section of the working-class population often received from classes higher than themselves certain belief systems. Sometimes, understandably, in receiving this culture, they varied it in their own way; but nonetheless, they received the impress of a cultural tradition which was of importance for their socialization into the society in which they lived.

In that circumstance, the office worker necessarily engaged with other persons in complex tasks which, however, in the nineteenth century and, perhaps in the early twentieth century, were still largely mediated through the texture of personal relationships. The office worker was involved with other persons in receiving orders and often in communicating them to others. He acquired a strong sense of hierarchy which very often appeared to the outsider as an enormous preoccupation with marginal status differences. Nevertheless, what he also acquired in this process was a sense of the nuances of interpersonal relationships. The office worker was often cut off from other workers, especially from manual workers, and was not regarded by them as really being a worker at all. The office worker, in return, did not wish to regard manual workers as people whose class, economic, and cultural circumstances had any similarity to his own. With the advent of the process of technologization and the development of electronic processing of data and other processes which affect the office, the human involvement of work in that particular context began to be reduced. The style of work changed and with it there occurred a diminution of the nuances, of the subtleties and sensitivities, of interpersonal relationship.

What I am really saying is that there were, in the nineteenth-century office situation, possibilities for the cultivation of a sense of reverence—and I use that word guardedly—for other persons. In other words, there was in that culture the possibility of interpreting the world in a way which was potentially religious. (I am not making any claim to special knowledge of the extent of religious practices among office workers; we know that in England they were an extremely important formative group in many voluntary associations including the nonconformist churches.) What is clear is that in their social circumstance there was a possibility for the interpretation of life-situations in terms that were conducive to the acceptance of moral imperatives and, perhaps, also to the acceptance of supernatural belief. When the office was technologized, those conductive circumstances that arise from an elaborate, complex, subtle, sensitive interplay of human relations began to disappear, and there is today much less likelihood of this work situation appearing to be relevant to the sorts of thing which the traditional religious belief system of the West has to say about man in his social circumstances.

I find it difficult to imagine how the Christian religion might reinterpret itself in order to make itself relevant to that situation of the worker in highly technocratic circumstances of today. I do not want to suggest that we should expect to find more than strong indicators of particular cultural tendencies in these changed social circumstances. But I think these are situations which the Secretariat for Non-Believers or sociologists interested in nonbelief would find well worthwhile to examine. One needs to look at context situations, at institutions, as well as to count the heads of individuals, to see what they tell you when you isolate them with a questionnaire. Our concern is the culture of unbelief and if I have been rather literal about the term "culture," I have been free with the concept of belief. It must include activities as well as intellectual assents, and the institutional religious context in which action is elicited. The investigation of individuals can provide us with only a part of what we want to know and not necessarily the most important part. If we do investigate individuals then I would also put in a plea that we investigate individuals somewhat differentially. Even in the democratic societies of the West not all individuals are equally important in terms of what they do and what they believe.

We should, for instance, look at certain elite strata and their beliefs specifically as well as looking at the mass of population. There are culture bearers and culture transmitters in our society. In part, these are of course intellectual strata;

but, much more important than the intellectuals are those who fasten on to the intellectuals, the journalists, the television producers, the editors and the entertainers. We live in a society in which recreation—which, because it was so unstructured, sociologists long treated as a Cinderella when they discussed social institutions—has become vitally important. The old-time Cinderella has really "gone to the ball," but the ball does not now end at 12 o'clock; it goes on all night, in the sense that entertainment is a continuously available facility of our societies. This is a new cultural condition which has very considerable relevance for unbelief because what is offered here is the possibility of deflecting people permanently from any thoughts about or any need to care about the issues with which belief is concerned.

If we are to undertake sample survey research, we might look specifically at those elite cadres of our society in which culture is transmitted and sometimes created and, if I can be permitted a value judgment, often corrupted. The role of these elites is important for our understanding of the attitudes that other men will have towards belief and unbelief. The type of research then that I should like to see promoted would also include collaboration and coordination of scholars who are not themselves highly technical and technologized men.

Now, it is true that most of the research institutes do in fact bring together, as Glock said in his opening remarks, people whose interests and skills tend to be similar. It is also true that problems which have been looked at in sociology and in social history of this kind tend to have been looked at by scholars working in isolation whose contacts with others in their field have come mainly through reading their books and articles, occasionally by attending conferences.

I see no inherent reason why there should not be established institutes which have a narrow focus on the world, in the sense that they take up a specific set of rather closely defined problems in which historians and sociologists and social psychologists and specialists within this field might work together. I have no doubt there are models in the United States; there is a model for this in the United Kingdom in the Institute for the Study of Psychopathological Politics, which studies Nazism and other political systems which give rise to destructive action. I would suggest that it is possible to draw together scholars in collaboration with each other who are prepared to devote themselves to rather specific themes of research and I see no overwhelming reason why we should not attempt to establish that sort of institute. Sociologists also live in a machine-dominated world, but we should not let the machines dictate to us what are the important questions and how we should investigate them.

PART THREE

.

VIEWS AND COUNTERVIEWS:
GENERAL DISCUSSIONS

9

TOWARD A DEFINITION OF UNBELIEF

·

LUCKMANN: I have tried to show that belief is a limited and restricted social fact, influenced by a combination of specific structural conditions. In archaic societies, and I am lumping together heterogeneous societies which however have a number of structural elements in common, we find that religion is diffused throughout the social structure, as part of the ordinary expanded processes of socialization. In this case, it would be totally useless and unproductive in any sociologically relevant sense to employ the notion of belief to describe certain overarching cognitive, interpretative schemes. To describe these interpretative schemes that integrate everyday conduct as belief would preclude any distinction between the social forms of religion in different types of society.

This notion of belief would not be terribly productive. In complex industrial societies in which institutional specialization produces a certain degree of autonomy of different institutional areas, religion too becomes institutionally specialized. The crucial moment when one can discern belief as a social fact occurs when a sort of official model is created by that institution, which provides a mode of socialization processes into overarching schemes of interpretation. This is what it would be useful to call belief.

As a historical social fact, unbelief is also institutionally defined as the opposite of that which is defined in the institutionally specialized official models as belief. The situation would be very simple in a society in which there is only one official model; unbelief then is what is beyond the institutionally recognized cutoff point of belief. The religious experts may have some difficulty to specify exactly where the cutoff point is in any individual instance; but they normally have no great difficulty in defining the cutoff point in general terms.

The situation is more complicated when in the same type

of society, there is a competing model in addition to the official model. The sociologist may define belief in relation to what is the "one" official model of religion, adopt the cutoff point again, and speak of unbelief in that area of interpretative, cognitive notions that lies beyond that cutoff point.

A rather simplified example that approximates a situation where there is only one official model in which religion is indeed institutionally specialized would be the Christian society of the Middle Ages. A postreformation, really capitalistic society would be an example of a situation in which there are competing official models, or some official models of belief in which again unbelief is a fairly well-defined social fact. Evidently this does not mean that the unbeliever lacks overarching interpretative schemes. My hypothesis is that we may be entering a new situation in which institutional specialization is no longer the one and exclusive form in which religion is a social fact. If this speculation can be validated, then there is clearly no intersubjectively verifiable way of defining unbelief.

Therefore, it might be useful to introduce a different set of concepts, all within the category of belief.

ISAMBERT: We are touching the core of the problem of the ambiguity built into the notion of belief and unbelief. Professor Luckmann has clearly taken a Durkheimian approach. Going beyond the common sense approach, he provisionally removes all subjective connotations from the notion of belief and unbelief and tackles the problem from an institutional angle. This, he suggests, is an indispensable approach. I feel uneasy about this, considering that often we come across institutions which are officially defined. The problem in this case originates from the imputation, or the ascription, of the notion of belief or nonbelief to these institutions, which the collective consciousness recognizes as specialized institutions of religion. An isomorphism is produced between belief and belonging, in force of which the believer will be defined not only by the subjective quality of believing in God, or in this or that dogma, but also by an objective affirmation which expresses his belonging to a dogmatic system characteristic of a given institution. To be a believer, in this case, does not simply mean to believe, but "to be seen" as a believer by

others—that is, belonging intellectually to an institutionalized system of dogmas.

Recent research in patterns of belief of French youth generates serious doubts concerning the categories we use when
speaking of belief and unbelief. We have come across young
people who belong to Catholic families that label themselves
as believers, but who in reality follow a belief extremely
heterogenous from a dogmatic viewpoint, completely lacking
the consistency of a dogmatic system of beliefs. There are,
to be accurate, a certain number of belief objects about which
all those who proclaim themselves Catholic agree, such as the
existence of God. Nevertheless, the whole system of Catholic
dogmas is not accepted, and often strange deviations are observed—for instance, concerning the problem of the relationship between this life and the next life. Our youth have
manufactured new dogmas, or they have adhered to different
dogmas presented to them.

This need for dogmatism which is observable among young
Maoists, or among young Trotskyites is an extraordinary
phenomenon of today. It is easy to understand, therefore, why
I have very strong reservations about the notion of a growing
skepticism in the world, expressed in the imagery of a world
where belief is gradually disappearing, swept by a wave of
progressive unbelief and brought about by a diminishing willingness to believe. Our problem, therefore, ought to be the
investigation of the degree of institutional consistency of a
belief system. We could hypothesize that the dissolution of
belief may lead to an effective state of unbelief by way of the
official belief, bringing forth phenomena, religious in nature,
such as the emergence of new micro-churches.

VERGOTE: Behind Professor Luckmann's arguments, I detect
the latent assumption that Christianity is a religious system,
or a world view in the Durkheimian sense. Considering that
we are interested in the distinction between the categories of
faith, belief, unbelief, and religion, I wish that Luckmann
had taken into account the fundamental fact that Christianity
claims to be a religion based on the proclamation of a divine
event. It may be said that this is only a theological category;
but the fact remains that this historicity is exclusive to the
church as an institution and to Christianity as a religion. It

is in this manner that Christianity finds its place among the world religions.

The attempt to make a distinction between belief, unbelief, and other religious categories runs the risk of violating objectivity, unless we take into account this fundamental fact. It is a questionable procedure, to say the least, when one attempts to differentiate faith from religion on the basis of cultural and historical factors. It surely does not account for the process by which Christianity became a religion.

LUCKMANN: The presupposition that Christianity is a religion is a presupposition that I, perhaps, stated explicitly, but that many sociologists would contest. That it is a religion with a claim to uniqueness does not distinguish Christianity from other religions with which sociologists deal. I admit that there are differences in the nature and specific characteristics of that claim, but I doubt that this is a circumstance which requires a total reformulation of the set of categories and concepts with which sociologists analyze religion.

There is a basic difference between religion in archaic societies and religion in complex civilizations. To use the notion of the social form of religion to describe one or another might be an idiosyncrasy of mine but I think it is useful, otherwise I would not have used it.

I am not sure that the evidence that can be adduced is strong enough to support the notion that we are merely dealing now with a situation in which the social form of religion is simply in a state of instability, aggravated by certain complications. Here I mean institutional specialization of religion in which, as Professor Isambert quite rightly pointed out, belief is part of the syndrome, institutionally defined, together with membership and certain performances.

O'DEA: It seems to me that one of the central problems is that of individual evasion. Our schematization suffers tremendously from simplification. When we think of what witchcraft was in the sixteenth century, of alchemy in the Middle Ages, and a number of questions like these, it becomes extremely difficult to place the Middle Ages in the Durkheimian scheme.

BERGER: Another profitable line would be to explore the historical implications of our problems and to ask how Durkheimian were the Middle Ages! But in Professor Luckmann's terms, how can we theoretically grasp the pluralistic situation which we face; what theoretical tools can we find which are useful for grasping what is actually going on?

PARSONS: There are both terminological and substantive questions involved in what seems to me like a difference between Professor Luckmann and Professor Isambert. Professor Isambert referred to community-belonging in terms of what would generally be called "dogma." The word belief has many ambiguities but one of them is between the pure assent to cognitively formulated propositions, on the one hand, and personal commitment, which, in the Durkheimian focus, is commitment to belonging in a collectivity, on the other hand.

Professor Bellah traces the problem back to the Greeks, or more accurately, to the special kind of Greek community, which came to be composed of citizens. This community in many respects was a fundamental model for the development of the Christian church. Somehow there was a synthesis between that community and the system of cognitive propositions which developed in Christianity; but these two need not stay together in the course of historical development.

My own view is that if the collective system moves away from certain sets of cognitive propositions, which we usually think of as religious in character, the collectivity may still survive in another form and with other kinds of belief systems.

KLAUSNER: There seems to be behind the paper a sort of prejudicial attitude towards the earliest societies whether they be archaic, medieval, or something else. They are said to lack the kinds of division of labor that we have in some later societies.

We have found that most primitive societies that we have analyzed with some care have shamans who stand out as separate kinds of people; these societies maintain very careful divisions among what the priests must do ceremonially, in the political structures, and so on. Historians would be disturbed by the suggestion that there was no deviance from norms in that kind of society, or at least very little of it.

Professor Luckmann suggests that we are going to see the rising of some kind of invisible religion. It would seem to me that, on empirical grounds, an invisible religion would be highly unlikely, in the sense in which he means it, under conditions of religious pluralism. Pluralistic positions existing side by side would force things from the invisible to the manifestly institutional. The key question which I should like to ask is whether or not we have to worry about the distinction between belief and unbelief and the substratum of the invisible things that lie behind it. Why could one not ask both questions? And why could a specific question not be put to the researchers in a particular institutional context—one which asks: Is there a greater deviance from the normative position of the Catholic church now than there was in some previous time?

LUCKMANN: While I do not believe that different sociologies must be developed for different types of societies, I do think that different methodological approaches may be more productive in the study of different types of societies. Indeed, certain differences between methodological approaches in sociology are not accidental. Community studies, for example, are a very useful approach in certain types of societies; but the same have a much more restricted validity and can be generalized only much more carefully in a complex industrial society. This is what I meant when I stated that in studying invisible religions, social psychological methods are probably not in use. The social psychological methods that are known to us might be more productive than institutional and organizational analyses, which might have been more useful in a situation in which religion is highly specialized institutionally.

I will readily admit that I have highly simplified the problems under discussion for purposes of presentation; I do not maintain, for instance, that in the Middle Ages there were no deviants. What I suggest is that deviance from norms was clearly recognized and defined, self-defined and other-defined, if you want to put it that way. This, again, is a relative statement and it by no means implies that nondeviance characterizes a less complex society. Norms in that type of society were more clearly integrated, and this integration was more easily perceived by the man in the street than is the case today. I am following other sociologists in assuming that institutional norms in various areas produce a sort of rationality of their own, when they achieved a relatively high degree of autonomy.

As to the complex question whether shamanism represents an institutional priesthood, comparable in any relevant sense to the priesthood within a classical civilization, it should be probably answered in the negative, but I do not think this is a point in question in our discussion.

Professor O'Dea raised the substantive question of "individuation." We all agree that a kind of individuation is a characteristic of all socialization processes. But I think that one can speak of a form of individuation in modern society which shows some characteristically different traits from individuation in different types of societies.

This is probably a question of crucial significance for our problem: How can we identify the conditions in the social structure which are responsible for this? Let me speculate for a moment that the social structure in modern societies has produced highly valid socialization processes responsible for a privatized kind of religiosity. The question, then, that I would like to place before us is whether there are institutions which are no longer necessarily (and certainly not exclusively) religiously specialized institutions, which play a certain role in this process of individuation.

GLOCK: Professor Luckmann has already indicated what questions arise in the light of past sociological theory about the role of religion and of belief in social integration. As we get manifest indications of the decline in what we have usually thought of as belief, there is a question raised as to whether or not there is some substitute for this kind of belief that will produce social integration, or whether indeed it is only this kind of belief that can produce social integration. What Luckmann appears to say is that invisible religion will become a substitute for visible religion, to provide some function in society, some kind of social integration. In terms of research, one would begin by asking: What do we mean by social integration? How do we measure it? In what ways, specifically, had we thought all types of Christian beliefs to be related to social integration? What kinds of notions do people have in their head in terms of their commitment to certain values of the society? What kind of ideas give support to these commitments? It might be useful, following Berger's suggestion, to begin to say what are the theoretical issues that lead us to be concerned about the phenomenon of belief and unbelief.

DE LUBAC: We are faced with very complex problems. Belief is an analogical concept, and this complicates further the question of the relationship between belief and religion. Let us take for instance the momentous phenomenon of Buddhism. The Buddhist ideal is precisely to transcend all order of belief and reach that enlightenment which can give direct knowledge of salvation. Buddha expressed this in the epigram at the end of his life: "Be your own enlightenment." Here we are faced with a belief system that is commonly known, a widespread religion, which states as its ideal the capacity to move beyond what we ordinarily designate as belief. The problem is further complicated when, over and above the distinction between belief and religion, we are forced to make another distinction, namely between belief and faith. This further distinction is unavoidable, especially when belief and faith stand in nearly opposed positions.

Christianity is not a religion characterized by a set of beliefs, however sacred. By its very constitution, Christianity is a response of faith to a saving event, divine in origin, which places man in personal relationship with God. It does not generate beliefs about God, but faith in God. The two are totally different concepts, and this cannot be ignored when studying Christian institutions objectively. For the man in the street the two notions may blur into a common thing. But when we are dealing with the substantial meaning and developmental history of an institution, we cannot avoid the distinction.

COX: In an effort to direct the discussion to stage C in Professor Luckmann's scheme, I should like to ask whether there is a muted, underlying assumption that man is not by nature, at least in the common situation, "homo religiosus." I think it was Professor Mandic who suggested that man will always need an explanation of the universe, the relationship of his species to it, and some meaning for the future which he anticipates, or hopes for, or fears. Professor Luckmann uses the term "sacred cosmos," but Professor Wilson suggests that perhaps there may be a large number of people, who, upon empirical investigation, are not conscious of, or feel no need for anything like either a cognitive scheme or a religious picture of the universe. Are we saying that there is implicit somewhere in their style of life a sacred cosmos or cognitive scheme? Is it an empirically researchable suggestion that there is emerging a kind of postreligious man, that is, a man who really feels no need for any kind of a sacred cosmos?

A theologian can obviously be expected to be delighted when scholars find out that men will always be religious, because that means that theologians will always be in business. There is, however, an interesting discussion among contemporary theologians about whether or not the category "homo religiosus" is in fact an accurate one.

MARLÉ: Earlier Father De Lubac opened a line of criticism which I should like to pursue. I feel uneasy about the fact that we are moving almost exclusively within the dichotomy of belief and unbelief. Linguistically the need to differentiate between faith and belief is very cogent in French, although it may be less so in English. I would dare say that the requirement of such distinction highlights, indirectly, the uniqueness of the Judeo-Christian phenomenon. It stresses the subjective element involved in religious experience, interfacing it with an institution which views itself as constituted originally by an act of faith. Belief is not located in, nor can be understood through, the notion of appurtenance (belonging) to an institution; rather the institution continuously becomes aware of itself and of its development (whatever its form) as the outgrowth of an act of faith, of an encounter, of an historical event. Ultimately we are speaking of an institution which traces its own dynamism to prophetic action.

It is at this point that the usefulness of sociological analysis in pursuing reality must be questioned. While reading Professor Luckmann's paper, it occurred to me that this formulation of religious reality which originated from an engagement of faith, took place in a relatively archaic society, the nation of Israel, not in a modern, differentiated society. In this society, for the first time, faith or belief were viewed as the outcome of a singular encounter between a man, Abraham, and God, a subjectivity responding to another subjectivity, and thus establishing a unique religious world view.

Religion, therefore (as the question of Professor Cox implies), differentiated modern society, but in a social context where everything had already religious connotations. And the starting point of this new religion is marked by a singular event consisting of intersubjective responses.

CARRIER: I agree that we have not been careful enough in relating belief to religion. The various descriptions or definitions of belief that have been given this morning indicate that to believe contains several aspects:

1. The aspect of cognitive process.

2. A participation in, and emotional adaptation to, certain values.

3. A participation in an institutionalized interpretation of the universe, of God, of man.

4. A set of attitudes vis-à-vis the beyond, the extraempirical, an assent, as it were, to the absolute.

I think that even an orthodox theologian, if we can use this term, would accept this description of "to believe," "avoir une croiyance." But this description of what it is to believe encounters a very serious difficulty when we relate belief to religion. Is the unbeliever a man who has no religion? Religion contains many other elements; it includes liturgical aspects, ceremonial aspects, behavioral codes, and so forth.

Anyone who has written on religious problems has encountered this crucial difficulty of how to define religion. I have tried to make a list of all these definitions, and have come to the conclusion that one should distinguish various attitudes in the act of defining religion. According to one such attitude, which I think prevails in the work of Professor Luckmann, religion is defined by a person's adherence to a set of beliefs, and his pattern of behavior related to the absolute.

This adherence is something which can be formalized and can be known objectively. For instance, one can say that he believes in this or that creed, and follows these or those commandments, within this or that church. This is something objective, and empirically controllable; and you can define who belongs, or not, to a religion so defined.

What strikes me in considering many definitions of religion

by philosophers, theologians, psychologists and sociologists, is that there is another line of thinking, whereby religion is defined subjectively. In this case, religion is more or less a fervor for something absolute, a feeling which cannot be formalized. It is a sort of a total commitment, a total engagement to some values that the individual considers not debatable. He is ready to give his life for these ideas, or speaking in religious terms, he is ready to become a martyr of these values. If you ask him to define what these values are, he will not be able to do it precisely. Is this man, therefore, non-religious? An unbeliever? From the normative point of view of a particular church, this is a deviation. But we have to realize that all our conceptions of religion are more or less normative.

Even Durkheim wanted to invent a special vocabulary for dealing with social phenomena and religious phenomena. When we say of someone that he is an unbeliever, we imply that there are people who have escaped the control of certain churches, that there are deviations in regards to certain churches, to certain institutional ways of conceiving God or the absolute. Thus we seem to admit that to be an unbeliever is to be in a category whereby membership in a social group has been lost.

PIN: Well, perhaps we cannot speak of a culture of unbelief unless we define belief by means of two conceptual coordinates and not exclusively on the basis of cultural evidence. Several speakers have pointed out the need to identify dimensions measuring individual modes of belief, side by side with historically established concepts that clarify the institutional significance of belief. I would like to suggest, therefore, that one of the two conceptual coordinates could be represented on the axis of belief/unbelief, which defines type and intensity of adherence and type of personality; the other coordinate could be represented by the various historical models, as illustrated by Professor Luckmann, which describe the overall characteristics of a given era.

MARTIN: In this regard, I want to suggest that we consider also another aspect of the post-Christian situation, namely, the Marxist one, which Professor Luckmann's scheme rather leaves out. I describe that system as the official "us," or the official "we," which is really the actual "they." Marxism is the system where religion is officially privatized, not where it happens to be privatized, but where it is officially restricted to the "I." Thus we have a monopolistic system, which is not a private system at all, which is run by the "they" in the supposed interest of the "we."

In his paper, Professor Bellah defines Christianity as a moving dynamism, not necessarily continuous, in any important sense, with its past, even with respect to its name. Therefore, there is not even within Christianity the possibility of defining unbelief, because there is neither a definable core nor a locatable continuity. I hold, on the contrary, that there is ultimately a continuity and a core, that this involves some degree of exclusiveness, and that in terms of such a definition the problem of unbelief is precisely the breakdown of those exclusive acceptancies and historical affirmations, if that has in fact happened.

Otherwise the moving center creates a new crisis of unbelief with every generation. That is to say, there have been successive waves of unbelief since the beginning, and there is therefore no special crisis at the moment; and there have been not only successive waves, but rival definitions of religion at the same time.

BERGER: I think I am correct in saying that we have been talking about three types of problems: a conceptual one, a historical one, and the empirical problem of the present stage of society. I would suggest that we become very concrete and discuss the nature of stage C, or whatever you want to call it—in other words, the contemporary situation, or what in fact the cultures of belief are in the contemporary world.

CAPORALE: We could try to see if there are wider dimensions to the problem of unbelief, I mean dimensions which transcend the scope of religious institutions. This would probably be much more fruitful in terms of our research, namely to find what common characteristics underpin different systems of belief, such as political beliefs, formal religious beliefs, beliefs in mass media, in public leaders, in the family, in friends, and so on and so forth. In other words, we may want to broaden our approach to the concept of belief and look for something recurrent, overarching, and transcending the religious dimension.

I am particularly intrigued by the socio-psychological process in consequence of which men believe, whatever the referent of one's beliefs. Considering specifically the two components of belief, namely the cognitive system of meaning and the identification with and orientation to a community, it would be very fruitful to know how the two are integrated, not only at a religious level, but at all levels. In a comparative study this approach would help to identify the characteristics of belief per se, particularly as it elicits an individual's commitment, or alternative responses to commitment, including deviance, indifference, and hostility.

PARSONS: It seems to me that the historical perspective is very important in view of the relativity of what we mean by belief and unbelief. In former times, the functional equivalent, if one may use that term, of what we now call unbelief was called heresy. It was not nonbelief, it was the wrong belief, from a particular point of view. The modern phrase was introduced with secularization, which I associate with the enlightenment of the eighteenth century; it constituted a mass phenomenon for the first time, which has continued ever since, and of which perhaps the most massive current example is Marxism. The whole complex of Marxism is in the plural, if you will, but we can speak of classical atheism as almost associated to one branch or another of this secularist intellectual movement.

Under the pluralistic heading I include two aspects, namely what we call ecumenicism and, on the other hand, individuation (or what Professor Luckmann refers to as privatization). Ecumenism, if it represents belief, has one very fundamental historical component, namely the conviction of exclusive validity. That is, you cannot be an ecumenical Presbyterian and really treat as heretics in the old sense not only all Roman Catholics, but all Congregationalists, Quakers, Baptists, to say nothing of the religiously practicing Jews.

There is a relativization of the meaning of belief if you accept ecumenical pluralism, and I think most versions of it include various forms of secular humanism as ecumenically acceptable, that is, as not meriting exclusion from the moral community, in the Durkheimian sense.

On the other hand, the tendency to dissociate belief from

any referent system of traditionally organized religion seems to be essentially a new phenomenon. Yet there is a considerable persistence of older patterns which often function not as positive models, but as definitions for antithesis. This is so important that I just do not think that a purely horizontal cross section of the current situation, analyzed without reference to historical genesis, could be very fruitful.

ISAMBERT: My question has to do with a basic problem behind Professor Luckmann's paper, whether unbelief can be considered, per se, as a consistent phenomenon and, consequently, whether we should at all conceive of a sociology of belief or a sociology of unbelief. Eventually we end up with the same conclusion, namely, that unbelief can only be defined with reference to a given belief. Even when we speak of unbelief that transcends the beliefs commonly recognized as religious and upheld by religious institutions, our referent is a particularly institutionalized set of religions, which never extends to include the religious universe, although it may include non-Christian religions. In effect, we find ourselves confronting different religions, diverse in part, but still sharing a common element.

True, unbelief begins at the very core of religion. As Parsons has indicated, mutual tolerance among religious bodies is the first phase of unbelief. In any case, it represents some detachment with reference to certain elements of dogma. If we attempt to outline a typology of unbeliefs, we can think of the above as the first type. A second type is represented by those who are partially detached with reference to a system of belief handed over to them by their cultural tradition. A third category of unbelief implies a positive rejection; it means not simply the abandonment of a particular belief, or a specific system of beliefs, but the rejection of religious belief per se as inadmissible. To give an example, the notion of hell may induce some Christians to either reject the idea of hell, or to reject the entire Christian system because it contains the idea of hell. This rejection can be easily generalized and frequently leads to another type of unbelief, namely, the rejection not only of a particular system of belief, but of all belief, because the doctrine is not empirically or rationally grounded. In this case, we have what we may call absolute unbelief, or the rejection of all beliefs.

To each of these degrees of unbelief there corresponds a form of substitute belief. Professor Berger has mentioned belief in the virtue of childhood as one of the typical substitute beliefs of contemporary society. We can also think of other nonreligious beliefs that are gradually taking the place of religious beliefs, often at the very moment when people think they have done away with belief.

PIN: There is a distinct opposition of viewpoints between theologians, sociologists, and psychologists on this problem, reflecting our different backgrounds and our distinct cultural heritage, particularly the Catholic tradition and the pluralistic tradition. Some of us still operate within the mental perspective of the emergence of modern secularism. In countries of uni-religious tradition, such as Italy, unbelief manifests itself in the rejection and the negative attack against belief as a component of the general culture rather than of a particular church. In this case, unbelief takes the nuance of negation of culturally established belief. In pluralistic countries, on the other hand, we observe an astonishing ecumenical climate in force of which one assumes a priori that the neighbor has some sort of belief. I refer to the advertisement that one observes occasionally in the United States inviting the reader to "go to the church of your choice." A similar advertisement would be inconceivable in a nonpluralistic country. This phenomenon, however, puts a serious problem to those of us who come from a uni-religious background. If we accept the model latent behind this mutual acceptance and respect between religious groups, should we conclude that these different beliefs have the same right to exist? Or should we think it possible to establish an empirical criterion on the basis of which we can rightly say that some of these people are real believers while the others are believers in functional substitutes of beliefs, such as the belief in childhood, the belief in democracy, or whatever?

BERGER: Father Pin makes a distinction between countries of Catholic traditions and countries of pluralistic traditions. This distinction can be made legitimately because there are important sociologic differences between the two. But I wonder if we may not be misled by this, considering that there are certain fundamental structures which have much more in common than appears at first sight. To be sure, it is most unlikely to see an advertisement reading "Go to the church of your choice" in Italy, but in fact people do—namely the choice to go or not to go to the one church available. This is an important difference when we consider the hundreds of churches that may be available in an American community. What I am suggesting is that there is a de facto pluralistic situation here, which is important to look at. There are competitors to the traditional religious institution. Etymology is frequently misleading, but it is relevant to note that the word *heresy* originally meant selection or choice within a tradition. In this sense today we are all heretical in that we have a choice in our kind of society which was not previously available. Although we come from different countries, culturally we all come from the Western world (I mean the political Western world as distinct from the Oriental), where there are very important common structures which are worth investigating sociologically.

O'DEA: We have tended to talk about belief being a kind of cognitive-affective phenomenon. When we say cognitive-affective phenomenon we mean two things: one, that it involves orientation, and two, that it involves relationship. I think that relationship is the truly important and significant aspect of the phenomenon. It is a certain kind of relationship to being, to the world, to one's fellow men. How that can be conceptualized is probably not the most important aspect of it. It seems to me, therefore, that one should talk about belief in the context of the community. I will give a small example of this community aspect becoming really quite important in relationship to the level of transcendence. When American Catholics and Protestants went to Selma, Alabama, during the civil rights struggle of the 1960s, to march, to be on picket lines, to face the police, what Catholics and Protestants discovered was something that it would be misleading to state simply in terms of belief. We talk about recognition that the other belief was a morally permissible one; but no matter what each of them would have said about it, they discovered a community that, in certain important respects, transcended the religious community to which they belonged.

A Catholic may have felt that he belonged to the universal Church, but a lot of members of the universal Church would not participate in the events of Alabama, while he and some Presbyterians and Congregationalists composed (so they discovered) a new kind of community. The relationship between this new community and what we are calling belief is a very important one and not always an easy one to define.

BELLAH: I see a danger in Professor Luckmann's position that, if institutional belonging no longer defines religion or belief, then everything might count as religion or belief. We have heard things like belief in the family, in sports, in mass media, in corporations, almost everything was mentioned here as possible institutions performing one or another of the functions that religion has had. In the interest of clarification I want to ask two questions: first, What about the man for whom various of these religious functions are performed by various agencies, who may not have all the functions performed by anyone, who sorts out, as it were, his religious functions into a number of different agencies, or cultures of belief, in which he participates with various degrees of seriousness or various degrees of provisionality? Is this beginning to happen? Is there any way in which this man integrates all of these various signals?

The other question reflects a theological interest. I do not think that we have fully discussed that particular function or aspect of the biblical religions which serves at certain levels in a disintegrative capacity. I can think of various aspects of Christianity, that would not fit easily into the Durkheimian definition of religion. Is this the problem, for example, with civil religion, or with other kinds of religion in which, perhaps, an overbalance of the integrative function of religion exclusively can occur?

BERGER: If we agree that the present situation may be characterized by the fact that quasi-religious functions are not performed predominantly, much less exclusively, by one specialized institution, we have done something very significant in terms of the traditional sociology of religion. In this case it becomes particularly difficult to specify research programs in the sociology of religion, because it is no longer easily segregated from occupational sociology, sociology of the family, or for that matter sociology of mass media, social psychology, etc. Despite the rather frightening thought of sociology of religion breaking up as an academic discipline with a specific subject area, it is a prospect that must be faced, if there is any validity to the hypothesis that religious functions are indeed no longer exclusively performed by religious institutions, but that they are performed by various kinds of institutions among which specialized religious institutions are still present.

On the social psychological level, a number of interesting questions, such as Professor Bellah's, which could be investigated (some of them with considerable difficulty) present themselves immediately. They are evidently questions which are even more complicated at the level of research operations, because it seems to me increasingly likely that religious functions will be performed in a rather diffused way by various kinds of institutions. At the same time through higher education, through the increase of the broad range of the middle class, for a certain number of people in western industrial societies the chances, on the average, of a higher degree of reflectiveness about problems has increased.

MARLÉ: I would like to comment on Bellah's remark on the disintegrative function of belief and, at the same time, comment on the statement of Parsons' concerning the ecumenical phenomenon today, viewed as an expression of weakness of belief or at least of a certain type of belief, or faith. I can think of a number of Christians to which these notions apply; but I regret to say that they still argue that our reference point is belief understood as belonging to an institution. This is tantamount to placing again the institution as founder and foundation of belief.

Among certain Christians, at least, the ecumenical movement is viewed exactly in the opposite light, namely, as an exigency of a faith which recognized that it has something more than what the institution represents, and which reaches the point of doing away even with the forms under which it is presented. This phenomenon should make us reflect on the singular characteristic of this faith, which does not define itself entirely in terms of an institution. This is, for instance, the faith that has made possible the centuries-old mutual understanding between the Oriental and Western churches. Although separated as institutions, these churches have recognized each other as being truly and definitively within the limits of the Christian faith with some minor differences, which at no time made an unbeliever of the other church. Which is to say that the institutionalized perspectives that constitute the core of certain beliefs are not coterminous with the reality of those beliefs.

BELLAH: I want to pursue this conceptual discussion a little bit further, because it seems to me that the issues involved are so enormously complex. Several times during the discussion I felt that we were not talking about the same things. Not that we are going to agree on terminology, but perhaps we might try to relate to each other in terms of various positions. The sociological conceptualization of religion, which was put forward by Professor Berger and developed considerably by Professor Luckmann, is a very valuable reference point.

The fact that the meaningful aspects of life are handled by various beliefs and indeed various institutionalized specialists is not unique to the present situation; it is indeed a normal situation in most of the world. In Japan, for example, the obvious fact that people are married in a Shinto shrine and buried in a Buddhist temple is nothing new; it is something that has taken place for centuries. It has not caused any split souls or anguish, except rarely, under special circumstances. Even in areas where we have to some extent a mythical conception of religious monolithic structures, not entirely dissimilar kinds of differentiation occur. For instance, anthropological studies of folk society, which are in some sense catholic, indicate a wide variety of "religious" specialists, which are a spectrum of closer and more remote relations to official church religion.

What is new about the present situation is not diversity, which I think is normal in human societies, but the element of choice, and this does create pressures and strains for individuals. In a situation where diversity is simply accepted, and everybody knows what it is and knows which specialist to go to, and for what particular need, if you can use such a term, there is no problem. Even in this case though, there is one point on which I am a little hesitant to go along with Luckmann's analysis, namely the privatization issue. When you have the institutionalization of choice, even as expressed on the rather vulgar level of "go to the church of your choice," you are already giving a kind of institutional support to the individual making his choice. Therefore, it would be a mistake to emphasize solely the individuation, without appreciating that permissiveness of society, which does not tell man anymore what to do, or which is not willing to provide an overarching framework, to the extent of permitting an individual to come to terms with ultimate issues. This, I think, is a positive institutionalization of a certain kind of human freedom. I do not want to emphasize it exclusively, because clearly the other side of the picture is there, but I think it needs to be brought out.

Finally, I should like to address the question about the disintegrative effect of religion. Here we run into a problem common in sociological concerns, namely, of what system are we speaking? Presumably for the Christian who is witnessing in Selma, Alabama, this is not a distintegrative act. It may indeed be a highly integrative act which confirms him in his own convictions, in the sense of living up to his religion, but it may also cause disintegrative consequences for the social system. Integration is a highly difficult word because, especially in some quarters, it seems necessarily to imply a positive value in any existing status quo. But when we bring in the religious element, and especially the element of meaning, integration becomes relative to value components which transcend any particular social system.

Sociological language can do justice to the theologians' insights by insisting that religious commitments may indeed be radically destructive given a social status quo, without denying that the religious commitment of the people undertaking this disturbing social task may have an integrative consequence, if examined from another system's perspective.

10

ON THE DEVELOPMENT OF UNBELIEF

·

BELLAH: Rather than present a summary of my paper, "The Historical Background of Unbelief," I will attempt to focus on some important issues. It seems, at times, as though we are in the final stages of a centuries-long dispute between philosophy and religion, in which nobody really cares who wins or loses. I happen to agree with Professor Luckmann, however, that we are in the presence of something new. I would also say that we are perhaps too old to speak with much authority about what is happening; we all had important formative experiences before or during the Second World War, and I think that something has changed since 1945. We are in the presence of a rapidly accelerating shift in the spiritual atmosphere that, I am afraid, few of us, including myself, are very well prepared to appreciate. Of course, history is seldom abrupt. People such as William Blake, and more recently Yeats, were but a few prophets in the wilderness of a new dispensation, which in the last twenty years has actually begun to arrive.

Further, close to religious man is death and hell. To be trapped in everyday pragmatic reality is precisely, and classically, to be trapped in hell. It is to live in the world of sin, the fallen world, the world of illusion. Religion has always been grounded in nonordinary experience; in nonordinary reality breaking into ordinary reality. If established religion can be seen as collapsing in the present situation, it is not because it is religion, but because it is religion trapped in ordinary reality, without transcendence, without manner, without the devastating power of the sacred. Even more, all the classical forms of nonbelief are collapsing. Neither enlightened rationalism nor classical Marxism command any significant loyalty among the young. If religion is faltering in the present encounter with unbelief, it is only because religion is unable to grasp its monumental opportunity. The world looks to the churches for manifestations of the sacred, but the churches are on the defensive.

In the present situation all cognitive structures have been rendered provisional. There is no way to prove Christianity, no way to prove rationalism, no way to prove Marxism. There is no way to test commitment or faith on cognitive argument. Though I know that most men are still caught in archaic or traditional modes of consciousness, I speak of the innovating vanguard, and I know that this will create problems for survey research. But history tells us that the innovating minority is always decisive. The alternative to the cognitive, in the narrow sense, is neither the affective nor the expressive, though both of these are very important. Both, in Parsonian terms, are constitutive of symbolism. This is the level of symbolism which I am trying to talk about as an alternative to the cognitive; I think it is closely related to what Professor Luckmann is implying when he speaks of overarching schemes of interpretation. I especially appreciate his remarks qualifying the rather highly conscious and intellectual sense that that phrase might have, and his indication that these overarching schemes may involve an unconscious dimension. It is important to see that these structures are constructive since they are symbolic and, in some sense, are a human product. Nevertheless, that word "constructive" could be misleading if it makes us overemphasize the conscious ego processes and overlook the great importance of unconscious creativity.

Religious symbolism is discovered, and in one sense is revealed, in experience. It is not artificially concocted according to formulas. Sigmund Freud was the culmination and the grave digger of the Enlightenment. He was the culmination because he brought even the unconscious itself into the domain of rational analysis, but he was the grave digger by revealing that the conscious ego is a frail mechanism, especially when it tries to defy the totality of the psyche. His work was the basis for a radical questioning of the Enlightenment and for a possible reunification of human consciousness. The ego cut off from the sources of its vitality is man outside the garden, falling man in the grip of the Principalities and Powers, man fratricidal and hellish. Insofar as we, as social scientists, live in the world of the ego alone, we are trapped in that hellish existence.

Now, on the contrary, for the first time, the choice is not philosophy or religion, as it was for Pascal and so many others. Our science, assigning a considerable part to Freud himself, is beginning faintly and crudely to be able to cope with the richness of reality, as religion, for so many centuries, has seen it. Therefore, I think, we do not need to make a choice; we can begin to translate between realms of reality, always recognizing the radical, problematic nature of such translations. We are beginning to be able to analyze man even in the realm of the encounter of the *mysterium tremendum*. This does not mean psychologizing or explaining away as it did even for Freud. Because we must now be able to give up the dogmas at the basis of our own endeavor, while remaining committed to enlightened rationalism as the foundation of our scientific work, we nevertheless know that this is only one road to reality, that it stands under the judgment of other modes. Finally, we know that the great symbols which justify science itself rest on much deeper levels of consciousness.

We are in a revolutionary situation, then, with respect to both science and religion, reason and faith. Dogmas of all kinds are questioned. We stand at the verge of a possible reunification of consciousness, not because of the imperialism of science, but because of the realization of the fallen nature of man and the perception of the eschatological possibility of new being.

ISAMBERT: Professor Bellah, you have indicated that your referent is basically America. How can one speak of historical approach to the problem of unbelief from a narrow viewpoint? After all, though the theme is essentially American, it has European origins. The question whether there have emerged elsewhere other types of unbelief has not been raised at all. In my little volume on *Christianisme et classe ouvrière,* I pointed out that in France, the unbelief of the working class becomes noticeable toward the end of the nineteenth century. At that time Senator Corbon, speaking in the Senate, attacked Dupanlou in these terms: "Why are we leaving? Because you have left us first." That is to say: the Catholic Church has abandoned us, and through the Church God has abandoned us; therefore, we will abandon God. Our future is no longer in God but in work.

It would be anachronistic to use these concepts apropos of unbelief in France today. All the same, we need to find out how things did change. I cannot accept the notion that in France unbelief is essentially a phenomenon of the intellectuals, and that the working classes have abandoned the Catholic religion and traditional beliefs because the intellectuals have preached atheism to them.

Unbelief has been deeply rooted in the French working class, particularly as a result of the rupture between the controlling class and the working class. Lately the trend has been in a less revolutionary direction, but characterized by utilitarianism and much deeper secularism than was the case of the atheistic workers of the classical period of labor unrest. This goes to show how difficult it is to make generalizations in this matter. It is my contention that this popular unbelief, which appears to me as a significantly different type of unbelief, transcends the parameters of the phenomenon of unbelief, as experienced in the American context. This makes it compelling to consider the phenomenon of unbelief on a worldwide scale.

If we want to place the notion of unbelief in its proper historical perspective, we must take into account its popular varieties. Instead of attempting to exorcise with holy water the problems that crowd the notion of unbelief, I would rather suggest that we endeavor to rediscover the drama of the antagonism, or whatever you may want to name it, that divides the world, not only with bombs and frontiers, but above all, by way of radically antithetic positions.

BELLAH: To even attempt an answer to this very important set of questions would take far more time than I feel I should take; but let me reply briefly on one point. All of us speak out of our cultural backgrounds. I think it is clear that my observations come out of an American situation which has been in some sense, in spite of the high figures for church attendance and other such indications, profoundly secular for a long time.

HOUTART: I should like to congratulate Professor Bellah on two accounts. First, for calling our attention to the link between the problem of unbelief and some of the gravest problems of society today; this linkage has been largely overlooked by us. Second, for suggesting the possibility of coexistence and manifestations within the same person of elements proper to the "organizational man" and to the "homo religiosus."

I would like to pose the question, however, whether we are not dealing in fact with the fundamental problem of the sociology of knowledge. I will not bring out again the criticism of the American frame of reference that predominates in his presentation; actually, I intended to show my appreciation for the attention he has paid to Asia. Yet the fact remains that his referent was basically Western society, and specifically American society, and his Protestant background of Calvinistic origin. This orientation comes through, for instance, in his pessimism about men, in the opposition between religious content and religious experience, in the conception of the Bible as opposed to Greek tradition, and in the opposition between institutions and personal styles of religious life.

MARTIN: I disagree so entirely with Professor Bellah that what I am going to say is going to be "wicked," and my manner of saying is going to be equally as wicked. He has been too existential in his approach. Professor Bellah seems to me to believe that there are no radical alternatives, no overall coherences in forming those alternatives. I think he believes this because he says that we have no compelling cognitive criteria for deciding between those alternatives. He also believes that this personal view, which is, as he says, a highly American view, is the way things are going to go in the world. In other words, we are going back to the Roman Empire, sideways to Japan, and forward to a situation where the Church of England has organized what will begin to look like a vertebrate institution.

I applaud the achievement of rational coherences and a radical opposition to alternatives in religion, and I do not think that these radical alternatives and the opposing of them is the same thing at all as having compelling cognitive criteria up your sleeves. I do not think that it was a perversion or an unhappy phase in human development; I believe it was an advancement. Obviously, it was not the whole story, but it is still a very important advance that will continue to be with us.

Now I am not surprised that Bellah has located a key group with a historical periscope—that is to say, a surrogate, in his terms, for the elite conscious segment of the working class in Marx's terms. I am not surprised that he appeals to anti-nomial, radical, subjectivist, child-heroes of our time—to the students; and yet, surely, there is a great paradox here, which is that they are the most intolerant, sectarian, exclusive group that I happen to know. He proclaims the end of theology to parallel the end of ideology. I am surprised that Bellah appeals to students, because they reject in politics precisely what he celebrates in religion, because they recognize that this value consensus in politics is just another ideology, another dogma, however syncretistic.

In other words, Professor Bellah puts all the rest of us in the American melting pot and presents us with the value consensus, not of the medieval village, but of the electronic city.

PARSONS: Professor Bellah's paper seemed at first to be a combination of historical and scientific assertions and eschatological visions. Now I see we have been treated to a large dose of the eschatological vision. I should like to reply religiously, and work back to see if I can discover some of the more scientific answers.

Bellah closed with the statement that the changes are coming about because of the realization of the fallen nature of man. This notion of "fallen man" has always made my ears perk up. I have never understood it; I have never known that it happened, and I am not sure that it has been realized today.

I have always had a rather optimistic view of man, or at least, one that coincided with man's behavior. Bellah has asserted that this particular religious symbolism is revealed in experience, but I thought that religious symbolism was revealed in community and not in private experience. Bellah has spoken of the importance of the unconscious in creativity, and I must agree. However, I cannot move with him from the unconscious to the weak ego. I have to identify with Freud, who said that where the id is, the ego has got to be. If I have to make a choice, I should rather trust the ego than trust the unconscious. Bellah has asserted that religion is grounded in the nonordinary reality which, sometimes, breaks out into reality. I have always thought that religion was the everyday, was the regular, was the aspect of the recurrent, and that somehow this breaking out into the unusual was a rather extreme version of it.

Let me move now into the paper itself. I will begin by commenting on a few points from the paper which are stylistic because the style of the paper shapes the ensuing content. Two quotations seem to move between the factually asserted and the rhetorical. I have picked out the statement that "The Bible was not, on the whole, created by a similarly self-conscious intellectual strata, but by religious and political enthusiasts much closer to the common religious conscience." As I read the sentence I wondered how important the phrase on the whole was; and I cannot quite grasp what is meant by "the Bible" since there are so many authors involved, coming from so many times, classes, and strata.

I am concerned about Bellah's notion of the self-conscious intellectual strata, as if it were not a social-stratification anachronism. We have these strata around today. We can differentiate the self-conscious, intellectual strata from religious and political enthusiasts; but to read this kind of a stratification system back into the biblical period is a bit strained. I wonder whether one could not say that any author of part of the Bible certainly fulfilled the function within his culture. This is the same role that the self-conscious intellectual strata fulfills in the present time.

The vast increase in literacy and education in the past few centuries has been intimately related to the rise of antiauthoritarianism as a major cultural theme of our times. The world does not look that way to me. Had we any possibility of measuring authoritarianism and antiauthoritarianism, I suspect that the authoritarians would have the edge on most accounts. Professor Bellah gets himself into the position of trying to account for a phenomenon which I do not believe exists in the first place. But even if it does exist, I am not sure that the coalition between increasing literacy and antiauthoritarianism would necessarily hold up. I am recalling some of those theoretical studies that used to go out in the old days, and I wonder about the correlation between education and social positions.

I wonder, in fact, whether the description of the American life and its outward directness may not be nearer to the true case than the preoccupation with personal experience. I do not know how Professor Bellah would maintain that these are necessarily innovative. In his discussion of the "black power" problem, Bellah shifts into a psychological mood, feeling that it is not the economic and political grievances of the black but self-hatred and the unconscious rejection of one's blackness which gives the dynamics to the movement. I have a problem here on the shifting of system references.

Professor Bellah also says that "Effective moral and political action can be carried out with widely different religious motivations." The notion here is that there is an integration of society around notions of effective moral and political action. I do not see current American society as being that integrated. I am too concerned with strife, conflict, and violence in our society to believe that we are moving to a point at which there is a mutual notion of moral action. The problem which is cutting right down through society is that we do not even know what effective moral and political action is. We cannot agree that we have different interests, that people make different decisions, and that different parts of the community support different parts of the moral code.

BERGER: I think I see a central problem emerging. There is some agreement here on this, namely, that we are dealing in the contemporary situation, where we can perceive two co-existing trends, which might be called secularizing or counter-secularizing, or perhaps (to use Professor Marty's terms) "operational" and "apocalyptic." This is of crucial importance, and I would wonder: (1) Am I correct in thinking that there is some agreement about it, because, if this is the case, it would be very important indeed? and, (2) If there is agreement, how do these two trends relate? and (3) Even more specifically, sociologically, where are these two trends located?

VERGOTE: In this regard, I should like to call attention to an element which to me seems very important for the changes in contemporary culture. I detect in Professor Bellah's presentation an insistence on personal experience as opposed to dogmatic faith. The search for personal experience is a major trait of contemporary men. The term itself is new, both in the cultural and in the religious contexts. I wonder whether this insistence on personal experience may not be correlated with another phenomenon: socialization. But what does personal experience mean? Bellah quotes Freud and psychoanalysis. What psychoanalysis teaches us is that the unconscious and experience are chaotic realities, full of contradictions and illusions.

In the history of religions we invariably observe that symbolic language preceded the individual experience. I have the impression that sociologists often think that symbolic language is an expression of experience. But if we pay attention to history we observe that symbolic language gives men the opportunity to make an experience. Man is a talking animal, and it is language that gives him the vision, the context, and the possibility to go through some experiences. This means that man internalizes certain symbolic language transmitted to him through culture.

A major characteristic of contemporary problems of unbelief and belief is precisely this opposition to all language that comes to us from the outside. It is a typical trait dominant in contemporary mentality, and its origin should be studied. For this reason I should like to propose that man experiences goodness, death, anguish, but that he never makes a religious experience. The current tendency, I believe, is to systematically reject the language that is being handed out by previous generations; and this, at least, is a sociological fact.

LUCKMANN: I suspect that Professor Bellah is being rather harshly dealt with in this discussion. I think that this might be due partly to the fact that neither he nor some of his critics explicated some of their presuppositions in their arguments and counter-arguments, and partly to the fact that they were not quite sociological enough. I do not know whether we can very easily identify all the causes for the social production of such phenomena as Bellah has identified. As sociologists, we would look primarily at social structures. I think that he was talking about a position which some of us took for granted, and therefore did not explicate sufficiently. This is what Pro-

fessor Parsons called "post-industrial society." I think we have
been extrapolating from phenomena which we find primarily
in the middle strata, more specifically, in the younger generation of industrial societies, with a distinct social structure and
with different socialization processes from those of the societies in the process of industrialization.

My second point is linked to this. Professor Martin spoke
of "operational man," and Professor Bellah spoke of the "new
religious man." If we are speaking openly of religiosity and
unbelief, we would be making a mistake in thinking that
these are two types of men that appear in our society; we are
actually speaking of the same man. The "operational man"
is only an abstract concept, a rarefied way of referring to
orientations and performances within clearly defined institutional contexts. The same man who is "operational" and
pragmatic within these institutional contexts may also be
"the new religious man" in the rather large interstitial areas
between the institutions, in contexts that is, which are not in
his orientation or his behavior, not controlled by functionally
rational institutional norms.

I must say I cannot conceive very easily of a contemporary
man, or of myself for that matter, as embodying the concept
of an operational man; but I know that we are pragmatic,
that we submit, that we conform with two functionally rational norms in any number of institutionally defined contexts. However, we are living outside of functionally and
rationally defined institutional contexts to a certain extent.
It would be probably an important, though difficult, task to
develop hypotheses as to how the dissonances of a cognitive
and an emotional kind are resolved by the fact that we are
both operational men and new religious men.

I should want to correct this picture; I think that some of
us are more operational, and some of us (for example, the
student expanding his consciousness in California) are more
the "new religious man."

CARRIER: I have read Bellah's paper, not as a "position" paper
but as a provocative set of suggestions, and I should like to
comment on two points, two phrases, two affirmations. Professor Bellah says that, "the conclusion grows ever stronger
that religion is a part of the species life of man as central to

his self-definition as speech." As a sociologist, a priest, and a theologian, I feel that this is a very worthy hypothesis and a crucial problem. The theologians and philosophers of old talked about "homo religiosus" and "homo christianus." I see many sociologists today coming back to that idea. It remains still a vague affirmation; I don't think it has been phrased into a workable hypothesis.

The idea of religion being a part of the social life of man, of man being religious more often than we thought in the old theological consideration of humanity, is a very fruitful idea. Bellah would exclude as nonbelievers those who are trapped in the immediate, in the everyday, those, to use the words of Tillich, "who have apparently no ultimate concern." I think this has to be explored with operational methods. But I don't know of any serious sociological study that would support this hypothesis. As a man interested in education, I think we have a problem which deserves more theological and sociological research. For the Secretariat for Non-Believers this is a crucial point: is humanity divided into believers and nonbelievers, or rather between those who believe like we believe and those who believe differently?

A second affirmation of Bellah's occurs where he speaks of religious institutions: "The effort to maintain orthodox belief has been primarily an effort to maintain authority rather than faith." I would agree with that affirmation if it were not for the adverbial expression "primarily." I think we have here another central and fundamental problem. I agree that a religious body, such as the Catholic Church, is capable of abuses through some of its organisms, through the sheer use of power. There is the possibility of confusion between the will of the religious body to maintain orthodoxy and the use of its power as power. This has been affirmed even at the Vatican Council.

But when we speak in these terms we are leaving aside something essential. Once we have conceded the abuse of religious power by sheer weight of structure, there still remains a dilemma: is the real issue whether the future belongs to institutionalized religion or privatized religion? If we put it that way, however, we are yet forgetting something important; for many believers the institution itself, or a certain aspect of it, is an object of faith. The alternative is not between the power-imposing institution and privatized religion. I would rather place the alternative between a power-imposing institution and an institution which is internalized whereby the believer accepts the institution as the expression of a tradition, of a common service, of a communion. In the creed, we say: "Credo in Ecclesiam," it is an object of faith. It is said also in the paper of Professor Bellah: "The Church is the body of Christ."

The phenomenon of growing unbelief might be viewed from an organized body not simply as a dropping out of the Church, a cutting off of those who simply separate themselves. It indicates a growing social or psychological distance between a man who remains a believer and the way he sees and believes in his church. These people are not simply outside; they are, as the Italians would say, *allontanati*. This point of view seems to be substantiated by current research, which shows that the greatest difficulties Catholics experience have to do with their dealing with the Church as an institution.

O'DEA: This line of discussion does raise the rather important problem of how we, as sociologists, put together our own existential stand on the one hand, with the necessity for scientific posture on the other. The role of the social scientist is analysis. In the past, analysis has been conducted in a theoretical frame of reference, which has stayed away from what I will refer to as existence, consigning that side of life to the emotional and, therefore, to the less important. In many ways, Bellah was reacting vigorously and with justification against this kind of theoretical presupposition.

However, when sociology becomes aware of existence, it must become aware of it in a cognitive mode as a datum; it cannot become aware of it as part of its scientific posture. There is a difference between overcoming objectivization in life and overcoming it in the analysis of the social sciences. To overcome it in life means being able to have some contact with that beyond which stands past the subject-object frame of reference. To overcome it in social sciences is to have some idea that there is a realm of relationship to transcendence in which people live, and to be able to do justice to people's actions as data in that realm.

The task which Professor Bellah has faced is indeed not an

easy one. Nevertheless, his attempt to bridge the subject-object split, the cognitive-emotional split, has not been really successful. One must face the "truth claims" of competing doctrines. Truth value will not mean the same about a scientific hypothesis as it will about a creed, although there may be some analogy between the two. Bellah, in contrasting "embodied truth" and "not known truth," tries to get out of the impass by resorting to rhetoric. I agree with the distinction he is trying to make—but the phenomena of the distinction are not all on one level. This raises the problem of cognition, as the forward edge of man as he moves into the future and into experience. It is true that, in certain Western writings, cognition has been split off from the rest of man and has been in certain ways objectivized, a process which seems to me to be a distortion.

The problems of the constitution of new symbolism are innumerable. It was Yeats who said that he didn't like the man who just thought with his head and didn't think also with the marrow bone. Yeats also said, "And what rough beast, its hour come round at last/Slouches towards Bethlehem to be born?" When Bellah speaks of the "image of Christ," this has to have some cognitive content if we are to distinguish it from the "beast slouching towards Bethlehem." My fellow New Englander, Ralph Waldo Emerson, said that he would live from the impulses that came to him. His idea of impulses was slightly different from Freud's. Nevertheless, there is a common area between them. When he was asked, "But what if the impulses are from below?" he replied, "If I am the devil's child, I shall live by the devil." Can we, two-and-a-half generations after Auschwitz, say if we are the devil's child, we will live by the devil? Are we to be that sufficiently uncritical of the unconscious? I feel that the unconscious is the source of creativity; what David Bakan has called the "agentive" side of man (against the "communal") has been terribly exaggerated both in life and in our analytical structures. Nevertheless, the role of reason and cognition remains a very important one.

I would like, therefore, to go back to Bellah's comment on authority: "The effort to maintain orthodox belief has been primarily an effort to maintain authority rather than faith." The statement will not hold up under historical examination. For instance, one cannot look at the Pontificate of Pius IX and think that this was primarily an effort to maintain authority. The effort to maintain authority was derived from an effort to maintain faith, as Pius IX and the people around him understood faith, which was in terms of the objectivized content. In the effort to do this, authority, having become functionally quite enhanced, became emotionally enhanced too.

In this type of situation, as one begins using authority to defend faith, if one is not careful, one can end up by using faith to defend authority. History is a matter of strain, of paradox and dilemma, of accomplishment and defeat, of tragedy and comedy. One cannot quite say these things about faith and authority as though the American denomination-alist evolution has brushed aside all those questions, and all those who were caught in them, who suffered them, who felt the "angst," the tension, and the pain. Again, with reference to internalization being the main direction of development, it is important that we do not take the development of Prot-estantism as normative.

Internalization is not the opposition of objectified institu-tionalization. That was the experience of Luther, but this is not the whole picture. The Roman Catholic Church did not continue to exist for four hundred years after the Reforma-tion merely because it was able to oppress people by author-ity. Let me just point to one very important institutional form, the confessional. Paul Tillich said that the confessional was the school which for centuries and centuries prepared for Luther and the Lutheran-Augustinian experience. In the con-fessional, we have a combination of the most cognitively stated kind of norm, the most objectivized personal relation-ship, and at the same time, the deepest internal conviction. It is possible to say this without implying that the confes-sional is a good or bad kind of institution. I am trying to understand this historical form with certain empathy and in-sight. There is in the confessional both an extreme objectivi-cation on the one hand and an intense subjectivity on the other, related together at a particular point of institutionaliza-tion. If one does not understand that, then one understands nothing about that particular form of sacramentalism which existed in the pre-Reformation church and which has per-sisted in the Western Church of the counter-Reformation.

DE LUBAC: I apologize to Professor Bellah if I do not make any remarks of a sociological nature, but I will not make any theological ones either for the moment. My reflections are historical in nature. There is a certain opposition between the Platonic world view and the biblical, even though this has become much oversimplified. I do not think that it is right to affirm, as a point of departure, a total opposition between faith according to the Greek model, a belief in objects, in truths, in realities, and a biblical faith which would involve no assent to knowledge.

If this is not entirely true of the Bible in the Old Testament, it seems to me to be untenable so far as the New Testament is concerned. For it is from this New Testament that the Christian churches derive their origin. If they call themselves Christian, it is precisely because the Old Testament is considered by them as a kind of prehistory. Thus, if the New Testament contains, in the minds of its authors, the faith in an event, this faith also contains objective elements. It is not, to be sure, a belief in abstract objects or impersonal ideas; it is rather, as in the Old Testament, a belief in facts, in events in which people are involved, people about whom something is known historically. I refer, for example, to the studies of Father Alfaro, Senior Professor and Dean of Studies at the Theological Faculty of the Gregorian University. This is not just a matter of personal ideas but of facts, which a very mediocre historian could verify with ease.

The position stated by Bellah somewhat forces this perspective. Consequently, we find much criticism thereafter of developments that occurred throughout history. No wonder that one will feel authorized to reject without any distinctions that which is labeled as dogmatic orthodoxy. An added advantage to this initial position, and Professor Bellah has availed himself of it, is that it allows us to eliminate the conflict between science and faith. But I believe that this conflict can be overcome in a completely different manner. The realities in which the Christian believes are of a different order than those of scientific knowledge, which is not all of human knowledge.

But the principal "advantage," perhaps, that one could derive from this position is that Christian faith thus becomes a sort of plastic material, completely fluid, amorphous, from which many different things could be molded. One would no longer see any borderlines between Christian faith, credulity, unbelief, types of belief, humanitarianism, and so forth, if there is no precise object of Christian faith. Once again, however, this does not seem to me to be in conformity with the data of history, nor with the texts themselves of the New Testament.

BELLAH: It is impossible to even begin to deal with the many points that have been raised. But fortunately, a number of people have focused on the same questions, so I will try to deal with some of the issues that have come up repeatedly. First of all, I accept fully the obligation, as a social scientist, to be analytical, to be in the broadest sense empirical, and to undertake a quest for knowledge which may very well undermine assumptions which I hold on extrascientific grounds.

On the other hand, particularly in the area of religion, I have simply reached the point where I find it difficult to sit through endless discussions which have no relation to the subject about which the discussants are apparently talking. Therefore, rather than trying to head off some of the questions which arose later, I deliberately attempted to strike a note which would bring the existentialist concerns with which we are dealing before us, and not allow us entirely to escape into the higher reaches of abstraction.

The necessary consequence of taking a polemical position is that one is immediately classed somehow in the opposite camp, whenever one makes a statement which seems critical of any given position. A whole series of questions focus around (1) my apparent down-grading of the cognitive, (2) my apparent implication that the unconscious is a more valuable source of insight than the ego, (3) my apparent lack of respect for reason, (4) my apparent assumption that a thousand and more years of theology is no longer of any value or relevance. These conclusions are certainly not the ones that I would wish to be drawn from my paper.

I pointed out the weakness of the ego when it is isolated or alienated from the rest of the total psyche. From that, I do not conclude that one must trust the id and not the ego. Rather, an integrated personality, in which the communication between deeper levels and unconscious levels of personality and the ego is open, is a fuller expression of humanity than one where those lines of communication are closed. The "pure operational man" also has an unconscious, even if the communication between his ego and his unconscious is very bad. I would suspect that some of his dreams are rather nightmarish. So the issue is not to take any one side of such dichotomy.

Theology, in my opinion, is a body of thought which in historic times has had by far the subtlest and most complex understanding of human motives and of the reality of the life of the spirit. We are today, in social science, only beginning very crudely and inadequately to be able to deal from the basis of social scientific endeavor with issues which theology has richly, subtly, and complexly been treating for many centuries. It is my feeling that anyone interested in religion, even purely from the scientific point of view, has an enormous amount to learn from theology. Needless to say, I feel that the theological enterprise is an essential part of the religious life, at least in the Western tradition, and is going to continue to be so.

The present situation is exciting because, for the first time in the history of social science, it is beginning to be possible to translate between the language of theology and the language of social science; not because theology has somehow grown up and been able to speak to the social scientist, but because social science is beginning to develop a conceptual scheme, and a terminology subtle enough for it to be worthwhile for a conversation to exist. I hope these remarks will indicate that I do not have any notions that theology as an enterprise is through.

The problems, however, of the level of discourse and of the kinds of cognition with which theology deals, and of the relation between cognitive symbolization in the narrow sense and what I have called "constitutive symbolism" remain very significant. From what I can see, many contemporary theologians are equally concerned with these issues.

Let me move, then, to what some people have felt was an overemphasis on the realm of experience, and particularly, private or personal experience. I do think that the Western religious tradition has a very serious problem in dealing with experience. Historical controversy and the difficulties which emerged from certain kinds of mystical movements, have an overdefensiveness with regard to the realm of experience. Direct or immediate experience in the realm of religion is never the whole story, is never adequate. That experience drives toward symbolization, and is not complete at the level of human action without symbolization. Man is a symbolic animal. To emphasize the significance of experience is not to deny the necessary nature of the symbolic formulation, the symbolic completion, the symbolic expression or even objectivization of experience, but to simply point to some of the dangers of which I think any sensitive person must be aware as when the symbols become totally alienated from any experience and do not express any inner reality at all.

I wish to push just one step further. Experience is not solely a private phenomenon. We assume when we say "experience" that we mean some very personal thing that happens to somebody when he is all set up in a little room somewhere, totally away from society. Experience is simply one dimension of human existence; it is as much a feature of collective life, of life in groups, as it is of individual private life. When Emile Durkheim spoke of "collective effervescence" and placed this phenomena as very central in his whole theory of religion, he was indicating that the experiential dimension is decisive in the collective experience. Therefore, I also want to stress that I am not arguing for a purely personal type of religious experience. It seems to me that we are tapping some of the new things in the religious world today. We can view a reemergence of a sense of authentic community, a search for a kind of religious immediacy in sympathetic groups, which may be sacramental or oriented to social action, but in which there is a genuine, human, shared experience and response, as decisive as any purely individualistic aspects of the realm of experience.

BERGER: All of us, particularly the social scientists, are too prone to fall victim to the intellectual's inclination to engage in endless clarifications of terminology and concept. I am not at all opposed to this, and in fact a good deal of my own work has been theoretical; but I would like to make a plea here for a more empirical thrust.

We have been trying to clarify the concepts of belief and unbelief, of secularization, and of religion. My experience is that we are not quickly going to reach agreement on any one of these. I take the liberty of offering a personal example. Thomas Luckmann and I have been arguing about the definition of religion for several years. I regard his as very unhelpful, and I feel sure he feels the same about mine. We have not reached agreement, and nevertheless, we have been able to do a number of things together which simply shelves this disagreement. I understand what he means, and he understands what I mean, and as long as this is the case, we can go on to other business. The other business I am suggesting in this case is the empirical business of trying to find out what makes people "tick" in the religious sense. Let me illustrate this alternative approach.

I think that one can make the statement that childhood in the modern society is a completely different experience from what it has been in any previous period in history. The reasons for this are structural; they have to do with the industrial revolution ultimately and more specifically with medical technology. The fundamental, and I think earthshaking, fact is that in modern industrial societies of the Western type, most children who are born live to be adults. This in itself is a revolution of unbelievable implications for the texture of human life. One could amplify this at great length, particularly with reference to medieval society, or to underdeveloped societies. Childhood in our societies is happier than it has ever been before in human history. This is a simple fact of staggering importance. What results from this is a quite novel process of socialization.

Now, in keeping with Bellah's comments about personal experience, these are structural facts which have obvious psychological consequences. But I would also contend that, in terms of the maturation and formation of individuals, they also have ideological consequences. It is very important to understand youth rebellion in this context. Today individuals move from this unbelievably happy childhood to confrontation with larger social structures which are not as bliss-producing and in some cases are very much misery-producing structures. We have today throughout the developed world what its opponents call a new utopianism, a radical demand for the humanization of social structures. I am not endorsing the youth rebellion; I am simply making a descriptive state-

ment, which I think can be understood as a very logical demand that the large institutions of society (the educational
system, the state, the economy, etc.) should continue at least
to some degree the benign character of the institutions which
are in charge of primary socialization in this society.

We are dealing here with a longing for a past Golden Age,
which is empirically valid in the biographies of most of the
individuals. A couple of years ago I reread the legend of the
childhood of the Buddha. You may recall that, in the legend,
the Buddha's father tried to shield him from the painful experiences of old age, illness, and death. It struck me that this
must have been very difficult in ancient India even for a
prince, which Buddha's father was supposed to have been.
Then it occurred to me that this was in fact the way in which
middle-class children in our kind of societies grow up with
little experience of illness, of death, and with limited contact
with old age.

Within such an institutional context of socialization, it
should not surprise us that death becomes a rather meaningless fact. Death is removed, bracketed in consciousness. In
America you can see this very dramatically in terms of funeral
customs. It is not only death, it is something much broader,
that is involved here. A philosopher used the concept of "the
sealing up of metaphysical concern," which is at any rate one
dimension of modern society.

Another element has to do with attitudes toward cruelty
and inhumanity. It is easier to kill today than it ever was before. At the same time there seems to be a sensitivity to suffering among large segments of the population, which is again
a staggering *novum* in human history.

I am not suggesting that this is a fundamental thing we
should all start talking about; I have just given it by way of
an illustration. We can look at this kind of phenomenon
while we bracket our terminological and definitional differences. We might move more successfully and more pro-
ductively if we make such a tentative agreement and ask
empirical questions of this kind, without hoping that we will
soon reach agreement on what is belief and unbelief.

PARSONS: I should like to amplify Professor Berger's very interesting point about the significance of death. Certainly,

throughout history, death has been one of the primary focusing points of religion. This is particularly true of Christianity where the sacrificial death of Jesus is the central symbolic event. However, a number of important changes have taken place in modern society. Not only is infant mortality enormously reduced, but the overwhelming majority of human population lives through a complete life cycle. They die of "old age" and, in spite of wars and accidents, they die peacefully. The child no longer has the kind of experience of death that was true of earlier generations, particularly not of his own siblings, partly because we do not have extended kinship households.

But an equally important change is the dissecting of different components out of the phenomenon of death, particularly the component of prematurity which is almost universally felt to be far more tragic and to raise more acute problems of meaning than death in old age after completion of a full life cycle. I am not saddened by the death of a man of ninety, even if he was a very eminent person. But the death of a Robert Kennedy or of a John Kennedy, in early middle age, is tragic in quite a different sense. Now, prematurity, namely, the violent and deliberate imposition of death by human agency on the whole has very substantially declined, and likewise the association of suffering with death. There are still a sufficient number of very painful terminal illnesses, particularly the various forms of cancer. Nevertheless, there has been a very major qualitative change.

The consequence of this is the differentiating of what we might call "normal death" as a much more salient part of the total death complex. No one who is at all schooled in modern biology can doubt the normality of the finitude of the individual life span. What is biologically normal in this sense must be a part of the human condition which sets certain fundamental limits to human control, but which must also be accepted in some sense as nontragic. It is not like wars, or accidental premature death, or various other phenomena of that sort. It is not that the individual does not have the experience of death although it comes later than it used to and, for the most part, after childhood.

Sociological speculation about the significance of the later phases of the life cycle and the roles of the older generation leads me to think that the fact of having experienced the death of a number of people who were close to the individual in question, is one of the most important bases of a special psychological maturity of older people, which the child in our society, or the adolescent, or the student cannot attain without that experience.

WILSON: It is interesting that we have turned to problems such as childhood, death, and socialization. If I interpret correctly what is happening, we have been recognizing that religion has its salience in the modern world at precisely these points in the individual life cycle.

If, then, we recall the comment of the last speaker, we see something which marks off a very sharp contrast between the functions of religion as well known to sociologists in the Durkheimian tradition, and the functions of religion in our own time. Without wanting to labor the Durkheimian functions, one could say broadly that, according to the classical tradition in sociology, religion functions for social cohesion, for social control, to legitimize the policies of the group, to explain the cosmos, to solemnize group values, and perhaps also to solemnize the events of the life cycle.

But, if we look at the modern world, we see that religion no longer expresses social cohesion in advanced societies, because that cohesion is not there in the experiential, existential, and structured circumstances of the society which is to be expressed. The whole process of religious differentiation in industrializing societies is an illustration of this process by which religion comes to express new solidarities, or to provide the ideology for new groups finding a sense of solidarity. We find here what I regard as our major error in our understanding of Durkheim, namely, that he was talking about a society that happened also to be a community, that is, where society and community were coterminous. By "society" I mean something which we can apply to a very large nation-state; by community I mean a persisting face-to-face group in which people share their lives together and some degree of collective involvement over a long period of time. It seems to me that we have picked up the Durkheimian analysis of an aboriginal community, and assumed that this would fit a nation-state, notwithstanding massive evidence to the contrary, especially in view of the process of religious differentiation. If we look at social control it is recognizable, at least in Protestant countries, that since early in the eighteenth century "hell" began to disappear. By the middle of the nineteenth century, even the Revivalists, who had to work on men's emotions vigorously in order to stimulate some religious response, let the concept of hell drop. One sees that very clearly with someone like Moody. He began to preach a God of love much more than a God of wrath, partly I suspect for the sort of purposes that our chairman, Professor Berger, has mentioned: that life was ceasing to be so fearful in so many ways, that what people wanted was the assurance of affection much more than the protection from the awful things that might happen in the world.

If one talks of the explanation of the cosmos, one sees even more fully that in all the operational, pragmatic spheres in which men are concerned, the religious explanation of the cosmos is a very remote one indeed for most men's needs, and most men can live in a day-to-day fashion without needing to invoke this ultimate explanation that religion can offer. It is when we talk about the life cycle, about childhood, about death, about the process of socialization that the functions of religion are in some measure evident. It is at this point that one sees the privatization element coming in to the modern world, in the sense that you contract into religious experience as you need it. If one wants to take Luckmann's point about the functions of many modern cults, or even of youth cultural unrest, one sees that people contract in at moments of the life cycle when they go through some emotional experience. The university has now become a place where emotional experience is more or less institutionalized for the population. Some religious response becomes an appropriate response at a moment of time.

I interpret religion very largely as necessarily a face-to-face, person-to-person phenomenon; when religion ceases to be that, it loses a great deal of its vigor and of the power it holds over the individual. In our role-articulated world, face-to-face relationships in the community have ceased to be the principal context of people's lives. The idea of a special relationship between an individual and a priest who stands in a permanent and most intimate relationship in some respects ceases to be one with which most men are familiar, particularly young people, who meanwhile are given new means of transport, new means of communication, and are becoming the most mobile section of our population.

In this respect, what has happened in our world is that there is a preoccupation with communication which has replaced the preoccupation with, or the experience of, community in the past. Many of the new sects emphasize communication as the real secret that men must break into. Scientology, Christian Science, and groups of this kind are concerned with providing a new language which will allow one to come nearer to the ultimate truth of the world. What they are in fact doing is diagnosing a basic condition of anomie in the wider society, in which they assume that, by instrumental and technical means such as better communication, they will in some sense restore the affectivity of the community. It is this search for affectivity, the search for a warm context which men only partially want while not foregoing what are the advantages of an instrumental, highly technologized world. This I see as the dilemma of religion; a dilemma about how far to rationalize religious procedures, how far to abandon community concerns and affectivity in the face of highly skilled technological agencies which compete with religions for men's time, money, and resources in the wider world. This dilemma goes to the very heart of contemporary society; it is here that our problems of belief and unbelief are really located.

LUCKMANN: I have been thinking about what Peter Berger said. I am afraid that we are getting "hung up" too much on that example, producing various examples on it, and even offering some theories, but not seeing what he had in mind. If I interpret him correctly, what he had in mind requires a research enterprise of staggering proportions. It would imply a socio-psychological investigation closely linked to institutional, structurally oriented, sociological analysis, of which we have a good deal.

I do think that on the whole the socio-psychological part of our enterprise is in dire straits. Necessary research would aim to investigate the typical ways in which our contemporaries, in different social strata, countries, and regions experience childhood, illness, and, taking into account normal deviations, experience death. It would also be worthwhile to investigate the ways in which they experience sexuality, in which they have a family life: we have a sociology of the family, but not a very good social psychology of life in the family. We had an occupational sociology of immense proportions, with considerable insight from various structural levels, such as occupational mobility, professionalization, and so forth. But again, we had relatively little of what I would call the "social psychology" of work, namely, the typical ways in which work situations are experiences.

These then are just a few of the more important areas in which investigations would be necessary to find out, first of all, how ordinary experience runs in this area; not to mention comparable investigations of attitudes toward our more anonymous institutions or loci of identification such as a nation-state.

Here the situation becomes still more complicated. Various attempts have been made to look for realities, or to define experiences of realities that are beyond ordinary experience. Certainly we find a relatively trivial—but for the sociologist, highly important—layer in these investigations in which experience is simply pragmatic. Our operational man would reappear again, pragmatically determined by experiences in these areas. What social psychology has not adequately produced so far is data on how the link between these areas of experience looks for ordinary men. We have some rather global theories (for example Riesman), and we have some social psychological theories on dissonance, and so forth. Yet, on the purely descriptive level, we know very little about how the various areas of experience in everyday life are linked in individual biographies.

This kind of program, one indeed of staggering proportions, could obviously use a great deal of what has been done and is being done in sociology and social psychology, and it could go on without any previous agreement on definitions on what is belief and what is not belief. One could afterward ask whether these experiences constitute cultures of unbelief, or whether they could be understood as cultures of belief.

MARTY: Several people have observed that almost all the time we talk about religion, and almost never do we talk about God, because we have forgotten the object of our study. The common man has not gotten the word yet that you can have religion without God, that we have these Durkheimian devices for interpreting his being religious. Unless he knows something about Zen or Christian atheism, this has not been communicated to him; and therefore, I think we are overlooking what is still the basic feature of the culture of unbelief, and that is the first event in the West, the death and disappearance of the God of explanation which begins at least with Copernicus. I recall that when John Robinson's book *Honest to God* came out, all the sophisticated theologians made fun of it, because it was still dealing with the crisis of Western man when he realized that God wasn't *up* there or *out* there. It was easy to deride this book, because Robinson simply relocated God *in* here and *down* there. If one should make a study of the vast majority of people who have taken on the culture of unbelief, I would surmise that this comes about, because they have never overcome the shock of the disappearance of spatial transcendence when they got a new physical world view.

Then came the secularization of philosophy, of history, of the state; God was no longer needed to sanction battles and we have seen him disappear. So, we are talking in terms of religion as a source of social integration, as a search for a system of relevance. Almost all the non-Zen people are having problems of an entirely different nature: they are getting into groups, but they think of themselves as unbelievers in a new way because of this. And psychologists observe that whether or not you use the word "God" you have no objective reference to verify it.

The question of death has arisen. Empirical studies of retirement communities indicate that when you finally come to face death, you do not start talking about religion. Church attendance, for example, is much lower in America's retirement communities, where every day they see the hearse, than it is in a typical suburb. One minister interviewed some people in a shuffleboard club, and asked why they took no interest in an Indian slum nearby or in their eternal destiny.

"What are you after?" he asked. One lady replied: "We are interested in keeping the ever-living juices flowing!"

So here again, the God-reference would not have made any difference, one way or the other. I would like to quote Eric Hoffer who said that, at some point in history, God and the priests seemed to become superfluous while the world kept going anyhow. I think that this is the fundamental experience in the culture of Western man's unbelief; not that God was to be raged against, but that he seemed superfluous; he no longer explained processes. One of our big problems in our study is that, by using definitions of religion from primitive society—Durkheim style—or from sophisticated sources—Durkheimian scholars in universities—we may overlook the actual phenomenological situation of most people who disbelieve because they no longer find the God who used to explain things.

DE LUBAC: If Professor Marty will so permit me, I will be very happy to offer him copies of the few works in which I have endeavored to bear witness to faith in God, to explain my reasons, to make belief understood insofar as that is possible.

Professor Marty remarks (this is something mentioned often nowadays and in the same terms), that the God of *explanation* is dead today. I will add, to be more precise, a *certain* God of scientific explanation has seemingly disappeared. As a matter of fact, for the believing Christian having a little consciousness of what his Christian faith is, this God does not have to die because he was never born, he was never living. You know that still today, in the twentieth century, Christians have the habit of speaking of Abraham as the father of believers. If we read what the Bible tells us of this father of believers, we see that the God of Abraham does not present himself as being a God of scientific explanation of the phenomena of this world.

Let us take the two great thinkers of the Western, Catholic, and Latin traditions: Augustine of Hippo and Thomas Aquinas. If we read what they have to say about the existence of God, we find that God's existence is never made into an explanatory device, to perform the function that modern science is now performing. We observe the same in the Christian tradition, in the teaching of the church, the official texts, the symbolism of faith, the liturgical prayers. In none of these is God presented as the God of scientific explanation of phenomena in the world. It is perfectly correct to criticize certain modes of thinking of God; but these have nothing to do with Christian faith. Because the God of the Christian faith was never proposed as the substitute explanation of the world.

I am not a sociologist but only a professor of history of religion; but I should like to insist on the distinction between general notion of religion and the notion of Christian belief. Historians of religion have for a long time accepted that religion cannot be explained as a prescientific device that conceived of a superior being to satisfy the scientific curiosity of man. This is the thesis of August Comte, according to whom man goes through a theological, philosophical, and scientific stage in the effort to find an explanation of the world's phenomena. Historians of religion, as Professor Bellah (to return, finally, to him) has noted, would agree that religion follows different mental categories and performs other functions than satisfying scientific curiosity.

11

UNBELIEF: CAN IT BE
SCIENTIFICALLY STUDIED?

.

HIGHLIGHTS OF THE DISCUSSION
OF GLOCK'S PAPER

BERGER: In terms of the presentations by Professors Glock and Wilson there are at least three directions in which we might proceed in our discussion. The first would be to engage in some further conceptual clarification and raise some relevant questions about some of Glock's conceptual machinery. The second direction in which we might travel would be to expound on Wilson's paper. In both Wilson's and Glock's statements there are some very stimulating ideas about the present situation of religion. We might proceed in this more substantive and empirical direction. Third, both Glock and Wilson are pointing to very practical operational possibilities about what this particular group might do.

PARSONS: I should like to pursue an issue which Professor Wilson has raised, because I think it may have research implications and may be capable of research clarification through actual data as well as through conceptualization.

Professor Wilson put forward a very prevalent view among social scientists, as well as other intellectuals. I would simply like to question the technologizing of the modern world and its implications. He used the term "dominate" several times in this context, seeming to wish to avoid it, but reluctantly having to confess "we probably are dominated by machines, technological apparatus, etc. of many sorts."

Looking at the development of both technology and social organization, they appear intimately intertwined with each other; but a more proper diagnostic indicates that we are conditioned by them rather than being dominated by them. I think we are conditioned in a sense which is very similar to the sense in which we are conditioned by the biological properties of our bodies. We can do certain things by virtue of those properties, and we are prevented from doing other things by virtue of those properties. Now, there is a curious history in the development of cultural reactions to advances of knowledge and to the advance of the technical application of knowledge. I might remark that advancement of knowledge even in the theological sense always produces new determinisms, which had not been appreciated before. The great seventeenth-century development of physical science, particularly astronomy, was an outstanding example of this. A religious storm ensued because it created the solar system as a deterministic system, whereas it was felt before that God made individual decisions about the movements of the planets from moment to moment. Very similar reactions were provoked by the nineteenth-century development of biological science which seemed to challenge the idea of completely free creation, by an act of divine will, of each species and of man in particular. This seemed to be a deterministic process which was out of divine control.

The same pattern seems to have held later in the nineteenth century in the economic field, with Marxism as its most prominent example: the idea that there was a deterministic order which could only be exploited by men but not determined by men. In this century the emergence of sociology into a position of considerable intellectual prominence extends the above pattern to the more intimate phases of social relationship.

In my view, the main correlate of these processes of increasing knowledge has been increasing freedom, not decreasing freedom, increasing self-determination by human beings of their own management of the human condition. "Management" is a revealing symbolic term; however, it seems to be continually perceived as restrictive of freedom. I wonder whether the relation between these perceptions and the spheres of actual autonomy does not provide a field of researchable problem.

VERGOTE: I would like to comment on what Professor Parsons just said about the condition of contemporary man. I doubt that we can compare the discoveries of the seventeenth and eighteenth centuries with the conditions of which Professor Wilson was speaking. Man has learned to understand his cosmic, biological, psychological, and cultural condition with the help of science, and the increased knowledge of his conditioning within the environment has increased his levels of freedom. Professor Wilson was saying that the technological civilization with its anonymity and its system of relationship between work and leisure creates an environment which man does not comprehend. There is a crucial difference between the science of environment and the type of environment imposed by contemporary culture and civilization.

One could say that man is conditioned by his religion; and it has been often remarked that the notion of God as Creator, for instance, is spontaneously associated with a prescientific vision of man. Science exerts a critical function with respect to spontaneous religion, as when the psychological or psychoanalytical study of the source of religious behavior affects the student's attitude to religion.

I interpret Professor Wilson as saying that a certain type of technological civilization conditions man against and beyond religion. The technological developments of our civilization has neutralized the problem of death and of ultimacies as viable systems of reference. I feel that the two must be distinguished. The culture of unbelief seems to me brought about by two factors: one, by the scientific criticism of spontaneous religious motivation because man is not spontaneously religious, but is made so, and two, by a host of other phenomena which represent the social conditioning within a virtually nonreligious context.

ISAMBERT: I shall step in to say how very interested I am in, and not just how profoundly I agree with, Professor Glock's paper. What appears to me to be most provocative is the manner in which Glock has us approach the problem: he succeeds in making operative even the oppositions we encounter. To put it rather simply, our difficulties concerning the functionality of religion, or of its content, tend to flounder on the question of the supernatural character of religion. Very skillfully Glock presents to us an operational typology, capable of supporting distinct inquiries.

He poses the problem thus: "one cannot define unbelief in itself; but only unbelief in relation to something else." His four types of unbelief, relative to four types of belief (supernatural, natural, objective, and subjective), cover pretty well the spread that can be observed. So we could very well plan to conduct inquiries on subjective beliefs in those areas when these beliefs prevail; and do likewise where objective beliefs prevail.

Having said this, let me go back to Professor Wilson's response, when he examines the difficulty which follows the crossing of subjective and objective beliefs. It seems to me that effectively there is a problem which perhaps complicates the need for operationalization a little, but which can be resolved. The problem is the search for a measure of unbelief and, I suppose, the necessity to formulate scales to measure it, or questionnaires with many nuances; well, it is that problem that needs to be faced and, however subtly, overcome.

LUCKMANN: I am afraid that we may pick up some of the "red herrings" in the presentation by Professor Glock and follow them up too much, and then in utter resignation accept his proposal! The "red herrings" are, for example, the subjectivist-objectivist distinctions. I think these are wrong distinctions. One criticism of Glock's scheme, put forth by Professor Wilson, must still be questioned, and that is the suggestion of a culture-bound starting point. I do not think there are any starting points that are not culture-bound, but if you follow through what Wilson says, then you come to the very sad observation that belief is still a social fact today, that indeed in our culture we know what we mean by belief, and that Wilson could rightly say that this was a convenient starting point. But a convenient starting point for what? For the study of belief, oriented by institutionally defined belief systems? Of course we can investigate the degrees of staunchness or laxity of this belief. If that were our purpose, I would see no real problem for research. But he simply jumps on to speak of those who have "contracted out," presuming that this would be a convenient starting point for investigating them. In my opinion, this is no convenient starting point for the investigation of the culture of unbelief.

I see no convenient starting point for the investigation of unbelief if we insist on the more or less officially defined configuration of belief. We will simply end up by investigating degrees of laxness or distance from belief systems, which would be a reduplication of what in the sociology of religion has already been done on a global and magnificent scale. We would have in effect a replication of a glorified parish sociology, perhaps in different social contexts. If unbelief is not a socially defined fact, then we cannot take up Wilson's suggestion of starting out in the middle range of operations and conceptualization, as it were, because we have no convenient starting point, no common-sense fact of unbelief. Glock is a bit too optimistic when he says that, in the early phase of operations, one would have to find out by depth interviews and open interviews how unbelief might possibly be defined. Again, I predict with a fair degree of confidence that in this preliminary phase the data will produce definitions and conceptions of belief, and only by contrast, something that is not that. In short, we would again be investigating almost everything that is not belief in the accepted sense. Here I see the most serious pragmatic as well as theoretical research difficulty.

Glock overemphasizes the yield of survey studies at this stage for our problem. Probably a much longer preliminary phase of a different type of study will be necessary before we can standardize our questions to such an extent that an instrument is produced that can be used in surveys. He does speak of participant observation at one point but he passes it over rather too quickly.

What I have in mind, then, is a supplementary proposal for an intermediate stage of operations, before any kind of survey research. We need a pilot study by way of participant observation and depth interviews to follow through individual experiences in their social context at home, at work, in leisure activities, for a rather lengthy period. I have in mind, by way of empirical reference, studies that in some ways are comparable to, say, *Street Corner Society* or, much more recently, David Sudnow's study of the social organization of death by participant observation in a hospital over a significant period of time.[1] The pragmatically dominating performances and the shift from work to leisure and from leisure to work would have to be observed in rather considerable detail. Complementary to this, I visualize studies of nonroutine situations in

1. William F. Whyte, *Street Corner Society: The Social Organization of an Italian Slum* (University of Chicago Press, 1965); David Sudnow, *Passing On: The Social Organization of Dying* (New York: Prentice Hall, 1967).

their social context, including the subjective meanings attached to these situations by the persons in question.

It may be an optimistic assumption to think that such study might yield a sort of provisional conceptualization on the part of the subjects of what is important, of what performs religious or quasi-religious functions in their lives. This might perhaps yield some common-sense conceptualizations that the sociologist might try to standardize and translate into questionnaires which could then be correlated with demographic data, class variable, and so forth, on a much larger scale.

In other words, I think that Glock's proposal jumps almost immediately into a kind of analytic morphology of something that we do not know how to define clearly. The method that I would suggest for the preliminary phase of investigation, to maintain the same image, would be a "physiology" first.

BERGER: I wonder if I might ask Professor Luckmann a question now. If I understand you correctly, you are not really rejecting Professor Glock's basic notions, except that you are suggesting a preliminary stage which would be in terms of more qualitative than quantitative research. Are you also assuming that these pilot studies would be cross-national?

LUCKMANN: I think they would have to be cross-national for the simple reason that their function would be to produce instruments for survey research. Obviously a pilot study could not give us incidence and frequencies. In order to get at the distribution of the phenomena in question, we cannot get around Glock's proposal. But I think that, first of all, we must be clear about what we mean by incidence of what. Were we to study belief in the traditional sense this would be relatively easy; and we could immediately jump into the stage of operations proposed by Glock. Since we do not know this exactly—this symposium has shown this fairly clearly—some preliminary investigation is vital.

CAPORALE: I should like to raise a fundamental question of focus in the object of possible research. It is one thing to analyze one's belief and another to reduce it to a researchable field. In his paper Professor Luckmann arrives at the conclusion that the notion of unbelief may be heuristically unproductive. I should like to suggest that we accept a substantial variation to the format of research proposed by Professor Glock, as well as to research on a psycho-sociological level, rather than on the institutional level, as proposed by Professor Wilson.

In a study so complex, three preoccupations need to be given priority: first, the promise of new methodological acquisitions integrated with theory; second, the inclusiveness of all relevant aspects of the phenomenon; and third, the possible productivity of the study in the form of theories with wider application and scope. Unfortunately, the explicit focus on unbelief may not do justice to these three requirements. A direct focus on belief, rather than unbelief in its widest comprehensiveness and variety, distinct from the sacred and/or religious context, would probably more readily provide empirical answers to some of the questions to which we have addressed ourselves.

As Professor Mandic pointed out, belief and unbelief cannot be confined to the religious dimension without running the risk of intellectual confusion, methodological difficulties, and frustration. If the boundary of our inquiry is too narrow and dictated by nonsociological categories (and I would think that unbelief is a nonsociological category), the wide spectrum of human experience that is encompassed by the notion of belief will be warped by oversimplification.

It has been frequently noted in the course of this discussion that belief and unbelief are not limited to the religious reference but include widely diffused modes of orientations, whether cognitive, symbolic, or relational, to use Professor O'Dea's concepts. They find their reference in the religious as well as the political, the aesthetic, the scientific, the organizational, or even the economic area of human pursuit. I, for one, would be deeply interested in a study which would permit us to identify the common denominators, or the constant factors that engender and sustain religious as well as secular beliefs, political beliefs, and so forth. It would be extremely important to find out what "belief pattern" underpins the functional alternatives to religion, such as astrology, psychology, psychiatry, games, chance, sweepstakes, including even the pseudocognitive mapping supplied by mass media and commercial advertising, or the system of meanings arrived at individually or collectively through a scientific process. This, of course, calls for the extensive use of psycho-sociological methodology of research which has already been suggested, and which may lead to establish, within satisfactory margins of accuracy, basic personality types, cross-culturally valid. The results of this study may produce a scientific validation and/or clarification of concepts and popular notions such as "the believer," "the unbeliever," "the skeptic," "the conformist," "the robot," "the operational man," "the metaphysical man," or if we want to use Glock's scheme, the objectivist, nonobjectivist, the natural believer, and so forth.

It has been said during this symposium that every affirmation of a system of meaning by individuals, groups, or institutions, elicits a variety of responses which may range from overacceptance to acceptance and rejection. This process, not the substantive reference, is of primary importance from a sociological viewpoint together with the structural configuration of the particular cultures which affect the probability of incidence of one response rather than the other. Such a shift in the focus of our concern might appear removed from the literal objectives of this symposium. But I believe it lends itself to far easier operationalization, to comparative cross-cultural designing, and to wider theoretical implications which may reach far into political processes, such as revolutionary movements, transitions to totalitarian regimes, processes of mass persuasion, diffusion of styles, mannerisms, and fanatic and millenarian movements.

Closer to a recurrent point of our discussion, this focus would permit a new approach to explain the dimensions of the privatization of belief which have been identified by Luckmann and Bellah as indicative of the contemporary scene. In fact, it would be extremely illuminating to identify the processes by which institutional antinomial situations, dissonances, and discontinuities are displaced from the cultural and institutional levels to the level of the individual, placing upon him the burden of developing mechanisms of conflict resolution and personality integration. We could hypothesize, for instance, that in the course of this research, side by side with the operational men, and with the *homo religious,* we will observe the "transitional man," "the prototypical pluralist," who has developed a high threshold of tolerance of dissonance and a low level of response to distinct solidarities.

As one case of the privatization of belief, this third type cannot be understood in terms of conventional categories having an exclusively religious reference. This "transitional man" represents the potential participant in the diffuse community of which Bellah spoke, and will ultimately transcend the categories of belief and unbelief.

STEEMAN: Pursuing what Professor Caporale has said, I suggest we do away with the term "unbelief" altogether and focus our research on what actually makes people tick. I think it is better that theologians make their statements after we have determined what people really believe, even if this has the effect of making theologians change their minds somewhat. Especially in the present situation of Catholicism, I would say that it is practically impossible to have any kind of orthodoxy at the moment and certainly not in terms of a functioning Christian community.

GLOCK: It is evident that each of us has different conceptions of how to distinguish belief from unbelief, and that running through some of our controversy are these latent and sometimes manifest differences. It seems to me useful to try to encounter the whole range of variation in which this phenomenon is viewed because I do not think that one can really begin to make belief and unbelief into useful scientific concepts unless one can get some consensus about how they are to be conceptualized.

A narrow conceptualization necessitates making a commitment ahead of time to one of a number of mental schemes. It turns out that, in my own research, I have made such a commitment. Professor Wilson disagrees with the idea I have operationalized; but whenever in the past my own research has tried to focus on the notion of belief and unbelief a major criticism of my work has been that this is too narrow a conceptualization, or too old-fashioned. Stimulated by this criticism and by Professor Bellah's paper in which it is evident that a somewhat different conceptualization can be proposed, I have attempted to explore how the various ways in which belief and unbelief are conceptualized can be ordered. On this condition we can begin to make nonabstract choices, because, in the end, you can only make the research choices after you have done research.

My general feeling is that one ought to see the whole before one begins to dig in on the parts; whereas I had the feeling that Wilson was saying: "Well, let's dig on this part, because history tells us it is important." The decision is partly a matter of taste. My preference is to look at the whole range of variation, try to specify it, and then slowly begin the process of making choices based partly on evidence and not only on opinion.

Several comments were made also about my distinction between subjectivist and objectivist beliefs. In a certain sense I borrowed that distinction from Bellah. I agree that the distinction is likely to be very difficult to pinpoint in a sort of black-and-white pattern in empirical research, because it is difficult to talk about variation. My paper was formulated in ideal typical terms: my guess would be that, in empirical research, we would find not so much four types as variations between types. A subjectivist believer, in some sense, could not escape the fact that he is in a milieu in which there is objectivist belief. For example, an Italian who is no longer a Christian in the usual sense could not escape the fact that he has been exposed to a lot of objectivist belief and, as he may formulate some belief of his own, part of this is likely to be a reinterpretation of what he has been taught in the Church. It is unlikely, therefore, that in the real world one would find it easy to distinguish what I would call "objectivist" and "subjectivist," but there would be a sort of movement between the two so that one could talk about people being more or less objectivistic in their beliefs.

If we consider survey research as a tool for collecting mass information, there are certain kinds of questions in which all of us are interested, the data for which can only be collected in surveys which are repeated over time. Most of our discussion about belief and unbelief had to do with the notion that there are changes going on in belief and unbelief and that these changes are going on in some kind of population. Let us say that for the last hundred years we have had something like the plan proposed in my paper, namely, sample censuses in selected countries every five years; and let us say that we were smart enough a hundred years ago to conceptualize phenomena adequately. Had this happened, today we would be able to pinpoint what now we can only surmise from rather obscure and rather secondary kinds of data. With regard to establishing changes, we should be in a very good position to have some further insight into change if we knew what populations were thinking over time. There is now in the United States a considerable coterie of sociologists and other social scientists who are trying to convince the government to extend their data collection operations beyond what is now collected on a periodic basis to get more than that attitudinal and value kind of data.

Frequently one comes across a diffuse feeling that surveys are mostly useful for social psychological research since the individual is the unit of analysis, and that somehow you cannot learn anything about social structure from a survey. I think that through analysis you can say something about people and you can talk about individuals who operate in certain milieus: lower-class people versus middle-class people; or believers of one kind versus believers of another kind. By aggregating data from individuals, you are really saying something about the contexts in which these individuals function; and indeed, much of the data, the information, and the characterizations that we make of units other than individuals are based on the aggregation of individual data. With political data, you will make statements about Socialists versus Communists, Democrats versus Republicans; and you will try to characterize Democrats, Republicans, or Socialists in certain ways. Underlying this characterization is the notion of aggregation of data about individuals. When we talk about Communists being this way, we really mean that if we had a survey and interviewed a sample group of Communists, we would find some high proportion to have these characteristics.

A lot can be said about what survey research is and what it can contribute but a lot more has been said about what it does not contribute. Still I think survey research is a tool which we cannot do without.

My judgment is that surveys of the kind I have described could satisfy interests that a lot of people have expressed. I could suggest that one way we might collaborate is in the invention and conduct of this kind of collaborative survey. I would certainly agree that a survey of general population samples ought to be complemented by surveys of elite samples.

But it seems to me that we might want to collaborate around an apparatus which would allow each of us to feed each other in theory and ideas.

Concerning Luckmann's proposal, I certainly would not want to go into the field immediately with a survey, but would want to take at least two years to work out in qualitative ways the whole problem of instrument development. I am a little skeptical about the possibility of participant observation as a major means to get at people's beliefs, because beliefs tend to be invisible rather than visible; and while sometimes they are made visible in interaction, this is not enough to rely on participant observation as a tool. Depth interviews are a more productive alternative, but this is a matter of taste.

Finally, concerning Professor Caporale's point, it seems to me that I am trying to incorporate his idea in the proposal. We are not really interested in belief and unbelief in some isolated way. From a descriptive point of view, we would like to know what is the distribution of believers and nonbelievers in a population, and over a period of time what changes occur in the people who are believers? Basically, we want to elaborate the notion of belief and unbelief. One of the questions we want to ask specifically is, what makes people one kind of a believer or another? The more important and abiding question that sociologists have been asking about belief is, what are the consequences of the degree to which a society is involved in some kind of belief? Much of the thrust of Marxist, Weberian, Durkheimian, and Parsonian thought is rooted in the notion that belief counts, and that it has an important role to play in the way in which society is organized and is stable.

WILSON: There is here the question of taking up a theological definition. I think that I did say that I did not want to put our concepts into the captivity of the theologians. If there is anything worse than asking sociologists to agree on a definition, it is asking theologians to agree on a definition! We could take a number of indicators. How often is God invoked to justify courses of action in the modern world? How often is God invoked in a particular institutional context? We could evolve a scheme to discover to what extent belief was explicit in a variety of social situations.

I will not pursue the "red herrings" I introduced about the

technological age, which I see as an age of secularization. In earlier ages of transition, we have seen new religions emerge in institutionalized forms in which there has been a specific supernatural reference. That seems less likely today. When we talked about the many things that Professor Luckmann mentioned as religious substitutes, we fall into a circularity trap. We define religion in terms of functions, and then we look at these functions and say that anything that functions in this way should be looked at as religious. I would prefer to see us work from the received opinions and ideas which exist in our own culture.

The alternatives of astrology and so on, which Professor Caporale mentioned, are certainly interesting in themselves; but I do not know that they are central to the problem as I conceive it; astrology, or dream analysis, or whatever it may be, is the equivalent of ancient magic. In different religious systems this kind of magic is sometimes incorporated into religious practice at certain points; in others it is rigorously excluded. Thaumaturgical concerns are widespread and orthodox religious practice often stands in uneasy relation to them. Priests may seek to claim monopoly of thaumaturgical power; or be content to circumscribe the activities of nonpriestly thaumaturges; they may simply treat them with disdain, or accept them in a complex division of labor—usually with consequent accretion of thaumaturgical practice within the dominant religious tradition itself. If we look around the world, especially in underdeveloped countries, we see the outcropping in new forms of these kinds of preoccupations in what is really a transmutation of magic. I do not think, however, that this is by any means as quintessential an item for us as is the broad thesis of secularization, or what I see as unbelief.

With regard to the extent to which our approach may be cross-cultural, I do not want in any way to suggest that we should not attempt cross-cultural studies. The point about comparison is that it must be comparison among entities which have sufficient similarity of structure to be comparable. There is no point in looking at unbelief in fifth-century China and unbelief in the contemporary Western world. We might look at unbelief in France, Italy, Holland, the United States, Britain, and so on, because there is sufficient similarity of cultural inheritance, and there is sufficient similarity of social structures. Perhaps this point modifies the impression that I reject any sort of overall conceptualization of our problem. Far from it! I think we can conceive our problem most usefully within the broad Christian and Western tradition.

Equally I did not want to suggest that I see no use for survey research. Rather I suggest that there are other forms of empirical enquiry which are certainly of no less importance. We tend too quickly to think that we can solve our problems if we can quantify them by looking at a population. This is a democratic fallacy. We assume the similarity of "yeas," and we regard them as items of equal weight in answer to questions. If you do ask people whether they believe in God, you may get a percentage of positive replies; but the relevance of their belief to their daily lives is a much more interesting question. I think that we should not end with survey research. I do not think that Glock wants to do that; but I see my own role to be that of one who throws up a number of alternative possibilities. What I would then suggest is that we might proceed by historical analyses, content analyses of literature, of the mass media, and the content of higher education in particular. Higher education and mass media are important because I see them as alternative systems for the communication of information or belief to the religious system itself which has always had a very important part in communicating ideas to a wider society.

I am in favor of participant observation as suggested by Luckmann, if you can find a situation in which to participate and observe. You cannot become the shadow of a man who walks home from work into the family and see what responses there are in this situation. You can observe and participate in small groups of some kind by joining them in a concealed way and finding out what happens. The difficulty for participant observation as Luckmann envisages it is that there is no structure in which to integrate oneself as a participant and as an observer. Broadly, then, I see as an alternative focus to survey research, a historical cultural institutional study which should not confine itself to religious institutions. The study of unbelief is to be made in other institutions of society, and it is this which should provide one of our major thrusts. This could be done by collaborative effort in specific institutions set up to look at particular problems.

BELLAH: Professor Glock points to the frequent, if regrettable, gap between theory and method in sociology. I have a feeling that we are exemplifying the gap of which he was speaking. It seems to me that we are in a new situation with respect to man's religiosity. This raises serious questions as to whether the accepted traditional way of looking at these matters is as adequate for certain groups who may be significant out of proportion to their sheer numbers. When we move to considerations that verge on the operational, we find that Glock's own scheme crosscuts the variables of subjective and objective with the variables of natural and supernatural, which is a way of making certain that you do not catch what is significant in the new situation because it is precisely these classic dichotomies that are decreasingly relevant in what I have tried to discern. If one adopts simply the conventional formulations of orthodoxy the convenient cutoff criterion is the notion of a supreme, absolute, independent being. I wonder whether this really will be an adequate criterion for dealing with the complexities of the contemporary situation.

It is possible that my perception of the present, and of the degree to which there is newness in the present, is mistaken; and that Professor Marty is right when he indicates that, outside of a few Zen Buddhists perhaps, there is nothing particularly new, and the scene is really represented more by old ladies in retirement homes who are concerned about their "ever-living juices"! This is an empirical question of sorts. It is my reading of the situation that there exists an honest frustration and revulsion against a whole cultural conception, a whole notion of human existence which is beautifully symbolized in that image which Marty gave us.

Quite a different strategy would be called for if it is deemed worthwhile to pursue the idea that new things are afoot. In this case, one would want to seek out strategic groups, voluntary associations of various sorts, spontaneous movements, arising in some respects on the fringe of established society, movements which may or may not have a tinge that would traditionally be considered religious. This means looking at various kinds of youth groups, students groups, all kinds of active, socially concerned people in Latin America, many of whom have a more or less tenuous relation to the Roman Catholic Church but who find themselves out of sympathy with many doctrinal formulations; groups again that would not be caught, or would be caught in only very tiny percentages in random samples, but may be suggestive of new modes of organization and new cultural forms very important for the future.

PARSONS: It is just as important in a group such as this to establish disagreements as consensus, and particularly if some of those disagreements are researchable even though they may not be resolved. The original ways in which the alternatives are stated in our discussion turn out to be secondary, or possibly irrelevant, or turn out to be postassumable under some more general interpretation.

We could supplement Glock's suggested frame of reference by the theme of autonomy or freedom versus constraint from the point of view of the attitudinal interpretations of the situation on the part of people who are involved in it. However, this theme may exist in other quite different traditions; in Western religious history this is a persistent theme, with claim and counter-claim on both sides. The concept "freedom" is a recurring one. Luther spoke of the "freedom of the Christian man." The French Revolutionary leaders spoke of their new kind of freedom, but in a secular context.

To this I would add another component, namely, religious innovation which is often conceptualized under Max Weber's concept of "charisma." These things ought to be thought of as researchable. Let me give only one very crude item that is much used in sociological and social-psychological discussion in the United States these days, namely, the concept of relative deprivation, which is sometimes spoken of as "the revolution of rising expectations." If we go back to studies of the French Revolution it is well known that the revolutionary spearhead had not been undergoing a degradation of their condition in the generation or two prior to the outbreak of the Revolution. Much of the dissatisfaction of the American Negro today can certainly be related to the fact that their position has in fact been substantially improving. Now, this might be applicable to the idea of the sense of constraint on the part of groups whose freedom had in fact increased. This is only one illustration of what could obviously be an extremely complicated area of analysis.

LUCKMANN: I think that Bellah was a bit too pessimistic in assuming that survey research would not produce any kind of information that would be relevant to our problem. At the same time I would join with him in pushing one point: if those of us are right who are theorizing that there is a qualitative change in religion, then it is entirely possible that, by survey research alone, we would not be able to discover that change very well. This nevertheless would not falsify the hypothesis.

Survey research is in any case justifiable in this situation precisely because many of us sociologists feel that nothing much has changed. Therefore, if we are interested in making an inventory of any kind about the present situation, we can safely assume that the established methods of survey research are going to yield significant information.

However, if we restrict ourselves in the end to that kind of analysis for which I have the highest respect, we may be missing an opportunity which this symposium presents. It would be extremely sad if it did turn out in the end, despite all the rhetorical statements to the contrary, that it is a question of survey versus other methods. I would be extremely happy if financial considerations did not force us to that decision because from certain points of view a decision for survey research to the exclusion of other methods would be defensible. It would yield certain kinds of information which many sociologists, including myself, would find extremely useful not to mention nonsociological, potentially fund-giving institutions involved in it. If it is not an alternative, I agree with Bellah that we will have missed an opportunity to verify or falsify certain assertions we have made which at least compare to each other.

Therefore I plead again for the possibility of combining certain kinds of approach. First (not necessarily in order of priority), there would be survey research, addressing itself primarily to problems which could be located theoretically and structurally in phase B. At the same time, and this indeed is the opportunity offered by this symposium, survey research would trigger off and possibly sponsor exploratory investigations, exploratory to some extent also in the research technology involved. Some of the problems cannot be investigated too well without a certain openness toward partly forgotten methods which produce data in the context of the social sciences. The method in this parallel action would be content analysis. This process, of course, would not break any new ground methodologically, because it relies on established methods to yield significant data on the occasions in which certain types of symbols of an explicitly or semiexplicitly religious character are invoked.

Second, there would be social-psychological methods which could model themselves on what have been rather recent developments in technology. This is an area where we would not be methodologically an avant-garde, but which would follow rather closely, in the sociology of religion, a development that is relatively new in a neighboring science.

Third, there are attempts at biographical analysis, a method which unfortunately, despite its importance in the classical period, has been somewhat neglected in contemporary sociology. I say "attempts" because I myself am not quite clear about the precise techniques of analysis to be used.

Last, there would be attempts at situational analysis in which modified versions of participant observation could be used. This analysis would focus on the various kinds of situations which we might theoretically postulate to be significant for our problem.

It would be entirely utopian to think that we could develop a research program in which all these methods, plus a rather costly enterprise of survey researching, could be done on a major scale. It is possible to be rather experimental methodologically, in combination with survey research, if one considered these as attempts of an exploratory kind which could be abandoned if one or two years of experimentation in the collection of data would prove that, while in theory possible, these attempts were pragmatically not manageable.

If any one of these additional approaches produced information that could be well used in the analysis of the problems of unbelief versus belief, then a larger investment of energy in one or the other of the methods would be warranted. In short, I am pleading not to make pragmatically an either/or decision.

Theoretically, we all know that it isn't survey research versus other methods; we might be forced to that decision, and that would be extremely sad. If it is at all possible, let us combine survey research with certain of the additional methods that I have listed.

GLOCK: I tried in my design to provide for some means to do two things in which both Luckmann and Bellah are interested. One is to describe the changes that are going on in belief and unbelief, and the second is to provide a belief to test some of the hypotheses. I think that Professor Bellah would probably not make the general rise of education a major theme in his causal sequence, but it seems to me that my design would test whether or not this change was related to the increase in education.

Bellah makes certain assertions about the role of belief in social integration. My paper is, I think, consistent with trying to test some of the propositions that he is advancing. Perhaps the cause of discontinuity between us is the fact that I passed over in one sentence my commitment to the notion that general population samples ought to be complemented with elite samples. Implicitly, I was in sympathy with the fact that the general population sample very often does not produce enough cases in significant cells, and surveys, therefore, require some overrepresentation.

KLAUSNER: I do not think that the division between Professors Glock and Bellah (and others) is as deep as it might seem at first glance. Bellah's critique about survey research is in a large measure a deserved one. Because of the size of survey research and the expense that is involved in it, survey researchers have tended to get involved in client-oriented work, and as a result a good part of the survey research which is available for inspection is quite third-rate. This has presented a stereotype not only of what survey research is, but has allowed the possibilities of survey research to be obscured.

Fundamentally, I think that most of us would identify with the contention of the best psychologists of the 1920s and the 1930s: that if a phenomenon exists empirically, it can in some way be measured. We are tied to the notion that measurement always has to be direct. We have learned that really what one needs are some strategic measures which are related by some set of observation sequences at some point in the theoretical network. Bellah has called our attention to certain very important caveats which all survey researchers should take seriously: we should not confuse the absolute frequency of a phenomenon with its social significance; we should not confuse statistical significance with substantive significance. Some of us seem to go on quite unthinkingly classifying populations by those variables that seem to be useful and easy to get (age, sex, urban-rural residence), instead of classifying by something that might conceptualize the work. Perhaps it is not the crude chronological age that is important; it may be position in the life cycle. One of the things we ought to use in classification is some technological aspect of exposure/involvement, the relation of technological aspects to the environment.

The only constraint of survey is that one needs to take measures on a large number of units and so attempt to derive some general propositions from this large number of measures. I am not sure whether one can derive general propositions without taking a large number of measures. The units on which one measures could be Bellah's Latin American youth groups. One could get the whole series of groups and sense the climates in the group by various kinds of measures. What one has to do is immerse oneself in the culture to find out what the significant things are. Survey research does not restrict itself to asking attitudinal questions; you can use any number of data-gathering devices. Situational analysis would fit very well within a survey system if one took a whole series of situations after one found out which could be regularly assessed over a large number of them. Bellah's attack is on vulgar survey analysis and not on what could be done if it were done in a sophisticated way.

BELLAH: I would just like to say that both Professor Luckmann and Professor Klausner have attributed to me an attack on survey research that was not intended in my remarks. I agree with much that Klausner said; I would simply ask for other approaches without demeaning the value of survey research.

GRUMELLI: Allow me to make some conclusive remarks. As promoter of the symposium, I am naturally sensitive to the prospects this symposium opens to us and, therefore, to all the ideas, to all the proposals that are made to further continuation of our work. I think it appropriate, therefore, to briefly highlight the accomplishments of our work, despite their shortcomings and difficulties.

In Professor Glock's report we have seen how it is at least possible to attempt to redefine our problem, which at first seemed varied and complex, overwhelming our modest resources. I would like to point out this result, which I see as very important, because it suggests, both operatively and semantically, the possibility that we can join in dialogue and truly understand each other.

One might have taken for granted that the notions of belief and unbelief would present a great variety of definitions. Nevertheless, the fact that the dimensions of the problem have been stated clearly in a meeting like this one, characterized not only by the abilities of the participants but also by their diversity—ideological and social—constitutes a gain of notable importance.

This brings me to emphasize the necessity for research which would test some of the diverse hypotheses here proposed, and define the boundaries of our problem, in the direction proposed by Professor Glock, or in whatever direction that allows us to operationalize our problem. It is certainly not irrelevant for the sociologist to highlight also the practical usefulness of his investigations. Positive science has far-reaching practical influences.

One can clearly deduce the importance these investigations can have for believers and nonbelievers. Aside from the difficulty of definition, we are more or less agreed that there are such things as believers and nonbelievers, precisely as manifestations of the latent potentialities of religious groups.

There is another problem which I should like to highlight— the encounter with the theologians. I have had frequent occasions in my writings to underline the necessity for the sociologist to adequately understand the reality he wishes to analyze. This is at times very difficult, as we have experienced again and again; but precisely for this reason it is so much the more necessary. I do not mean that the sociologist should abdicate his perspectives and accept those of the theologians. But, as Father De Lubac observed, the complexity of religious phenomena requires specific competence which is scarcely evident in some of our investigations. There is a need, therefore, on practical ground, to increase the creative opportunities for similar meetings between theologians and sociologists of religion.

PART FOUR

·

POSTSCRIPTS AND NEW FRONTIERS

12

BELIEF, UNBELIEF, AND DISBELIEF

·

TALCOTT PARSONS

As a general commentator on the Symposium on the Culture of Unbelief, there are two aspects of my position which should be made explicit at the outset. First, I am not a Roman Catholic, but a somewhat backsliding Protestant of Congregationalist background. Second, I am not a theologian, but a sociologist by profession. My commentary will not attempt a summary of the discussions—though the Agnelli Foundation has kindly made a copy of the transcript available to me—but rather will be critical in the sense of ranging about some of the principal issues which figured in the papers and discussions in my own terms, hoping in the process to help to define the situation for future stages of discussion and research in this field.

Belief, Disbelief, and Unbelief

The relevant context of the use of the terms "belief" and "unbelief" was of course religious. It does not seem useful here to attempt discussion of "What is religion?" in general terms. At certain points aspects of that question will arise and can be dealt with on those occasions. Since, however, the concept belief is so central, a brief commentary on it does seem to be in order. First a point of logic. In Western culture at least there has been a strong tendency to think in terms of dichotomies, often accentuated in their mutual exclusiveness by such expressions as "versus." Thus we have rational versus irrational, heredity versus environment, *Gemeinschaft* versus *Gesellschaft*.

If members of such dichotomous pairs are to be treated as types, however, they have frequently turned out, not only to admit of intermediate or mixed types, but to be resultants of a plurality of variables, so that study of the possible combinations of the component variables might at the typological level, yield, not a single dichotomous pair, but a larger "family" of possible types, which differ from each other, not on one, but on several dimensions.

I think—or "I believe"—that this is true of the concept of belief itself, at religious and at other levels. I might suggest that stating the problem in terms of belief-unbelief is already a start in this pluralistic direction in that the alternative to belief need not be simply disbelief but might be some way of avoiding being placed in the category either of believer or of disbeliever. The logic here is similar to that involved in the history of the concept of rationality and its antonyms. Namely, it was a major advance when rationality was contrasted not with irrationality but with nonrationality; there could be types which, though nonrational, were not irrational.

Certainly in the Western tradition, the concept of belief has a cognitive component. This is to say that however difficult this may be in practice, beliefs are capable of being stated in propositional form and then tested by standards of "truth" or cognitive validity. It is true that most propositions of religious belief are not subject to what we generally call empirical verification. But they still must, ideally, be tested by standards of conceptual clarity and precision, and logically correctness of inference.[1] The equivalent of the empirical component in science is the authenticity of the nonlogical components of religious belief, for example, revelation, or some kind of religious experience.

Another aspect of the problem, however, is brought out by the distinction which was discussed early in the conference, namely between what is meant by "belief *that* . . ." and "belief *in* . . ." In my view, it would not be appropriate to use the term belief in the latter context if there were *no* cognitive content involved, that is, if the action referred to were completely nonrational expression of emotions. The little word "in," however, suggests a noncognitive component which is not included in "that," which may be called commitment. The "believer in . . ." of course must, explicitly or implicitly, subscribe to cognitively formulable and in some sense testable propositions, but in addition to that, he commits himself to act (including experiencing) in ways which are, to put it in the

1. The aphorism of Tertullian, *"Credo quia absurdum est,"* could not prevail in Western religion.

mildest form, congruent with the cognitive components of his belief.

An important, perhaps the premier, example here is the Protestant doctrine, especially associated with Luther himself, of "salvation by faith alone." This is faith *in* the Christian God. The formula as such contains no reference to the cognitive set of beliefs, but it clearly implies them in the sense that faith is faith *in God;* with no cognitive conception of God the commitment would be meaningless. The alternative, for Luther, to salvation by faith, was clearly that by works through the Catholic sacraments. The definition of these alternatives did not challenge the general strictly *theo*logical conceptions of God and his relations to man.

From the point of view of the Catholic Church of his time, Luther was a heretic. But his disbelief in the mission of the historical church and in the sacraments, was only one form of unbelief. Surely in many ways he was not only a believer in some vaguely general sense, but he was a believer in Christ and the Christian God. This is to say, he accepted much of the cognitive framework of the inherited tradition.

Professor Bellah has spoken of a strong cognitive bias in Christian religious tradition. That the emphasis on the cognitive component has been strong does not seem to be seriously open to doubt. That it has been a bias in the sense that over the long run it has distorted Western religious development is a question on which I prefer to withhold judgment. Prior to rendering a necessary basis for arriving at such a judgment, it seems to me more urgent to attempt to clarify the nature of the components, both cognitive and noncognitive, rational and nonrational, of religious orientation, and certain aspects of their relations to each other.

That there must be a major set of noncognitive components is a view which has been accepted in the introductory statements of this commentary and is indeed very widely accepted. This noncognitive component is, to my mind, what distinguishes religion both from philosophy on the one hand, and science on the other, both of which are intellectual disciplines. While theology may well be considered to be such a discipline, clearly religion is not. Durkheim's famous dictum about religion, *c'est de la vie serieuse,* is one way of stating that difference and seems to be more or less adequately expressed in the term commitment which I have used above.

The Rational and Nonrational Components of Action

Bellah, in a paper presumably written almost immediately after the conference,[2] discusses explicitly the prominent role of the noncognitive and nonrational components of action in the work of the three great transformers of thinking about man and society in the generation of the turn of the century, namely Freud, Durkheim, and Max Weber. All three were prominently unbelievers in our sense though not unequivocally disbelievers, and all three were deeply concerned with religion. Bellah suggests that they were "symbolic reductionists" in that they granted a certain "reality" to religion, but held that the content of explicit beliefs must be taken to be the symbolic expression of something else.

It is in the realm of that "something else" that, according to Bellah, all three formulated the decisive noncognitive categories, namely in Freud's case the *unconscious,* in that of Durkheim, *society,* in a sense which in this context of usage clearly requires much interpretation, and in that of Weber, *charisma,* which also requires interpretation. Though these three formulations are by no means directly congruent with each other, they all constitute in some sense "residual categories" which are defined mainly by contrast with their antonyms, rather than positively.

In order to formulate a more adequate conceptual scheme it seems necessary to introduce at least two further distinctions in addition to that between the cognitive and the noncognitive. One touches the interpretation of the status of the noncognitive categories introduced by Freud and Weber, whereas the other concerns the interpretation of Durkheim's usage of society as a referent of such symbolism.

In the intellectual setting in which he introduced the concept of charisma, Weber had worked out what seems to the author a major clarification of certain aspects of the structure of the cognitive world. This occurred mainly in his famous essays on *Wissenschaftslehre* and eventuated in a special

2. Robert Bellah, "Between Religion and Social Science," chapter 14 of this volume.

version of what is usually considered to be a "neo-Kantian" position. One aspect of it was the full extension of the cognitive paradigms, which had basically come to be established in the natural sciences, to what Weber called the *Kulturwissenschaften,* a category which included both the social sciences and the humanities. The second, however, was the introduction or clarification, in the area which Kant had left cognitively unstructured under the rubric of "practical reason," of a category of cognitive knowledge concerning values, and the underlying "problems of meaning" in reference to the human condition. Here Weber's contribution is the establishment of this category—of course he by no means stood alone—as a category of rational knowledge.[3]

This was the basis on which, in his classification of "types of action," Weber was able to introduce two rather than one rational type. Since the context was action rather than knowledge as such he called them *Zweckrationalität* (which I have translated as "instrumental") and *Wertrationalität* ("value") respectively. From the beginning Weber's classification assumed that the rational types would be complemented by nonrational—not irrational—types. The duality on the rational side, however, strongly suggested the usefulness of a corresponding duality on the nonrational. In his actual classification Weber did indeed introduce two such categories, namely "affectual" and "traditional" action.

The line of distinction between the two rationalities of Weber's classification clearly concerns the direction of orientation, on the one hand downward to the empirically given conditions of human action, physical, biological and on certain levels even social and cultural and, on the other hand, upward toward the "grounds of meaning" of action and their modes of symbolization. In the paradigm we are outlining, this line of distinction should be extended onto the nonrational side. The nonrational category corresponding to instrumental rationality is that of the motivational components which are rooted in the biological nature of man, his needs and their affective modes of expression, modified as these have been from pure biologically inherited propensities,

3. Talcott Parsons, "The Sociology of Knowledge and the History of Ideas," in the *Dictionary of the History of Ideas* (New York: Charles Scribner's Sons, forthcoming).

by various features of the processes of learning and socialization. Though the references of the term are highly complex
and raise difficult theoretical problems, Weber's term "affectual," though perhaps not quite in the sense in which he
defines it, is probably as good as any.[4]

The other category of the nonrational, like value-rationality,
is a mode of orientation to the grounds and problems—in this
sense interpreted in a largely noncognitive sense—of meaning.
Here, curiously, Weber utilized the logic of the residual
category in a special way, and placed here the concept "traditional," which was clearly nonrational, but oriented wholly
to stability. He then introduced that of charisma as specifically
a nonrational orientational force of innovation, but did not
explicitly relate it to the types of action. Once, however, that
it is seen that a typology of the components of action at
the most general level should include their contribution to
both stability and change and the balance between them,
including the fact that Weber himself used the concept
charisma outside the context of change,[5] charisma emerges as
the appropriate concept in Weber's terms for the meaning-
oriented category of the nonrational side.[6]

4. It will be noted that Durkheim also used this term. See the
introduction in Emile Durkheim, *Elementary Forms of the Religious
Life,* trans. Joseph Ward Swain (New York: The Free Press, 1965;
first published in French in 1912).

5. Cf. Talcott Parsons, *The Structure of Social Action* (New York:
The Free Press, 1949). The distinction between the rational and
nonrational components of *action* does not in any direct way concern the problem of "irrationality." Put slightly differently, the
problem of irrationality does not reside in the nature of any of
the components of action, but in their combination. Rationality is
in one aspect a normative category. There are rational components
of action because knowledge is so essentially involved with it. But
rational action or deviation from its norms is always a function of
the combination of all the components, including both rational
and nonrational. Irrational action, then, is the outcome of tensions
and conflicts within the organization of action, in which, it is
essential to note, what at the more analytical level here have been
called rational and nonrational components are involved on both
sides (or several) of the tensions and conflicts. The exigencies of
combination will of course vary according to the types of action,
and their organization in systems, which are involved.

6. For Durkheim perhaps the nearest equivalent was sentiment
which appeared in his original definition of the collective conscience.

Seen in these terms, Freud's concept of the unconscious was definitely a residual category, originally formulated by contrast with the naïver versions of the conception of rationality of action, at both cognitive and behavioral levels. This is not the place to follow through the complex developments of Freud's theoretical thinking. Originally, however, the content of the unconscious was overwhelmingly interpreted to be focused on instinct. This, however, proved to be unstable and Freud himself eventually placed the superego mainly in the unconscious and distinguished it from the id. The extent to which the superego was exhausted by its unconscious components and how it articulated with internalized culture more generally remained problematical, but in a rough sense it can clearly be said that Freud's distinction between id and superego paralleled that of Weber between affectual and charismatic components of action. Hence we may say that in both Weber and Freud the analytical basis for studying a nonrational aspect of religious orientation had been laid down in the great tradition of emerging social science.

Durkheim and the Moral Component of Society

For both Weber and Freud, the primary direct referent of their symbolic reductionism, as Bellah calls it, was values; references to the reality by virtue of which values were rendered meaningful, remained in different ways problematical for both. There is a major overlap in this focus with Durkheim's position, but the difference is of great significance for the problems of the symposium. Durkheim made a great deal of the thesis that sacred things were symbols, the referents of which should be sought out by research.

The basis on which he established the connection with society was the common attitude of moral respect. In his earlier work in areas quite other than the study of religion he had gradually come to give a special place to what we can now call the internalized and above all institutionalized structure of norms and values carrying what he called "moral authority." Indeed, when Durkheim presented his famous

See Emile Durkheim, *Division of Labor in Society*, trans. George Simpson (New York: The Free Press, 1964; first published in French in 1939, second edition with additional preface, 1902).

definition of religion in the *Elementary Forms of the Religious Life*,[7] he featured the crucial phrase "moral community." The normative regulation of secular life, for Durkheim, was interpretable in terms of Weber's value-rationality. The set of beliefs and practices which he called religious, constituted symbolic expressions of the same moral community.

Weber would emphasize the consensus on values which at least in considerable part derived from the belief system, including both the cognitive component and that of commitment. Durkheim, on the other hand, did not really go beyond the existence, as institutionalized, of this moral community; Weber's was thus the deeper analysis. In stopping where he did, however, Durkheim brought to light—or to explicit attention—a most important concept which has flowered in Bellah's conception of the civil religion.[8] For Durkheim, the society was never only the community in which its members participated but was also, precisely to them, as well as to an outside observer, an object. As such the moral, and as another aspect the sacred, quality of it constituted one of its major constitutive properties.

In the French situation of his time Durkheim was a "laicist"; though of Jewish origin he was not a religiously practicing Jew and he belonged to the anticlerical left. These circumstances help to explain his views about the Church as that concept was included in his definition of religion. From his own normative point of view he repudiated two primary institutional developments of the Christian world. The one was that of the established Church, especially in the Roman Catholic form, but with differences in some Protestant cases, where the church, though established, was differentiated from the secular social order, with both the laity and the secular priesthood participating in both—members of religious orders, however, minimally in the secular world. The

7. In my translation into English it reads that, a religion is "an integrated (*solidaire*) system of beliefs and practices relative to sacred things, that is separate and taboo, which unite in one moral community called a church all those who adhere to it." Talcott Parsons, *The Structure of Social Action*, p. 412.

8. Robert Bellah, "Civil Rights in America," reprinted in William McLaughlin and Robert Bellah, eds., *Religion in America* (Boston: Houghton Mifflin, 1969).

second is the institutional form which was first clearly developed in the United States but has increasingly become the dominant institutional form for the noncommunist Western world, namely denominational pluralism with religious freedom and toleration, and in the more logically developed cases, separation of church and state.

Such processes of differentiation, however, have been deeply grounded in the structure of predominantly Christian societies, with either Establishment constitutions or pluralistic ones, and doubtless further steps of differentation are likely to occur, some of which will be suggested below. Hence we cannot accept Durkheim's identification of the societal moral community with a church. Bellah, however, has still been able to show, most clearly for the American case, that these differentiations are by no means incompatible with the societal community at the same time being secular and yet having a religious aspect. In that sense, of course, Durkheim was right.

Clearly these considerations are highly relevant to the discussions of the first day of the conference, which centered on Professor Luckmann's paper. In the course of those discussions there were many references to a Durkheimian point of view, which it is perhaps fair to say on the whole Professor Luckmann himself took. It is quite clear, however, that Durkheim did not have an adequate basis for the analysis of Luckmann's stage C, except perhaps rather vaguely in his analysis of the phenomena of collective effervescence.

The Concept of Secularization

The main Durkheimian position, however, sharply raises the question of the meaning of the concept of secularization about which something needs to be said before returning to the problems of belief, unbelief, and disbelief in the current sociocultural situation.

In this commentary and for many years, the general view which I have been espousing is that, in the socio-cultural sphere, and indeed also the psychological, what has come generally to be called "religion" stands at the highest level in the cybernetic hierarchy of the forces which, in the sense of defining the general directionality of human action among the possible alternatives permitted in the human condition, controls the processes of human action.[9] This is a view obviously shared with Max Weber, but also I think by Durkheim and Freud, though Freud has been widely interpreted to hold directly contrary views.

The question of secularization should be approached on this background. The term clearly refers, even etymologically, to concern with the world by contrast with the transcendent. It is clearly its claim to some kind of contact with the transcendent which is the hallmark of religion, whether the contact be conceived or felt as "knowledge of," as some noncognitive "experience of" or as being instrumental to the "will of" some transcendent entity. One suspects that all of these components, and probably others, are involved in an authentic religion, though in different combinations in different religions. It is in the nature of the case that there should, if the concept of transcendence is meaningful at all, be a sense of tension between the transcendent referent and the worldly. But just as there are various ways of experiencing or having contact with the transcendent, it is also true that the world is not to be conceived as a constant given entity, the properties of which are in no sense a function of human action and history.

If there is a generic meaning of the concept secularization it is probably a change, in this area of inherent tension, in the direction of a closer relation of the one to the other. The concept has, in the Western world and especially in religious circles, been widely interpreted to mean a one-way change, namely the sacrifice of religious claims, obligations and commitments, in favor of secular interests. The other possibility, however, should not be forgotten, namely that the secular order may change in the direction of closer approximation of the normative models provided by a religion, or by religion more generally. The tension seems to have been particularly pronounced in the Judeo-Christian religious tradition, or at least has been defined in ways familiar to most of us there. On the one hand, we have the conception of man as irrevo-

9. It should be made clear that exercise of authority or power constitutes only *one* mode of control in the present sense, and in the context of this discussion, by no means the most important mode. There is an unfortunate tendency, which is by no means justified, to equate control with dominance and coercion.

cably sunk in "sin and death," whereas on the other hand we
have the conception of man as created "in the image of God"
and hence as the "lord of the Creation." Indeed the very center
of the constitutive symbolism of Christianity would be meaningless without this duality—to put it in one way, if man were
totally "lost" why should God make his "only begotten son"
a *man* of flesh and blood in order to make human salvation
possible? [10]

It was Weber, perhaps more than any other recent Western
mind, who seriously began to explore the possibility that the
second alternative should be taken seriously, namely of change
in the world in the direction of institutionalization of religious
values, though of course Troeltsch, in his conception of
Christian Society, also moved in that direction about the
same time, and they both had many antecedents. Put in
sociological terminology, there is the possibility that religious
values should come to be institutionalized, by which we mean
that such values come to be the focus of the definition of the
situation for the conduct of members of secular societies,
precisely in their secular roles. The processes by which this
occurs are highly complex and would require an elaborate
treatise to analyze at all fully. That it has in fact happened,
however, seems to be indisputable. When it happens, however,
tensions do not disappear, but come to be restructured; the
world as such is in its very nature *never* the transcendently
defined ideal.[11]

10. On the general relations of moral order and original sin see
Kenneth Burke, "The First Three Chapters of Genesis," in *The
Rhetoric of Religion* (Boston: Beacon Press, 1961).

11. In writing in the present context for what is, sociologically
speaking mainly, though by no means wholly, a nontechnical reader-
ship, it is difficult to know how far to go in the exposition of underlying sociological frames of reference and paradigms. In part I am
being deliberately paradoxical in attributing to the concept secularization what has often been held to be its opposite, namely
not the loss of commitment to religious values and the like, but the
institutionalization of such values, and other components of religious orientation in evolving cultural and social systems. This latter
process, with which the remainder of the present paper is primarily
concerned, has often, especially perhaps in religious circles, been
held to constitute secularization in the former sense, though when
seen in the larger perspective this turns out to be a misinterpreta-

The Institutionalization of Religious Values

It is by this path that a society—and in different ways its various subsectors—comes to be a moral community in Durkheim's sense, and hence acquires religious significance so that

tion. Such misinterpretations have, however, been extremely prevalent and have appeared repeatedly at various stages of the larger process.

Secularization in the second sense constitutes a dual process, on the one hand, of the differentiation of religious components from the secular—as in certain respects was the case for the differentiation of the Christian Church from both the Jewish ethnic community and the society of the Roman Empire. Such differentiation clearly involves a diminution of the religious value of the social and cultural components from which the newly emergent religious one becomes differentiated. Thus, while Roman society was in a certain sense quasi-sacred, for Christians it came to be, for the time being, entirely deprived of this quality.

Once this process has occurred, however, the questions which are crucial to us are not resolved by the process of differentiation alone, but concern a complex sequence of sequels which are, at various stages, contingent on inherently variable factors. In a very schematic way, the following seems to be the central one: The initial process of differentiation is very generally associated with sharp antagonisms between the newly emerging complex and that from which it is coming to be differentiated—thus early Christians versus both Jews and Romans, later, Protestants versus Catholics. If, however, the conditions for a successful process of institutionalization are present—which is by no means to be taken for granted—then three further modes of change must occur, in roughly the following temporal sequence, though clearly this is by no means rigid.

1. What will later be referred to as *inclusion*. By this I mean that the older order from which the new religious movement has come to be differentiated, will regain positive religious significance and be included within a broader sacred order. The medieval synthesis, as it has just been sketched, is a major case—secular society, the state in the medieval sense, came to be part of the same order as that of the Christian Church and incorporated many components of both Jewish and Roman institutions, e.g., both the Old Testament and Roman Law. The modern civil religions are cases of this phenomenon.

2. *Adaptive upgrading*, by which, in this context, I mean the reevaluation of the older, previously downgraded components to constitute assets from the point of view of the broader system. In the above case, the accord of a new positive religious value to secular life, as distinguished from the view that members of the segregated orders were the only groups which were in any real

at least some of its institutions are, within certain limits of course, sacred things in the quite literal sense. If this is the case, then the totally concrete dichotomy between sacred and profane entities, transcendentally meaningful and worldly, becomes untenable. A particular human society, in different aspects, is both sacred and profane, both an embodiment (to use a specifically Christian image) of the transcendent and part of the secular world.

There is another of Durkheim's fundamental contributions the understanding of which is essential to our analysis. This lies in the implication of his decision to devote his basic analysis of religion and society to the case of the most primitive religion, as well as society, about which he thought there was adequate record, namely that of the Australian Aborigines. The fundamental contention is that there is no human society without religion. The two are concretely, though not analytically, indivisible. It follows that both the religious and the secular parts of the complex are involved in a process of evolution and that this process always involves interdependence between them—and human personality as well.[12]

It is, I think, fully established that one major aspect of any process which can be called evolutionary is differentiation. In the course of such processes it is to be expected that both the religious and the secular aspects of both cultural and social systems should undergo differentiation within themselves and that there should be processes of differentiation between them. It is in this frame of reference that I should like to see the two-way aspects of what is frequently called the "process of secularization."

Where we of the Judeo-Christian tradition now stand on

---

sense Christian, constitutes a massive phenomenon of upgrading.

3. *Value-generalization.* If both inclusion and upgrading, as outlined, are to be legitimized, this cannot take place literally in terms of the value-orientations of the religious movement which previously declared the excluded elements to be in principle illegitimate. There must be a restructuring of the valuational base at a more general level, according to which, in our example, both religious and laity are in some sense really Christian.

12. See Robert Bellah, "Religious Evolution," reprinted in his *Beyond Belief* and also my own *Societies: Comparative and Evolutionary Perspectives* (Englewood Cliffs, N.J.: Prentice Hall, 1966), chapter 3, on "Primitive Societies."

these matters is perhaps best made clear in terms of an exceedingly schematic sketch of the main historical stages by which we have arrived where we are.[13] First, the early Christian Church became differentiated, not only from the people of Israel, but from the society of the Roman Empire. The latter was defined as pagan, the former perhaps as sacred, but in a kind of a "quasi" sense. The great structural innovation, however, was the establishment of the Church as a religious association of individuals. In the early period, of course, in part buoyed by eschatological expectations, the church remained as aloof from both the Jewish community and Roman society as possible.

With the process of proselytization, however, this aloofness became decreasingly feasible. The process of growth ended with a dual change, namely first the acceptance of Christianity as the official religion of the Roman Empire and, within the Church itself, the differentiation between the religious orders and the laity (see Paolo Tufari, forthcoming Ph.D. dissertation, Harvard University). This development set the stage for the Catholic pattern which culminated in the Middle Ages. Another major development was the split between Eastern and Western churches, connected with the decline of the Western Empire. Our concern will be with the development of the West under the jurisdiction of the Roman papacy.

The medieval system, theologically defined above all by St. Thomas, interlarded, in ideal conception, a stratified church-state system—an internally stratified secular society (state in the medieval sense) and an internally stratified Church. In terms of the religious values the Church was clearly higher than the state. It was the field for the implementation of spiritual as distinguished from temporal commitments. But the significant new element, by contrast with the early Church, was the inclusion of the secular society, the state, as temporal arm in a Christian collective system. The layman then inherently came to play a dual role. He was a member of the church conceived as the "Body of Christ" but at the same time he was a member of the secular social order. To mediate

13. See my article "Christianity," in David Sills, ed., *The International Encyclopedia of Social Sciences* (New York: Macmillan and the Free Press, 1968).

between them there developed the secular priesthood, precisely as distinguished from the religious orders. The former were implementing the Mission of Christ at one level down, as it were, in that they were both consecrated and members of the secular community, indeed its spiritual leaders.

This meant the basic moral and spiritual upgrading of secular society, on a basis which justified Troeltsch in calling it a "Christian Society," a designation which no Christian would have applied to the Roman Empire in the time before it became "Holy." At the same time the hierarchy relative to spiritual values was preserved in institutional structure at three levels. First, the priority, not in power but in legitimacy, of church over state. Second, within the church, in the priority of the still aloof religious orders over, not only the laity, but the mediating secular clergy. Third was the priority of the aristocracy, to which the medieval system certainly gave a fundamental moral sanction, over the common people. This sanction was predicated on the presumption of higher levels of spiritual and moral commitment on the part of aristocracies as compared with the populace.

This inclusion of secular society in the religiously legitimated system could not occur without profound theological changes from the early Fathers. It was Thomas who brought these to a culmination with the conception of a stratified Christian Order, in which spiritual and temporal, divine and human, Church and state were interlarded. The crucial point, however, was the religious legitimation of the secular order in a sense which could not be asserted of the early Christian view of pagan society. It was on this basis that medieval society could, in Durkheim's sense, be considered to constitute for Christians a "moral community" by virtue of its institutionalization of the sacred order.

From the Reformation to Ecumenicism

Grandly architectonic as it was, the medieval system proved not to be stable. The great crisis at the level of constitutive symbolism, and hence of belief, came with the Reformation. Whatever the causal factors leading up to it, Luther and other Reformers launched a fundamental attack on the Thomistic system. The crux of it of course concerned the status of the Church, especially through the sacramental system, as the machinery of salvation, and with it the status of the priesthood. The sacraments came to be by-passed by the direct relation of the individual believer to God through faith. The true church then became the invisible church of the faithful in communion with God, with no spiritual necessity for intermediary structures. The clergy then became spiritual guides and teachers but were deprived of the "power of the keys."

The reaction of the Church of course was to outlaw the Reformers as heretics and to assert the integrity of the "catholic" system more militantly than ever in what is usually called the counter-reformation. The full reestablishment of the older system was widely considered to be the sole condition on which Western Christendom could be viable. On the other side, the more radical Reformers maintained that the total destruction of Catholicism was equally essential from their point of view (some of my ancestors were in this category). Neither position, however, prevailed, but rather a quite different one. Many will still call it a dishonorable compromise, but I suggest another interpretation.

The first stage, signalized by the Peace of Westphalia, seemed to be one of resignation dictated by sheer exhaustion from the terrible costs of the Wars of Religion. But the formula *cuius regio, eius religio,* proved not only to be a formula of truce but also the beginning of consolidation and extension of a new process of differentiation and attendant related changes in the Western socio-religious system. First the coexistence within the same system of both Protestant and Catholic Principalities meant that there were common interests, for example, in maintaining peace or in promoting political alliances, which cut across the religious line. In the longer run, the effect of this was to confirm the differentiation between religious and secular collectivities by dissociating secular political interests from religious affiliation—as, for example, in the eighteenth-century political alliance between the France of Richelieu and the Prussia of Frederick the Great. It was not a terribly long step from there to the conception of the legitimacy of a pluralistic religious constitution internal to the principality, a step first taken in Holland and England after the Reformation. This of course is the origin of the system of denominational pluralism within the politically organized society, and hence of the differentiation between churches as primarily religious bodies and the moral community in Durkheim's sense, which is also in the civic sense a religious entity.

Eventually, through many conflicts and struggles, Protestantism and Catholicism have come to constitute differentiated sectors of the same ecumenical religious community. The inclusion of Jews in such a community was, again, not a very long step. There is a parallel with the growing tolerance, in democratic polities, of differing political parties, where choice among alternative party affiliations does not jeopardize the individual's status as a loyal citizen.

With this change in the underlying structure, gradually the definition of each of the plural denominational groups began to attenuate their initial tendency to define each other's members radically as disbelievers and often as heretics. Only in our own time, however, has the ecumenical movement reached the point where a new position is being widely institutionalized or approaching that status, namely where the individual is held to have a right to the religious adherence, including beliefs, of his own choice and, whatever the element of stratification in the religious system, that right includes recognition of the religious legitimacy of the adherents of other faiths. The great steps of our time have, of course, been those taken by the Roman Church with the Papacy of John XXIII and Vatican Council II, which he called into being.[14]

14. In the United States, which has played a rather special part in these developments, the new ecumenicism was very sharply symbolized by the funeral of the assassinated President John F. Kennedy in November, 1963. This was particularly significant because Kennedy was the first Roman Catholic to be elected president of the United States. Since he was a faithful Catholic, the services were conducted in the Catholic Cathedral of Washington by the "parish priest" of the Kennedy family, Cardinal Cushing of Boston. The attendants at the funeral mass, however, were persons of all faiths, starting with the new president, Lyndon Johnson, very much a Protestant. Burial, finally, was in what Bellah calls the most sacred place of the American civil religion, the Arlington National Cemetery.

An almost equally symbolic event, which I personally attended, occurred in Boston, Kennedy's home city, two months later. This

It is not, I think, too much to say that ecumenicism, however incomplete and, indeed, in certain respects precarious its institutionalization still is, represents a stage where belief can clearly no longer be assessed in terms of cognitive or non-rational (or both) commitment to one religious collectivity at the Church level. The contemporary Catholic, Protestant, or Jew may, with variations within his own broader faith, even for Catholics, be a believer in the wider societal moral community. This level he does not share in regard to specifics with those of other faiths. He has, however, as I have put it, come to respect the religious legitimacy of these other faiths. The test of this legitimacy is that he and the adherents of these other faiths recognize that they can belong in the same moral community—which may be a predominantly secular, politically organized society—and that this common belongingness means sharing a religious orientation at the level of civil religion. Hence we must speak of at least three references of the concept of believer, namely (1) full adherent of an established denominational religious body, usually though not always called a church; (2) the status of an adherent of another such denominational body (from the point of view of believers in (1) those in category (2) are clearly disbelievers, or at least unbelievers); (3) common membership in a moral community which is characterized by a civil religion. In this context members of both categories (1) and (2) can in common be believers.

The Enlightenment and Radical Secularism

Clearly, however, the complications do not stop here. As early as the seventeenth century, thought about man and society began to appear which purported to be wholly secular, repudiating the entire religious tradition. Perhaps the earliest

---

was a memorial Requiem Mass, held in the Cathedral of the Holy Cross in Boston with Cardinal Cushing officiating. What was new, however, was the fact that, as part of the service itself, the Mozart Requiem was played by the Boston Symphony Orchestra, a citadel of Boston Protestant "Brahmanism." It was the first time that the Boston Symphony has, as an orchestra, ever participated in a religious service. The ecumenical character of the occasion was further emphasized by the fact that the clergy of all faiths marched in the procession and sat in the sanctuary.

represenative of the highest intellectual stature was Thomas Hobbes, who was an especially thoroughgoing materialist. This movement of secular thought gathered force and came to play a highly salient role in the Enlightenment of the eighteenth century, then underwent still further developments in the Positivism, especially of the nineteenth century, which are still reverberating.

This movement tended to repudiate traditional religion, Catholic, Protestant, or Jewish, specifically from the point of view of the status of the cognitive component of religious belief systems. Over part of the world of cultural sensitivity in the West, this movement led to a genuine polarization, perhaps most prominent in the secular anticlericalism which has been so prevalent in many predominantly Catholic countries.[15]

Positivism, of course, purported to make of empirical science the only valid mode of cognition accessible to man at all. Starting as early as Rousseau and certainly conspicuously with Comte and somewhat later Marx, though the belief component in the cognitive sense was purportedly held to the level of science, the commitments to action which were so prominent in these movements certainly came to include noncognitive components, as perhaps most vividly obvious in the connection of these rationalisms with the Romantic movement.

It is perhaps safe to say that a purely secular, positivistic counter-system to traditional Western religion reached a kind of apogee in the nineteenth century and then began to break down in a sense parallel to that in which the Protestant counter-system to Catholicism has broken down into ecumenicism, a process which of course required major modifications in the earlier Catholic system itself.[16]

Within the positivistic system, clearly the major modification is the abandonment of the closed materialistic determinism which was so prominent in intellectual circles over a long period, perhaps culminating in the later nine-

15. In this connection Weber spoke, with a certain awe, of the forms of "extreme rationalistic fanaticism" which appeared in the course of the French Revolution and in various connections during the nineteenth century. He clearly felt that such fanaticism was not a simple matter of cognitive beliefs alone.

16. I am quite ready to acknowledge that the pattern of sequences outlined here, closely resembles that of the Hegelian-Marxian dialectic.

teenth century. The alternative could not, however, be philosophical idealism of the Hegelian variety, nor an idealism too closely Kantian. Many other participants in the conference are far more competent than I to assess the significance of a wide variety of these philosophical movements. Let me only say that for me personally, from the philosophical side, a particularly important figure was A. N. Whitehead.

The positivistic systems, to an important degree in the very process of transcending their scientism, reintroduced, in modified form, both nonempirical cognitive components and nonrational components into the picture. On the cognitive-rational side what was important was the reintroduction of components which are, to say the least, exceedingly difficult to treat as purely empirical. Perhaps the most conspicuous example is the dialectic of history of the Marxian system, which is a kind of restatement in secular-rationalistic terms of the Christian eschatological myth that, after the expulsion from Paradise (primitive communism), there have been many agonies of subjection to the sinful powers—both feudalism and capitalism—but that finally the, this time, *collective* savior, the proletariat, is born in the humblest of circumstances and mediates between the contemporary man and his sinful past, history, and is destined to bring about the imminent "second coming," the state of communism.

This intellectual (or symbolic) construction has occasioned problems of validation and indeed interpretation which are in important respects parallel to those confronted by the theologians of the Christian Church. It was suggested above that the early Church was confronted with not only one but two foils, namely, the historic, and clearly to it, sacred socio-religious community of the people of Israel, and the world of the gentiles, namely the rest of the population of the Roman Empire. Perhaps it is not too fantastic to suggest that the secular religion movement, culminating in Marxism, has faced, on the one hand, the partly "sacred" religio-moral community of capitalism, from which it has felt a special urgency to differentiate itself, but beyond that a much diffuser "pagan" world, namely that of the underdeveloped societies. Perhaps Moscow has become the "Rome" of one part of the new system, very clearly differentiated from the "Palestine" which might include the Rhineland, Paris, London, and New York.

In this context, however, events seem to have moved much faster than in the earlier developments. If the socialist movement was a kind of functional equivalent of the Reformation, in certain respects sanctifying the secular social world, then the ecumenical phase seems to have begun to develop with surprising rapidity. These conflicts and tensions are much farther from being resolved than are those having to do with Catholic-Protestant relations, or those of both Judaism and Jewry—though in the latter connection it should not be forgotten how recent the demise of Nazism is. Nevertheless the current difference in the Catholic case, especially since John XXIII, from the many pronouncements especially of Pius XII about "atheistic Communism," parallels in secular society the attentuation on the part of American political spokesmen of the not-so-distant past, of the virulent "cold war" ideological confrontation, the accusation, from the capitalist side that there is a communist conspiracy to conquer the world.

It may seem farfetched to set up the Communist movement, as the most politically effective outgrowth of Marxian theory and the socialist political movement, as a kind of culmination of the conception of the ideal of the totally secular sociocultural order. I think, however, that this view is defensible. Making allowances for the relevant differences in the stage of evolution of the Western system, the Communist societies are very closely comparable to those dominated by strict Calvinism, especially Calvin's own Geneva, John Knox' Scotland for a brief period, the apogee of Cromwell's ascendancy in England, and very early New England. The difference has not lain in the basic pattern, but in the level of secularity of the system idealized and subjected to drastic controls.

The new religio-secular ecumenicism is not, however, grounded only, or even mainly, in the intellectual confrontation between Christian theology, and Marxism, or other secularist, theory, but also in the emergence of emphasis on essentially noncognitive components. Perhaps because of my special intellectual standard, it seems to me—and I am happily in agreement with Bellah on this—that the especially important intellectual mediators have been Freud, Durkheim, and in somewhat different ways, Max Weber.

As I have already noted, the decisive factor was the

emergence of the conception of the moral component, both in the structure of societies and in the personality and motivation of the individual. For Weber, it was exemplified above all by the internalization and institutionalization of the concept of the calling in ascetic Protestantism, and with it the new level of sanctification of secular callings. For Freud it centered on the concept of the superego and its intimate involvement with the unconscious. It was Durkheim, however, who most clearly and definitely saw and characterized the moral aspect of society, both as seen by its members as object, and as defining their orientations as participants. This, combined with Durkheim's conception of religious evolution, opened the door, as we have seen, to Bellah's fruitful conception of civil religion.[17]

This seems to me to be the main path by which what are often called "secular humanists" have been brought into the moral community of modern society, including the religious implications of its existence as such a community. Both the separation of church and state in the American tradition, and the inclusion of a lay component in full citizenship in continental Europe, seem to me to imply this. Many of these secularists never had any connection with Marxism; I have concentrated on Marxism because it is the most salient grandscale antireligious (in the traditional sense) movement.

In terms of the paradigm of contexts of belief and unbelief outlined above for the ecumenical process of inclusion, one can say that secular humanists in this sense are not even believers in the "faith of their own choice." At the level of the moral community and civic religion, however, they must be accorded the status of believers. At this level it may be sug-

17. In this respect, it has long seemed to me, Marxian theory has been notably ambivalent and vacillating. On the one hand materialism seemed to dictate a conception of the real forces of history as totally independent of any normative component. On the other hand the collective voluntarism of the social movement went far beyond extending opportunities for its members to satisfy their interests. On the contrary, it allegedly generated genuine solidarity and thereby imposed moral obligations on participants. In a sense, in between lay what Marx called the "relations of production" as distinguished from the "forces of production." The key component here was the system of legal norms, to which we may say Marxians have attributed a kind of semi- or pseudolegitimacy, as part, no doubt, of the more general semilegitimacy of capitalism as referred to above.

gested that disbelievers are the revolutionaries who basically challenge the moral legitimacy of modern societal communities, and commit themselves to their overthrow, and unbelievers those who, though not actively combating such communities, are alienated from them and seek to minimize participation.

From the point of view of the traditional Western religions, the most important epithet aimed in this direction has been "atheism." It is now relatively commonplace that preoccupation with this issue is at least partly an expression of Judeo-Christian religious parochialism since other advanced religions, notably Buddhism, have been said to be atheistic, but of course nonetheless religions for that reason. This, however, seems to be too simple an argument in the present context. A much more important point is the emergence, as defined explicitly as such, of the "civil religions"—the American is clearly one variant in a wider complex.

This is the result of a process of inclusion directly parallel to that sketched above in relation to ecumenicism. Durkheim's equation is here, as we have noted, decisive. Those who recognize and participate in a moral community may or may not, according to matters of definition, constitute a church, but they must share in what in some sense is a common religion. Conversely, those who share what can properly be called a religion must to some extent and in some respects, constitute a moral community.

The crucial point is that, in the development of modern societies and cultures, memberships have come to be pluralistic. There is not one moral community which is an undifferentiated unity after the manner of Rousseau, nor is there one true religion outside of which nonparticipants, or disbelievers, are cast into the "outer darkness." In its secular version Rousseauism led to exclusive nationalism and the Terror; in the religious versions, counter-Reformation Catholicism to the Inquisition, Calvinism to the execution of Servetus, and Communism to the great purges of Stalin's time.

Of course in this process it is highly significant that the great mediators, the three we have named (Freud, Durkheim, and Weber) and doubtless others, were neither believers in the traditional denominational senses, nor "principled atheists." Their roles have been more closely analogous to those of an

Erasmus, a John Locke, a Thomas Jefferson, a Tocqueville, and indeed, if we stretch a point, a John XXIII.

The mediation process by which old dichotomous polarities have come to be mitigated, and new inclusions facilitated, in general has not only promoted new integrations, but has also opened new possibilities, which from many points of view have constituted versions of Pandora's box. From the medieval point of view, the Reformation did this, and from that of even relatively ecumenical Christianity, the Enlightenment did it again.

The New Resurgence of the Nonrational

With all the salience in these previous phases of problems of the nonrational, notably in the case of faith in the Lutheran sense, and of both personality needs and collective urgencies in such fields as nationalism and other forms of community, the main line of Western religio-social restructuring has centered on the cognitive component of religious commitment or "belief in. . . ."

The new phenomenon in the present generation, as very much preoccupying the discussions of the symposium, for example, in Luckmann's stage C and in Bellah's oral statement and many comments on them, seems to me to be the emergence, perhaps for the first time in a comparable way since the early Christians before the Alexandrian Fathers, of the nature and significance of the nonrational components of religious systems and all their complex relations to the secular world.

There have, of course, been many outbreaks of the non-rational in Western religious history, such as perhaps the Children's Crusade, the Waldensian disturbances, and the Anabaptist outbreak in the early Reformation. There is, however, a sense in which the extension of the differentiation and inclusion process which we have been outlining, to the "sancti-fication" of a whole series of levels and aspects of secular society, starting with that of "worldly callings" in Weber's sense, has now reached something approximating an end of the line. There is indeed now a sense in which church religion has come to be largely privatized, but concomitantly religious or quasi-religious significance generalized to an immense range of what previously were defined as more or less purely secular concerns, such for example as racial equality and the elimination of poverty.

A particularly good indication of this end-of-the-line situation from the religious point of view is the fact that what, in its terms, has for nearly two centuries been defined as the most subversive cultural movement, namely materialistic rationalism, now seems to be in course of being brought "into the fold." Furthermore, from the societal point of view, perhaps it can be said that we are witnessing the last throes of the disappearing institutional legitimacy of aristocracy; the demand for inclusion of all human classes on a basis of some kind of fundamental equality has become irresistible.

From the point of view of the conventional criteria of progress, in spite of the turbulent vicissitudes of recent times, and the very present threats of engulfment by the Nazis, of victory of the Communist conspiracy or of mutual destruction in nuclear war, the story has been on the whole still one of progress, namely higher levels of welfare, of education, of health and longevity, of access, for the previously disadvantaged classes, to the good things previously monopolized by the privileged.

For partisans of the new movements of dissent and revolt, the refusal to be impressed by these achievements of modern society and the tendency to declare the latter to be basically corrupt indicates that the tensions underlying the current cleavages have taken a qualitatively new turn.[18] Far deeper than this, however, lies the problem of what in some sense is legitimacy. The questions are becoming such as "If now we have unprecedented facilities for attaining whatever goals are

18. The above negative evaluation of contemporary industrial society and its dangers for community were most fully expressed in the symposium by Bryan Wilson. As the transcript shows, I took rather sharp issue with his diagnosis of the situation, and I could have said a good deal more. There is, however, no doubt about the prevalence among intellectuals of these views, and probably of their strategic importance, whatever their status by standards of sociological correctness. In terms of the argument of this paper it might be said that they have the function of defining aspects of the world which can be religiously and morally condemned, thereby facilitating the acceptance and eventually the sanctification of other worldly elements, some of which are now present, others in process of emergence, and others which will necessitate directed attempts to bring them about.

desired, how will the relevant goals be defined?" and second, "Among the goals professed in a liberal society, by what processes and criteria will priorities among them be set?"

The conflict over legitimacy, however, does not rage most fiercely over the failures of modern society with respect to these more or less classic problems of social justice—with perhaps the critical exception of commitment to the elimination of war, which I think has progressed considerably in recent decades. They come to focus, rather, on the legitimacy of areas of expressiveness in behavior, one major aspect of which, on the historic background, is a new permissiveness, in areas where highly restrictive codes have been institutionalized for many centuries.

In attempting to designate this focus we immediately run into terminological difficulties of the kind noted above. Probably the most widely acceptable term for the main thrust of the new striving for liberation is for affective concerns. These run all the way from the grossest levels of eroticism, and indeed aggression, to the most highly sublimated levels of love. Here, however, the critical thing is to remember that on the nonrational as well as the rational side of the action paradigm we have set forth, there is a dual, not a unitary reference. Only in one respect is everything expressive the same, namely by contrast with the nonexpressive.

We can then presume that, within the expressive rubric which is contrasted with the rationalism of the modern establishment, there is involved a charismatic component in Weber's sense, as well as permissiveness for the expression of nonrational motivational components. In Freud's terms, there may be superego as well as id components.

The New Religion of Secular Love

The current new movements, of the "Christening" of which Bellah so eloquently spoke, seem to have one very important kind of relation to early Christianity, namely their immense concern with the theme of love. So far as I can see, however, there are two especially prominent differences from the early Christian case, directly in this connection, and certain others on its boundaries.

First, the source of inspiration of reorientation is not seen in the same kind of theistic terms which linked Christianity

with Judaism. In this connection probably another phenomenon of ecumenicism is important, namely, the increasing interest in and acceptance of the legitimacy of non-Western
religions, notably those of the Hindu-Buddhist complex. It is of
course well known that these have had a particularly strong
appeal, often in seriously garbled form, in socially and
culturally radical circles.[19]

Probably, however, the most important motivation for an
avoidance of theism concerns the desire to emphasize the
this-worldly location of the valued objects and interests. From
one point of view, then, the new movement may be a kind of
culmination of the trend of secularization we have traced
which has sanctified, by inclusion, and moral upgrading component after component of what originally was conceived to
be the world by contrast with the spiritual order.[20] If, as
Weber stressed, the order of secular work could be so sanctified, why not the order of human love? The immediacy of this
orientation pattern, however, is too oblivious to the need for a
transcendent anchorage which must somehow include both
affectively adequate symbolizations and some elements of
cognitive belief. So far the dominant tone seems to be the
repudiation of the inherited symbols and beliefs, but that
may well prove to be temporary.

19. An interesting and important index of this new trans-Western
ecumenicism is the rapid decline of interest in Christian missions,
both Catholic and Protestant. In the nineteenth century and the
earlier part of the present one we quite literally believed in the
urgency of converting the "Heathen Chinese," as the only half sa-
tirical phrase went. Now there is probably a disposition toward
romantic overevaluation of exotic religions.

A related point is that we have had a strong modern tendency
toward a cynical interpretation of the past, e.g., to the effect that
the Europeans involved in the exploration and exploitation of the
extra-European world were motivated only by concerns for money,
profit and power, especially through slavery. That there were genuine religious concerns involved is, however, clear, not only in the
American mythology about the settlement of New England, but
also of Virginia—cf. Perry Miller, *Errand into the Wilderness* (Cam-
bridge: Harvard University Press, 1956). Clearly very similar things
were true of Catholic, Spanish, and French settlements; they were,
in substantial part, missionary enterprises.

20. With all due allowance for the basic differences, when a very
central Christian aphorism is "For God so loved the world that He
gave His only begotten Son . . . ," it is perhaps understandable that
mere humans should "love the world."

The second central feature which is different from early Christianity is closely related. It is that the community of love is not felt to be properly defined as a separated entity concerned primarily with the afterworld (a *Heilsanstalt,* as Weber called it) but as an integral part of human society in the here and now. It is set apart only by the conflict between such movements, vague and relatively unorganized as they have been, and those elements of society which resist them and are unsympathetic to them. There is no clear equivalent of the Christian church's self-definition as separate and apart by virtue of its transcendental mission.

Though, as suggested, even expressive symbolization, to say nothing of belief systems, is still incipient, probably the master symbol has become that of community, that is, of secular collectivities in the organization and solidarity of which the dominant theme is the mutual love of the members. In the more radical versions, the ideal is that not only the national level of societies, but world society should become one vast concrete community of love. It seems to follow, to what Pareto called the "logic of the sentiments," that any other motivations and mechanisms of social control are inherently immoral and should not be accepted on any terms. This obviously is a Utopian ideal, certainly in Mannheim's sense, with a vengeance. It can, however, be said to be a legitimate socio-cultural descendant of Christianity.

Objectively, so far, the trial institutionalization of the new religious orientation is confined to small, more or less self-isolated groups, which in some respects resemble the conventicles of early Protestantism. Whether or when it will crystallize into an organized mass movement depends on many factors, not the least of which is leadership. In the sense in which Luther and Calvin were the major prophets of the Reformation, Rousseau of the Enlightenment, and Marx of socialism, it does not seem that a major prophet of the new religion of love has yet appeared. Perhaps, in retrospect, Gandhi will appear as a kind of John the Baptist.

Moral Absolutism, Eroticism, and Aggression

The above two characteristics of the new, presumptively religious ferment help to explain, if their designation is correct, three aspects of the fermenting mix which are disturbing to those who are not themselves caught up in the ferment, but who are more disposed to be sympathetic with it than to condemn it out of hand. These are its tendency to moral absolutism, to forthright, indeed flamboyant eroticism, and to a seemingly new attitude of permissiveness toward or even legitimation of aggression and violence which seems difficult to reconcile with the stress on love.

The key to understanding these disturbing phenomena seems to me to lie in the phenomenon of regression and the understanding of it which has been attained in the last generation and more of the development of social science. The essential framework lies in the great principle of evolutionary biology, that "ontogeny repeats phylogeny," however complicated the empirical application of that principle may be. In terms closer to our own, the process of differentiation and its related processes, are critical to the evolution of human action systems, including their cultural, social, and personality and organic subsystems.

Regression then means that under pressure, a system will revert to patterns which have been dominant and appropriate in earlier stages of its development. Perhaps the most graphic demonstrations of the phenomenon have been provided in the field of psychopathology, especially through the insights of Freud. Fixation on and at particular levels of regression is the primary hallmark of psychopathological states, but the recognition and understanding of such fixations is the starting point of successful therapy. Therapy in turn is the first cousin of creativity. New creative developments in the personality or the cultural or social system are overwhelmingly associated with phases of regression.[21]

Throughout this paper I have stressed the importance of the moral aspect of the interface between the transcendental and the worldly references of the human condition, between religious commitments and coping with the given situation of action. What I here call moral absolutism is the product of dedifferentiation of the inherently pluralistic moral com-

21. An already classical explication of this phenomenon is presented in Erik Erikson's *Young Man Luther* (New York: W. W. Norton, 1962). See also his paper, "Reflections on the Dissent of Contemporary Youth," *Daedalus,* Winter 1970.

plexity of evolutionarily advanced social and cultural systems, to the point of fixation on what seems, under stress, to be the one essential moral commitment which not only must outrank others in a priority scale, but to which all others must unequivocally be subordinated, as presumptively the only way in which the treasured central value can be asserted and protected against abandonment.

The phenomenon itself is of course by no means new. It, in fact, characterizes charismatic movements rather generally, including early Christianity itself, the Reformation, Jacobinism, and Communist socialism. It is clear, however, that it generates severe conflicts in the course of developmental processes of the sort we have been analyzing, because of its incompatibility with the moral bases of structural pluralism. It challenges the legitimacy of the moral commitments of all elements in the system which will not give the demanded priority to the one absolutized value and hence escalates the conflict to the level of a value-conflict, which can be much more serious than the usual conflict of interests. Proverbially, religious wars are particularly bitterly fought.

This circumstance, combined with the centrality of the valuation of love in the new movement, helps to make understandable the complex set of relations among love and the erotic on the one hand, aggression and violence on the other. The involvement of religion with erotic themes is of course as old as the history of religion itself. Modern psychology and sociology, however, have made it possible to gain better analytic insight into the reasons for this interrelation than have previously been available. One such insight concerns the continuities between the erotic component in child care and its functions for socialization of the child, with the nature and function of genital eroticism for the adults.

In one sense the primordial solidarity is that between mother and child—as beautifully symbolized in the Renaissance Madonna theme. This is at the same time ideally a relation of mutual erotic gratification and of love. This critical feature is repeated at the adult level. There are many variants as a function of variations of kinship systems. The modern isolated nuclear family, however, precisely because in this case the family is highly differentiated from components of social structure with other functions, presents a particularly

concentrated case of the relationship. Here, especially as
analyzed by the social anthropologist David M. Schneider,[22]
it becomes clear that sexual intercourse between spouses has
become the primary cultural symbol of what Schneider calls
their "diffuse enduring solidarity," which may well be translated as love, and not only as between themselves, but in their
sharing of mutual responsibility for their children since they
constitute the senior component in the family.

The incest taboo has an important bearing here, in that it
draws a sharp line between the erotic relations of the married
couple and, after early childhood, the prohibition of such
relations between parents and children and between siblings.

I should postulate that love in a nonerotic sense must be the
core concern of a religious movement in the sense suggested
above. There is, however, at the same time the deeply rooted
relation between eroticism and love, which in an important
sense is a major bridge from organism to personality. Under
the kinds of pressure which have been discussed, I should
argue that there is a strong tendency to regression, in precisely
the above sense, from the level of sublimated love, as Freud
would have put it, to that of erotic attachment, and indeed a
tendency to absolutize the significance of erotic experience.
Especially as it occurs between two persons—autoeroticism is
something else—it can seem to be almost the ultimate in
genuine solidarity.

There are, however, two problems about a primarily erotic
basis of the wider solidarities which, if we are to believe
Durkheim, religions must involve. One concerns the regressive
relations of the erotic complex in its significance for individual
personality development. To give too great primacy to erotic
relations in this sense is to skate on the edge of acting as a
child and treating partners as children. The binding-in of the
erotic component of motivation to adult capabilities and responsibilities is clearly a major function of the incest taboo.

The second problem derives from the fact that mutual
erotic solidarity is bound to intimate bodily contact, by far
most fully expressible in the diadic relation. Though group
sex has certain attractions, its serving as a primary symbolization, even, of wider solidarities seems to be severely limited.

22. David Schneider, *American Kinship: A Cultural Account* (Englewood Cliffs, N.J.: Prentice Hall, 1968).

Putting it simply, the wider the circle of erotic relations and the more casual that to any particular partner, the less is it possible for erotic experience to symbolize diffuse enduring solidarity. A full, culturally generalized language of love must be couched in terms of other media. Such languages have, by and large, been predominantly religious rather than carnal.

It seems to me that early Christianity solved the problem by drawing a very sharp line between religiously significant love and carnal appetites. The Pauline dictum "it is better to marry than to burn" was not exactly a glorification of conjugal love. The religious orders then, on their emergence, adopted full celibacy as a matter of principle and this was later extended to the secular priesthood.

Luther's marriage, however, in violation of his monastic vows and, significantly, to a former nun, was a symbolic act of new legitimation of the erotic complex and could not very well be interpreted, in the morally rigorous climate of early Protestantism, as simply "surrendering to the flesh." The fact that the institution of a married clergy was universalized in all branches of Protestantism is of course critical.

Various of the movements which led to the institutionalization of new sectors of religiously legitimate secular society have been accompanied by movements toward sexual liberation. This was true of the French revolution and also of the socialist movement. But where political freedoms and release from economic exploitation are felt to be the main stakes, neither love nor eroticism is likely to be central. In the current situation, however, I suggest that the institutionalization of love at some level of community has become central, and that regressive pressures operate strongly toward the erotic emphasis. These emphases, however, I also suggest, lead to unstable states because unsublimated erotic motivations do not form a sufficiently firm and generalized basis for solid attachments to ground a religiously legitimate and viable network of units and of moral community—remembering always that modern community must be pluralistic.

The early Christian pattern of radical segregation between love and the erotic component thus seems not to be viable nor, I should venture to say, even legitimate in the modern situation. At the very least the erotic relation of husband and wife, independently of the procreative function, must be legitimized, or it cannot function, in Schneider's phrase, as a primary symbol of diffuse enduring solidarity. What extensions beyond the conjugal relation may come to be legitimized I may perhaps be pardoned for not entering into here, not only because of the delicacy of the issues, but because this is already perhaps an overly long concluding paper. I do, however, think that there will be others.

The deepest reason why the early Christian pattern is not acceptable now, I hope has been made clear. This is that the new religious movement, which I feel will almost certainly prove to be largely Christian, cannot define itself as a separated collectivity outside of what has been called secular society, but must be defined as an integral part of the latter which hopes to permeate its moral and spiritual qualities. Not only the love component—which is not the same as the moral—of solidarities, but the erotic component, is too deeply intertwined in the texture of society, especially at the level of the interpersonal intimate relations which are coming to be so highly valued, for it to be extirpated. If, indeed, this extirpation were possible, which I doubt short of major convulsions, the price would be the postponement of any new community of love, probably for many centuries.

Finally, perhaps these considerations throw at least a little light on what to many of us seems to be the most irrational aspect of the new movements, namely the resurgence of aggression and violence. Important as these may be, a very large part of it seems to go beyond natural resentment or anger at being unjustly discriminated against, exploited, subordinated to dubiously legitimate authority, blocked in pursuing legitimate goals, or simply not listened to. In making any such judgment of overdetermination it is of course essential to bear in mind that when we speak of the aggression and violence of the proponents of the new presumptively religious groups, they do not stand alone. There is also aggression and violence in other quarters, and there is little hope of disentangling who is guilty of aggression and who is understandably reacting aggressively.

Psychodynamically by now the interconnections between love and hate have become familiar. In one aspect they are the positive and negative sides, respectively, of the bonds of emotional significance of objects, in Freud's term of cathexis.

As Freud put it, cathexis means an investment in relation to other persons—or groups as such—in social interaction, and failure of positive reciprocity can readily flip over into negativity, that is, hostility, hate, and aggression. The bitterness of family quarrels attests to this—far from it proving that the members do not in some sense love one another it is evidence that they do.

From this it seems to follow that he who makes a special commitment to love, by that very fact becomes especially vulnerable to hatred, where his expectations of reciprocation are frustrated. It takes an especially elevated level of love to transcend this dilemma, one which Christianity did in fact attain, but never succeeded in fully institutionalizing—it was most poignantly put in the injunction "love thine enemies."

Again, there is an enormous difference from early Christianity deriving from the fact that the current movements are so integrally involved with the affairs of secular society. When combined with moral absolutism, as it very generally is, the love-orientation disposes its proponents to aspire to political effectiveness, that is to power, which necessarily means coping with opposition at many levels. Where resort to violence, or confrontation, seems effective, the temptation is enormous. But in addition to the temptation of tactical effectiveness there is the emotional seduction. If you can convincingly think of your opponent as really wicked he must deserve to be hated, not loved—and isn't the mere fact of his opposition almost sufficient proof of his wickedness?

In a situation where political stakes were very high, Gandhi's nonviolent resistance movement achieved remarkable discipline in maintaining nonviolence, but when the British finally left India, there were disastrously violent clashes between Hindus and Muslims with many thousands killed. Perhaps one can suggest that in nonviolent movements aggression in the motivational sense is by no means generally absent. If the discipline of nonviolence is impaired, the aggressive component may easily break through into violent action and, short of that, of course verbal abuse and humiliation of opponents and the like may figure very prominently.

If, as many of us feel, there is enormous creative potential in the emerging religion of love, the danger of lapsing into aggression and violence, along with that of moral absolutism, which are of course related to each other, seem to me more serious than the danger of regression into eroticism—or the related retreat into dependence on drugs. The point about the former two is the extent to which they serve as triggers to mobilize, not only legitimate opposition, in the sense of adherence to values somewhat different from those absolutized, or of defense of rights against violence or insult, but they release the irrational affective factors which lie back of the tensions inherent in such conflict situations, factors which in general in relation to creative movements operate repressively.

I may perhaps end this discussion on a Durkheimian note. The affective-charismatic components of a religiously innovative movement are likely to be self-defeating and to lapse into some sort of antinomian anarchy if they are not somehow combined with the factors of the discipline which goes with moral order. I even venture to think that a substantial component of cognitive belief is an essential ingredient of the stabilization of religious innovation.

Conclusion

The basic structure of the belief-disbelief-unbelief problem in the contemporary phase just sketched is the same as in the earlier phases. Two differences, however, complicate the too literal reference to precedents. The first is the overwhelmingly this-worldly orientation of the new religion of love, if I may consolidate a little the use of that term. The other is the salience, indeed primacy, in the movement of the nonrational components. Here there is a temptation, on the side of the proponents, to declare that problems of belief are totally irrelevant, and of opponents, that the movement is a simple case of disbelief in a sense which implies an obligation to combat it with the utmost vigor.

Deeply rooted cultural precedents predispose many in the West to the feeling that the only truly religious love is profoundly other worldly and must be sharply contrasted with any basis of worldly love, even though it is love of "thy neighbor." In the other context, far more than in the past, the reaction is against the rationality complex in very general terms. There is a crucial sense in which the most immediate antagonist is not the traditional organized religions, but the most secularized rationality systems, notably though perhaps ambivalently, Marxian socialism, but ramifying much more broadly into nonsocialist aspects of rationality, both in cultural systems and in social institutions, in the latter context, notably bureaucracy, but also clearly academic professionalism.

We have, however, argued that belief systems prominently involving cognitive components are essential ingredients in all religious systems which have a prospect of stabilization. For the principled antirationalist the construction of a viable cognitive belief system presents peculiar difficulties, which are not altogether unprecedented, but which becomes especially acute in these circumstances. I venture to suggest, however, that certain resources essential for this task are available, at least incipiently, in some of the social science sources which have been reviewed.[23] It is interesting to note that, from the point of view of the incipient religion, these sources are predominantly secular in a sense parallel to that in which the Greek intellectual tradition was secular from the point of view of the early Christian church. Clearly Freud, Durkheim, and Weber were not prophets of the religion of love any more than the Neoplatonists were prophets of Christianity, but what they, various of their successors, and others not associated with their names have done may well prove essential to the new movement. The fact that, in a profound sense, especially the latter two understood but rejected Marxian socialism, seems to me critical in this connection.

There has been much discussion of the role of youth, especially student youth, in this movement. This is, in my opinion, indeed crucial as a kind of spearhead, but this is not the place to go into the reasons why such appeals are so attractive to the contemporary student generation on a nearly worldwide basis. Social science, in my opinion, has progressed toward making such understanding possible.[24] It should, however, be clear that a student base is not a sufficient anchorage in the structure of societies for the institutionalization of a major

23. Robert Bellah, chapter 14 of this volume.
24. Talcott Parsons and Gerald Platt, "Higher Education, Changing Socialization and Contemporary Student Dissent," in Matilda White Riley, et al., eds., *A Sociology of Stratification*, VIII of *Aging and Society* (New York: Russell Sage, forthcoming) and Erik Erikson, *Young Man Luther*.

religious pattern. Students remain students for only a few years, and they must face the dilemma of either relinquishing their legitimacy with relinquishment of student status, or extending the basis of legitimacy from the student phase to later phases in the life cycle. The slogan "Never trust anyone over thirty" is a typical "chiliastic" aphorism which manifests a sentiment but cannot be stably institutionalized.

Each additional step in secularization, in the sense of the institutionalization of Christian patterns in the secular world, which we have traced adds a new set of complications to the belief-disbelief-unbelief problem. A most important point then needs to be emphasized. When the institutional resolution, inclusion, and upgrading has in fact occurred, the older patterns do not disappear, but continue to function, though in modified form, which often means in more restricted circumstances than before. Thus to go way back, Christianity did not extirpate Judaism, but the latter is now persisting ecumenically together with a wide variety of Christian churches and sects. Protestantism did not extirpate Catholicism, nor vice versa, and they not only coexist peacefully but have become integrated into a more general religious structure. Then, very recently, I suggest, rationalistic secularism has not only failed to extirpate church religion, but has gone far toward becoming included with it as a still broader religious framework, in which all the older religious groups—with some qualifications—survive.[25]

I see no reason why the general pattern of emergence of a movement, starting in acute conflict with its most immediate predecessor in the role of institutional establishment, moving to truce in that conflict on the pattern of *cuius regio, eius religio,* then eventually to the process of resolution by inclusion and upgrading, should not be repeated in the present case, as well as those which have gone before. I am sure that we are barely entering upon the phase of acute conflict, which

25. Indeed, I look forward to the day when, in a Jewish, Catholic, or Protestant high ceremony like the Kennedy Memorial Mass, the Director of the Institute of Philosophy of the Soviet Academy of Sciences—a post which I interpret to be the equivalent of "Dean of the theological faculty of the religion of Marxism-Leninism"—will march in the procession and sit in the sacristy as one of the assemblage of the clergy of all faiths.

we can only hope will not eventuate, for the next century, in a new cycle of wars of religion which might indeed be fatal to civilization, but most particularly to the religion of love, because, however partially justified their accusation of hypocrisy against their opponents may be, they simply cannot afford to let hatred and antagonism prevail over their central orientation. This factor and, among other things its cognitive understanding, plus of course the antiaggressive components of the whole great religious tradition of the Western world, give considerable hope that the sense of conflict will not be escalated to the point of the most serious threats of mutual destruction.

I have been so bold as to suggest that the contemporary situation, in which the problem of the meaning of unbelief has become so salient, may constitute both an end, and a turning point leading into a beginning, of a major cycle of human religious development. The key connecting symbol, which may, in Bellah's sense, be interpreted realistically as well as in the framework of symbolic reductionism, is clearly love. This was certainly the keynote of the Gospels, and has become so again today. The cycle, however, is not a simple return to the beginning, but a spiral, in the course of which much has happened, which, schematically, may be called the Christianization of the world.

Though in the current turbulent stage, it must be expected that conflict, confrontation, aggression, and hatred will be exceedingly prominent on both sides, the orientational content points to a pattern of resolution, which is inherently precarious in its initial stages, but which, if it materializes, may well usher in, not paradise, for this is not given to human societies, but a new phase of religious and social progress.

However important, on the one hand, insistence by the proponents of the new on their claims, at the risk of over-reliance on moral absolutism and aggression, on the other hand by the defenders of the, after all not totally bankrupt, older values on their legitimacy—again at the risk of refusals to concede and insistence on discipline which will be interpreted as intolerably punitive—there is a basically solid foundation in Christian tradition for the resolution of these conflicts.

This frame of reference will necessarily, I think, apply on both sides of the conflict. There are, it seems to me, three main components of the essential orientation. The first is humility, in the historic Christian sense, which is inherently incompatible with moral absolutism, as the arrogation of the right to punish because the other has sinned and you are pure.[26] Note that I apply this on both sides—the proponents of love have no better moral right to punish their opponents than do those of the establishment. The second orientation may be called the sense of tragedy. Moral dichotomization into the "good guys" and the "bad guys" is proverbially unproductive. The nonrational sense, as well as the cognitive understanding, that the good are always engaged in a struggle with the evil elements within them, and that conversely the bad are always in some sense trying to overcome their evil motives, is an essential ingredient of resolution. Human history is not a morality play in which the good are rewarded and the evil punished, but a struggle for salvation, enlightenment, progress, or community in which many, indeed most, of the participants have been and are caught up in tragic conflicts and dilemmas. The third component, compassion seems almost to follow from the importance of the first two. If we love a person—or a group or a symbol—we must at the same time understand and empathize with his difficulties and his conflicts, including those which from our point of view are destructive of our values, and still love him, not only in the sense of particularized affection, but of giving him support for the implementation of the value of universalized love.

It seems to me that this was the basic message of Pope John XXIII. It was that Christian humility, a sense of tragedy, and compassion form the essential basis for a much greater extension of the regime of love than we have ever known before.

26. There are, of course, other bases of the legitimation of punishment. The arrogation referred to is a version of the Donatist heresy.

13

UNBELIEF AS AN OBJECT OF RESEARCH

BRYAN WILSON

Unbelief may or may not be a new social phenomenon. We simply do not know of the past what proportion of men actively subscribed to, passively acquiesced in, or quietly dissented from the formal belief systems institutionalized within the societies in which they lived. Occasionally we know something of those who actively challenged official beliefs, and even in some periods, of those who simply refused to conform; we know of them because officials, whose business it was to ensure that ideological and ritual conformity prevailed, recorded something of the time, energy, and resources they spent in seeking to induce or coerce acceptance of the faith, and in cataloging the evils of heretics. Of the actual incidence of unbelief, however, we know very little.

There is a sense in which our ignorance is appropriate, for the idea that we could know about the incidence of unbelief in the past is to impose contemporary conceptions of belief and unbelief on social conditions to which they almost certainly are not applicable. Our ignorance of the past incidence of unbelief is not merely a consequence of the fact that techniques of investigation have themselves only recently become available, but also reflects the modernity of a socially recognizable phenomenon which we label "the culture of unbelief." In the past, it simply did not matter in the way that it is now possible to say that it matters, what individuals believed nor how strongly they believed it. Society relied on its collective, usually communal, agencies to enforce compliance and to elicit conformity in behavior and, as far as behavior was predicated by belief, to demand intellectual assent to socially established ideologies. But, in such conditions, conformity and assent cannot be adequately ascribed to the power of individual convictions; opportunity for an individual to choose what he would believe was either not available or very much less available than now.

Over most of the historical past, belief may be readily regarded as a matter less of individual choosing than of the culture in which individuals lived. For the mass of men, belief was not associated with any conscious adoption of an intellectual position. It was at most a set of unchallenged axioms built into expressive and instrumental action, and into procedures and institutions, rather than a matter of private reflections, speculations, assents, and dissents. It is by recognizing this distinction that one might resolve the contradiction that is sometimes found in respect of primitive societies, when it is simultaneously asserted by different anthropologists that such societies are suffused by religion and, on the other hand, that primitive men are sometimes skeptical and even secular in their orientations.[1]

The highly integrated and cohesive type of culture has gone. It was rooted in the communal life of traditional societies (and was sometimes given elevated expression in "the great traditions" of such societies), to use Redfield's term. In consequence of its passing, unbelief—as an individual act of choice—becomes a recognizable phenomenon, and one that is open to investigation. Contemporary societies not only do not impose belief, they equally do not even underwrite it in their procedures of socialization and education, and in their wider institutional frameworks. Even more, they increasingly withdraw explicit support from those agencies—the churches, in the typical western case—that sustain a culture of belief. Thus, if individual unbelief can now be recognized, so, too—and this is more socially significant—it can be related to the decline of the social institutions that used to provide the cultural contexts in which belief was sustained.

We ought not to suppose that changes in individual choices about belief have themselves produced a culture of unbelief; for individuals to have developed the consciousness of choice there must have been significant changes in social and cultural institutions. The culture of unbelief is primarily a matter of culture, not simply a matter of randomly distributed beliefs. (For cultural institutions themselves to change there must, of course, be some change in the action-patterns [perhaps even in

1. For a recent discussion of the religiosity of primitive peoples see Mary Douglas, *Natural Symbols* (London: Barrie and Rocliff, 1970), in which, however, ritualism is taken as a primary criterion of religiosity.

the decisions] of strategically located groups or individuals, but changes made in institutional arrangements need not in themselves be specifically concerned with religion. There is likelihood that the effects for religious belief are in most instances quite unintended consequences: changes may follow a pattern inimical to religious belief and practice without any of those involved in altering institutional arrangements being aware of such consequences, and without any possibility that they could be foreseen.)

Social Choices and Methods of Enquiry

It is evident, therefore, that whatever discoveries may be made by the highly individualistic methods of investigation that have been developed in modern society, and that are specially well suited for the study of advanced society—namely, survey research—nonetheless, the culture of unbelief will not be explained solely by those procedures. Survey research is peculiarly appropriate to modern conditions because industrial societies, as they have advanced, have given special prominence to individual choice: in politics (democracy); in economic consumption (the competitive market); in moral attitudes (the permissive society); and in religious belief (denominationalism and tolerance).

But we deceive ourselves if we suppose that the culture of unbelief can be extrapolated from attitude surveys. Choice is not the only feature of the situation; choices are structured, and at times the structure may put certain choices at a premium while virtually precluding others. The philosophy of choice may persist as a necessary ideology for advanced society; it is not necessarily closely related to the persistence of conditions of effective choice, as such. It is a commonplace assertion of cynical consumers, cynical voters and, in an ecumenical age, perhaps also of cynical worshippers (if such an animal is possible) that the proffered choice is often illusory, that labels and publicity that are designed to emphasize differences, in fact, conceal similarities of commodities that compete for choice, and in consequence, conceal the unimportance of choices, because the frameworks within which choices can occur are socially circumscribed. Official forms in the United States that ask the individual to state "the religion of your choice," or even "your religious preference," simultaneously emphasize that diverse choices are permitted and also that there is official indifference to what is chosen—that these permitted choices do not really matter. The cynicism of the age is not unrelated to the manipulation of apparent choices combined with the progressive realization that there is often a complete absence or a nearly complete absence of real choices. In consequence, it may be that choice is far less important than the overall quality of the—rather similar—things that are on offer as the range of choice.

In the religious sphere, as elsewhere, only by examining this quality can we penetrate the substance of belief and unbelief. It may be that in contemporary society firm commitment to beliefs has less consequence than lax commitment in the past; or that in a pluralistic society firm believers become a more sharply distinguishable class than in earlier periods of history. Whatever the case, we shall discover it not by the analysis of attitudes to choices, but by the analysis of the culture itself.

All this is not to deny that there is a sense in which outright unbelief is a matter of individual choice, and that information about such choices might be important data for an understanding of contemporary society and religious development. But without an appreciation of the cultural and institutional circumstances in which men come to make choices, and an extensive knowledge of the quality of the commodities that they choose, the structural constraints on choice and the cultural circumscriptions of it, survey research alone could provide us with no more than a superficial analysis of the symptomatic. Despite their prestige as the technically most advanced and most accurate form of sociological enquiry— and to some they represent the high point of the discipline's development—attitude surveys are in fact now the most thoroughly routinized procedures of sociological research. It would be a pity if the ease of mounting such investigations, and their reputation for precision, were to eclipse the more basic nature of more difficult and less routinized analysis of institutions and the content of culture.

I have already dissented, in my remarks at the meetings of the symposium, from the assumptions made by some participants, that this basic analytical task is best conceived as the preliminary elaboration of a highly abstract conceptual framework. Such a work of abstraction is scarcely a corrective for the frank empiricism of survey research. We do not need universally applicable abstract definitions of belief, unbelief, religion, and so forth, before we can commence work on the real historical problems. No formulations of such concepts have as yet commanded majority or even wide assent among sociologists—much less have they established themselves as of wide applicability in the real world. Generations of scholars have sought a universally acceptable definition of religion that covers all cases, without success.

To postpone research until agreed conceptual frameworks are formulated might be to retard its beginning for a very long time. Sociological research, while it should certainly be more than data collection through questionnaires, does not need to proceed operationally from perfectly elaborated logical structures that are valid for all times, places, and collectivities. We may content ourselves with the fact that we belong to a given cultural context, that we inherit traditions and know, in greater or lesser degree, the circumstances of change within this cultural tradition. Our insights and our analytical procedures are heavily indebted to this same culture, of course, but we have sufficiently freed them from specifically ethically committed ways of thought to have the simultaneous advantage of both neutrality of procedure and *verstehende* comprehension of the phenomena with which we are concerned.

It is historical analysis of social structures, of theological systems, and of religious institutions in their relation to the social order in which they have arisen and within which they have been sustained, that appears to be most essential to augment the social survey. For we know, to take but a trivial example of the limitations of survey research employed on its own, that many men effectively choose unbelief without being conscious of the choice. As there were probably many passive believers in the past, when the cultural activities of society proceeded on built-in religious premises, so we may assume that there are, at least in respect of previously institutionalized belief systems, and despite educational advance and growing consciousness of intellectual issues, nonetheless many passive unbelievers now. In making them conscious of unconscious choices, survey research risks the consequence of stimulating a range of spurious rationalizations to account for them.

Definitions

The assumptions that underlie the foregoing comment self-evidently rest on a certain understanding of the term "belief." It must be assumed that all men entertain beliefs of some sort and hence a working definition of unbelief should be clarified at the outset. It is necessary to make clear the extent to which sociological inquiry might detach itself from, or conversely, must base itself upon, certain existing social and cultural conceptions.

Men evince certain convictions and in large part act in accordance with them—whether acts are consequences of beliefs or whether beliefs are rationalizations for actions is an issue that can for the present be left aside. It is clear that unbelief carries no absolute meaning. As a concept it depends on some specifiable system of belief. The word "system" is important, since the rejection of random beliefs by equally random individuals is of little significance: unbelief becomes important when it is the rejection of a system of beliefs, or a way of thought. The system of belief has significance for even unthinking men, however, because it is entrenched in social and cultural practices and institutions.[2] Practice enters into our considerations because it is in the fulfillment of the obligations required by beliefs that belief systems acquire their corporate significance and their objectivity in the culture. Whether those practices preceded the formulation of beliefs, as anthropological tradition suggests, is a question that we can leave aside.

Certainly, however, whatever incidental beliefs men may randomly have entertained in the past, it is only those beliefs that received sustained social support and institutional expression that can be properly regarded as relevant to society. It is the rejection of, or disregard of, these beliefs that we may label "unbelief." Unbelief does not necessarily imply outright hostility or activity to destroy the belief systems of others,

2. An issue that the symposium skirted but did not really take up—much less resolve—was the matter of acceptable variation of belief. Would, for example, a Methodist be regarded a believer in a culture predominantly Catholic—would a Jew, a Muslim, or a Jehovah's Witness?

however, nor to disrupt belief-dependent patterns of action or the institutions created for the expression of belief. A minimal criterion is at least a disregard for the socially established conceptions of the supernatural order and the practices associated with them.[3]

Belief, then, is taken as more than a mere intellectual assent to a set of propositions: it is an orientation to the world that is determined by faith in a well-defined supernatural order. Any particular believer need not himself know the details concerning that supernatural order. It is enough if he accept the socially established formulations concerning it, and "believes in" those who do know about it, and accepts their guidance in regulating his own activities in regard to it, and all those actions which experts declare to be of significance in connection with it. It becomes evident that the role of the professionals of belief systems is a particularly important element in understanding the culture of belief and unbelief.

Preliminary Considerations

The culture of unbelief is in itself a new social phenomenon that may be said to arise only as those agencies and institutions that were supportive of socially established belief systems progressively lose authority, influence, and eventually relevance within a given society. (This formulation allows us to set aside the vexed question of the extent of individual commitment to religion in different historical periods.) [4] Two broad perspectives are necessary for a thorough comprehen-

3. In this formulation we are faced again with the need to determine what is "socially established." In England, this was at one time the Established Church, but in the nineteenth century one might have to admit that the major denominations were also established, as they were, much more fully in constitutional terms, in the United States. But how ought the intense fundamentalist revival movements to be regarded, since their members believe much the same as orthodox Protestants, even though they believe it more intensely? It might be argued that precisely because of the variations in degree of commitment (quite apart from variations in kind of commitment) a culture of unbelief comes into being, since there is no uniform set of expectations about what belief means and what implications it has for behavior.

4. For very divergent views see the works on the one hand of Peter Laslet, and on the other of K. S. Ingliis.

sion of the culture of unbelief: one that seeks to delineate the process of institutional and cultural change and to lay bare its causes; the other that seeks to discover the degree of internal coherence among new, uncommitted institutions that facilitate the culture of unbelief, the intellectual premises of that culture itself, and the extent to which such a culture is integrated with particular elements of social structure. The former perspective is historical, concerned not simply with the decline of belief, but with the displacement of particular belief-sustaining procedures and social arrangements. The latter calls for a thorough functional and structural analysis.

Clearly such a research program could easily assume unmanageable proportions, and we might first determine the scale on which the phenomena are believed to exist, the social units that might be investigated, and the possibility of designating strategic areas of inquiry. Is the culture of unbelief seen as a general, if unevenly spread, property of Western (or world) society? Or is it the property of some distinct state societies rather than of others (of Sweden, for instance, but not of Italy; of England, but not of Scotland)? Or do we consider that a culture of unbelief is rather a system of ideas, symbols, and values that can flourish in particular regions or districts, or in particular collectivities or institutional orders (among scientists rather than among farmers; in universities rather than in armies or hospitals; in economic activities rather than in socialization activities)? Do any social systems or subsystems persist in which there is no very extensive consensus of belief in a supernatural order or a sacred value system? Might there be unbelieving cultures that are well integrated with established and stable social systems, whether such cultures are coterminous with total societies or exist merely as distinct entities within total societies? Or do we see the cultures of unbelief as, at least as yet, no more than random, socially inconsequential distributions of motley beliefs and disbeliefs that lack any enduring institutionalized structures?

To deal with these questions we do not, of course, need to ask whether social systems can now sustain themselves without common adherence to substantive values. All we need to ask is whether they can persist without subscription to supernatural values, that is without sacralizing the dominant orientations and procedures discernible in their operation.[5] It may be that the culture of unbelief finds expression only in limited contexts—in subsystems or in regional and local cultures, or in particular institutions which, even if conspicuous, are, nonetheless, sustained in a society, the stability, order, and inner coherence of which may depend either on the general consensus concerning transcendental values, or on highly technical and, indeed, technologized, regulatory procedures.[6]

Areas of Research

For immediate purposes the foregoing questions need not be directly posed, but the fact that these issues have emerged indicates that investigation of the culture of unbelief should yield important conclusions about the maintenance and continuance of any type of social system in the future.

A number of related research areas present themselves for attention: the determination of the role of belief in culture itself; comparison of matched contexts distinguishable by belief and unbelief, and by contexts in which believing and unbelieving cultures coexist; [7] analysis of changing patterns of belief, and the correlation with them of other cultural configurations; the distribution of attitudes within selected populations; the replacement of established belief systems by new

5. The background assertion of importance here was expressed by Edward Shils and Michael Young, "The Meaning of the Coronation," *Sociological Review*, 1 (1953), pp. 63–81. For a brief comment on this position, see my essay, "Social Values and Higher Education," in Bryan Wilson, *The Youth Culture and the Universities* (London: Faber, 1970), pp. 234–266.

6. In Western society the dominant institutional sphere is the economy, where rational, not religious, precepts for action clearly apply. (A religious leader who advises his followers to forsake the ninety-nine sheep that are safe, in order to seek the one that is lost, is, by rational economic criteria, no more than a feckless sentimentalist!) Yet may it be said that societies dominated by the economic order really rely on such religious values—values that are transmitted especially in socialization as the basic social and moral ideas that underlie all orderly social procedures.

7. Evon Z. Vogt and Thomas O'Dea, "A Comparative Study of the Role of Values in Social Action in Two Southwestern Communities," *The American Sociological Review*, 18 (1953), pp. 645–654.

patterns of belief, and presumably, the process of destructuring of the institutional frameworks on which earlier patterns of belief depended, and analysis of incipient institutions that house and diffuse new beliefs. Some of these areas of inquiry, particularly the analysis of the role of belief in culture, may be studied as a process of social change or, at least, as a comparative study of a given social system at different stages of its development—itself the most fundamental form of comparative study.

Even the much more static investigations of particular societies, however, will necessarily be a type of historical study reliant on historical materials, since cultural systems and institutional orders can be thoroughly known only as entities existing in the past, even if the relatively recent past. This is not to deny that survey research, extended interviews and life histories may at some points have important contributions to make to our knowledge of culture and society, but even these methods are likely to uncover information that has a strong past reference, and this should be acknowledged in relating them to broader studies of social structure and culture.

The analysis of the culture of belief is a precursor to the analysis of the culture of unbelief. Studies of past and contemporary societies in which a culture of belief has been, or is still, maintained, must be collated. This work is primarily a matter of bringing together already existing materials, or abstracting from historical and sociological works that are usually concerned with some subject other than unbelief. The beginnings of research into the culture of unbelief are the historical, theological, literary, and social accounts of particular societies. From these the broad contours of a culture can be traced, and change in the patterns of belief and its social role might be discerned. These will be the necessary first indicators of the more specific research that will follow into strategically chosen sectors of past or contemporary society. It is in the context of these studies that survey research may come to play a much more clearly specified role in sociological analysis than it could were it undertaken as if nothing were known about the subject and as if there were nothing to guide its operation except highly abstract conceptual schemes lacking every specific historical and cultural reference.

A neglected but important factor in the maintenance of belief systems has been society's dependence on religious institutions for the performance of a number of functions that are ancillary rather than intrinsic to religion itself but which, in some cultures, have traditionally been closely associated with it. The role of monasteries in economic development in pre-Reformation Europe, for instance, has certainly been explored, but churches have fulfilled a wide range of other social functions—in education, social welfare, charitable enterprises, hospital work, moral rehabilitation—either for the whole society or for particular sections of it (for example, for the military). These functions have had distinct significance in the maintenance of a culture of belief. An analysis of the concessions granted to religious agents in particular societies, and the services rendered to government, political parties, trade unions and in the promotion of religiously inspired voluntary associations for a variety of ends not strictly religious, would take us a long way to understanding the functional alternatives to formally organized and consciously institutionalized belief systems. These functional alternatives might not, of course, be represented only by nationally planned welfare systems, even though that is the case most likely to interest the student of unbelief. The ancillary functions undertaken by religious agents in some societies, may never have been engrafted onto religious institutions in other societies—particularly where an extended family system has continued.

The role of religion in promoting voluntarism and in undertaking functions performed in other times and places by the family or the state is perhaps a distinctive feature of Christianity. The accretion of these ancillary concerns may have been far from incidental for the consolidation of religion in society in particular historical periods, and their attrition, a significant aspect of its disintegration at others. Societies in which religious agencies never acquired ancillary functions on the scale on which that occurred in Christianity may have avoided the risk of depending on temporary ancillary concerns for the social integration of religious activities themselves. In Christianity the transfer of these ancillary functions to secular agencies may have precipitated the decline of religion, which never undertook these ancillary functions and were probably unaffected when they were assumed by the state.

An analysis of voluntary associations might also focus on a

somewhat different issue. Religious motivations in stimulating voluntary association and voluntary action have been of considerable importance in advanced social systems. The extent to which these motivations acquire autonomy and persist once commitment to particular ideologies has gone, and in particular when supernatural belief no longer underwrites a civic ethic, could be an important area of inquiry for both contemporary society and for an understanding of new cultural patterns.

Obviously the specific contribution of particular religious systems has varied from one case to another, and perhaps also in association with different state systems. Catholicism may have played a bigger role in the maintenance of hospitals through the specialist religious virtuosity of religious orders; Protestantism may have been more important in communicating a more even commitment to civic order and voluntary charitable endeavor. But in this respect the role of new religious movements (which must, in any case, be a specific study for any comprehensive analysis of the culture of unbelief) cannot be omitted. The commitment to good works of the new sects in Japan, the development of medical and welfare clinics by the Kardecists in Brazil, and the powerful thrust in similar directions by the Seventh Day Adventists are examples of the importance of this orientation in at least some new religious movements.

In respect of both of the foregoing perspectives on the involvement of religious agencies in the maintenance of ancillary ends, governing and elite classes are likely to be of considerable importance. In circumstances in which religious agencies are acquiring new ancillary functions it is likely that governing classes transfer (or impose) these functions, and provide the facilities that are associated with them. In periods when concessions and facilities are being withdrawn, and when new forms of social organization are emerging, it is ruling elites who curb the activities of religious institutions. It is then within these classes that bargains are struck, or currents of thought are expressed, or new concepts of social organization developed, which may have considerable consequence for the role of religion in society and, perhaps through the intermediation of ancillary concerns, consequences for the social image of religion entertained by the masses.

The examination of the role and orientation of secular

elites (and the relative influence of different elites or differentiated sections of the elites) must be complemented by investigation of religious elites, the professional groups whose primary concern is the dissemination of supernatural beliefs and the staffing of religious institutions. Apart from obvious issues such as the comparative study of the social composition of the clergy, the processes of primary motivation, recruitment, education, secondary socialization, role performance, social status and the professional reward structure, their access to other institutions and facilities, and their part in the various departments of social life must also be subject to review.

Survey research can certainly provide us with information on the status-ranking of priests in comparison with other occupations, but this information needs to be augmented by historical analysis of the role, composition, and social image of the clergy. There must be analysis of the extent to which priests are regarded as being able to cope with human, social, physical, and other problems; their relevance for decision making in advanced society, for inspiration, leadership, maintenance of morale, and the provision of education. We need to know not only how much priests are "looked up to"—accorded high status—but also the extent to which they are "looked to"—regarded as useful and relevant—since status may in itself be merely a deference pattern inherited from the past. Deference as a survival may be not without importance, but its relation to functional reliance should not be overlooked. Deference is an attenuated form of reverence, and reverence is itself perhaps the most significant aspect of the posture of religious men, at least in advanced religious systems.

In an increasingly egalitarian society, deference may be expected to diminish since it is a disposition that corresponds to normative differential ascriptions of social honor. As priests divest themselves of honorific symbols—the pious and saintly demeanor, separation from the world, the priestly habit of dress, a distinctive religious language (and style of enunciation) —and seek other sources of contemporary social approval (involvement in political action and nonreligious social movements) so we may regard this as an indication of the diminution, if not of formal subscription to received beliefs, at least of dispositions and postures that were conducive to its maintenance and its communication to others.

The clergy are crucial because they are expected to be the

section of the population most committed to the received system of belief and responsible for the socialization of others to it. Yet the clergy also "drop out" and sometimes even abandon the faith itself. The study of the clergy, through life histories, institutional socialization, and by attitude survey might afford unique insights for the pressure of the culture of unbelief on society. The clergy should be the most invulnerable section of society to the culture of unbelief, and yet most sensitive to its incursions into social life generally and into the religious sphere in particular. Aware of their own loss of purchase, the clergy may well illustrate a range of responses to a situation which they experience even though they may not be sociologically articulate about it. They are one strategic group for investigation; prominent laymen (compared with matched samples of nonchurchmen in the wider society) might be such another.

Intellectual Systems and Communications

Even though I have emphasized institutional analysis as a primary focus of research, and have interpreted belief rather broadly, the structure of idea systems and their intrinsic content must not be overlooked. The central propositions of theology, ecclesiology, and soteriology must be examined both in their refined form as held by professionals, and in their popular formulations current in the literature and other presentations provided for the general public. Comparison of these idea systems with secularist, scientific, business, and entertainment ideologies would be instructive. Again, were all this to have to be begun from the beginning the task would be immense, but we have an extensive literature on all of these ideologies, supernaturalist and other, and sociologists might begin their work by synthesizing existing knowledge and relating particular supernaturalist and secular ideologies to each other and to social structures.[8]

Assessment of the relative plausibility of theological prop-

8. This is not the place to indicate the bibliographic range of these areas, but immediately important works come to mind: for example, L. Schneider and S. M. Dornbusch, *Popular Religion: Inspirational Books in America* (Chicago University Press, 1956); Reinhard Bendix, *Work and Authority in Industry: Ideologies of Management in the Course of Industrialization* (New York: Wiley, 1956).

ositions in different social circumstances may, in the first instance, be a somewhat speculative exercise. But sociology has not in the past eschewed such imaginative reconstructions, and from this *verstehende* perspective perhaps the richest insights have been obtained. Such reconstructions would be appropriately undertaken in advance of any survey research that might go some way towards testing them. It would be over-intellectualist to suppose that internal coherence and logical plausibility alone determined acceptance or rejection of idea systems, of course, both because we are aware of the extent to which men are tolerant of cognitive dissonance and ideational compartmentalism, and because each idea system must be reviewed in relation to more specific variations of social circumstances, intellectual competences, age, sex, and other basic variables.

The circumstances in which particular theological concepts were evolved and their relation to particular social conditions is basic for an understanding of the culture of belief and unbelief. The sociology of theology has never been adequately undertaken, and it might need a team of scholars with rather varied intellectual skills, and with wide-ranging historical knowledge to complete such an analysis. Research teams are necessary not only for highly technical quantificational research procedures, but (and the basis of group relationships in what have been previously regarded almost exclusively as the task of individual and isolated scholars is itself an important exploratory enterprise) also for the comprehension of the extraordinarily wide range of knowledge that is not readily encapsulated in neat mathematical formulae. Such teamwork could probably lead to important reinterpretations of the emergence and persistence of theological systems, their transmission and acceptability. The most important tasks in respect to the culture of unbelief might be work on contemporary religious movements the idea systems of which are recent, and knowledge of the spread of which might yield most for an understanding of the culture of unbelief.[9] Of these new movements more will be said below.

More extensive and pervasive, if less readily identifiable and less socially bounded, than new belief systems, however,

9. A recent outstanding example is David F. Aberle, *The Peyote Religion Among the Navaho* (Chicago: Aldine, 1966).

is a climate of ideas—part traditional and supernaturalist and part secular and scientistic—that is widely and progressively diffused, but the specific content of which is vague, mercurial, and at times, contradictory and even inarticulate. To identify the elements in this constellation—even to suggest that any sort of pattern might be discerned—might be to impress too much of the analyst's sense of order on the real world, yet the importance of grasping the content of this ideational cluster in readily defined categories is all too apparent.

Perhaps the best procedure would be to take a sample of ephemeral literature as well as of more enduring works of fiction and social commentary for limited but sequential periods, to discover the frequency with which supernatural ideas and other alternative ideas and values find expression. Both high cultural and mass cultural materials would necessarily be included, and the procedure would be one of strategic sampling rather than extensive coverage. A well-codified content analysis might yield a significant indication of the extent to which traditional belief was invoked in recent and contemporary cultural products, and the extent to which it had given place at different cultural levels to other beliefs and values.

Clearly the written word is not, in itself, an adequate indicator of the values of contemporary society; and this more traditional medium of communication might be more readily a vehicle than others for traditional beliefs, through the association of style, idioms, past educational association and the past involvement of religious elites in literary activities.[10] New media of communication, advertising, radio, cinema, television, that have evolved their own procedures, without such overt religious influence, may have always been far less committed to, and have adopted more varied stances toward, traditional beliefs.

It is clear that the dominant character of communication has changed in modern society, and the most dramatic aspect

10. Certainly in Anglo-Saxon countries both the clergy themselves and the members of their immediate families were, in the eighteenth and nineteenth centuries, much more important contributors to serious literature (including fiction and poetry) than perhaps any other single profession.

of this change has not been from the written to the spoken word, but from the personal spoken word to the impersonal. Such a change at once affects the extent of what is known; more people share a certain body of fact, but the source of that fact is no longer located in the community structure as —for most people—it was in the past. Even religious knowledge, although acquiring objectification in extracommunal structures ("the church"), is built on local folk tradition. Much more significant, the idiom which it employed, the issues with which it was primarily concerned, were themselves derivable from life in the small community. The model of relationships, the moral prescriptions and the assumptions about human life embraced in traditional religion are heavily dependent on personal experience of community structure and are adapted to it.

But in modern society, communication and fact transcend the immediately apprehended and the local. Much more abstract categories, wider generalizations, extensive comparative knowledge (and its consequent relativism) characterize communication in the modern world. Role structures have replaced natural communities, and increasingly life is planned, consciously organized in systems that are themselves based on abstract principles rather than on received folk morality. The language of religion, and a great deal of its prescriptive matter, feeds on, and informs—perhaps necessarily—personal rather than role relationships, deals with natural communities of men rather than with formal organizations.

Analysis of communication systems and their relation to social structure is clearly crucial to an understanding of the culture of unbelief. Much more extensive bodies of knowledge are today shared by much larger groups of men, and awareness of the relativity of values and beliefs is widely diffused. In this circumstance the resolution of the apparent paradox of great uniformity of knowledge and wider diversity of privatized belief and value-commitment, is perhaps to be sought. The social psychological aspects of contemporary belief appear to be of far greater importance today than they could have been in the more solidified societies of the past. Privatization, opportunity to utilize knowledge to support private beliefs, suggests both the likelihood of established traditional supernatural belief systems becoming discredited, and the possibility that men will work out their personal neuroses (one might say "exorcise their devils") in their own ways.

Of Time and Leisure

The constitutional and formal aspects of the organizational structure that characterizes modern society are important contexts in which belief may be sustained or undermined, but attention must also be given to the assumptions that men in different situations make about their own social participation. As traditional community structure has given place to technological society, the time dispositions of men have changed. This may be assumed to have reduced the congeniality of supernatural ideas, which make very distinct assumptions about time and its social significance that diverge sharply from those entrenched within the implicit operation of the modern world. The time scale in which eschatological prospects are worked out, the importance attributed to past and future, differ from the attitudes to time and the allocation of time once society evaluates time in material and monetary terms. The use of time for ritual activities is another facet of the same phenomenon.

In community-based social systems, time, movement, and change were differently experienced and understood from the common experience and understanding of men in societies dominated by role relationships. The significance of a cultural inheritance that puts both the mythological past and the transcendentally projected future at a premium and the present at a discount, becomes obscure. What men need to know about the past, and how much they need to speculate about anything beyond the future that they can instrumentally effect, both diminish. Thus, although there has been a great growth in leisure time for at least the masses of men, there has also been growth of activities, impressions, contemporary knowledge and instrumental demands which render affective, nostalgic dwelling on the past, and speculative contemplation about the future equally irrelevant. Whereas communication of ideas of the past and promises and propitiatory actions in respect of the future were powerful ideological patterns of social control in traditional societies, the shifting locus of operation of social control in contemporary society results in a much more technologically manipulated work sphere of activities and a liberation of leisure time for use according to private dictates.[11]

The foregoing is no more than speculative comment—unresearched, but one hopes not unresearchable. From such speculation research hypotheses are to be evolved. The growth of leisure time, the increased separation—in space, time, context, activities, and psychological orientation—of work from leisure would alone mark out this area for special attention: it is all the more important because it can be fairly readily demonstrated that religion, concern with the supernatural, has shifted from being central to the whole way of life of men (work included) to being for the vast majority in all advanced societies, no more than a leisure-time pursuit. When life was unremitting toil for most men reward was conveniently located in a transmundane sphere, about which therapeutic promises and psychic reassurance were the immediate temporal benefits.

As promises, rewards, reassurances, and threats lost their purchase on men's minds, religious activity became a leisure activity: its intimate connection with work and the rhythms of life diminished as men's work activities came to have less direct concern with nature and more with man's own material and organizational products. The goals of working are now located, both in the minds of men and according to the assumptions on which modern social systems operate, and by which motivation is mobilized firmly in the after-work sphere of men's lives. It is "after-work" not "after-life" which looms large in the thinking of industrial man—the arena in which reward is to be realized.

Because religion has been relegated to the leisure sphere it has become volatile in its character. Consequently it is today frequently regarded—by its own professionals in particular—as a ready-made agency for any one of a variety of goals: the diffusion of legitimated status; get-togetherness; civic action; political protest (recognizable, perhaps, in that sequential order of fashionability in recent decades). But, if religion

11. For expansion of this point see my essay, "Technology and the Socialization of the Young," in Bryan Wilson, *The Youth Culture*, pp. 204–217.

is no longer significant as a fundamental activity of social life, even in the leisure sphere it faces at once the competition of a variety of other, increasingly powerful, technological and dynamic agencies that have a vigorous profit motive behind them and that seek to command more of men's attention, energies, and material resources. Paradoxically, precisely because these leisure industries are known to operate primarily for their own profit, and because they are uninhibited by traditional moral restraints, they become immediately more comprehensible to modern man and congenial to the climate in which he lives: religious agencies, which seek no material reward and which emphasize their moral, educational, socializing mission, become, because of these very items, suspect.

Religious Tension in a Rational World

Tension is endemic between religious thought systems and the rational procedures of modern society, and this clearly constitutes an important element in the culture of unbelief. One need not suppose that modern man is, in his thought processes, implicitly more rational than primitive man (although this may well be the case), but one must recognize that the canons of rationality are firmly entrenched in his social circumstances, that his world is predominantly organized by rational precepts and elicits rational responses from him.[12] Rationality is encapsulated in the machinery and the technological control of modern everyday life, and in the empirical, pragmatic, and instrumental orientations upon which it depends. The "external constraint" of the modern world is no longer nature, or, as Durkheim hypothesized, the totality—unrecognized by individuals—of society, its customs, mores, and traditions. External constraint is increasingly the rational organization of production, consumption, distribution and decision-making in the world of man's own conscious making.

In principle this is an intellectually comprehensible world, but it is not a world with which man can readily establish emotional rapport. It is a world that may be comprehended, but which cannot be understood: a world where individuals feel that they have no influence. Whereas men were once at

12. This issue is discussed in Bryan R. Wilson, ed., *Rationality* (Oxford: Blackwell, 1970).

the command of arbitrary but affective others, in both their social experience and in their apprehension of the workings of the divine, now they are coerced by a much more objective, hence less resistible, power, which lacks all emotional appeal. Thus deities that are projected as embodiments of human emotions—love, fear, destruction, jealousy, goodwill—are less relevant symbols to express the forces of order and constraint in a world manifestly governed by nonaffective structures that seek to draw from men responses that are as rational in character as they are themselves.

The growth of rational procedures in society and the search to control social action and social process by the imposition of rational mechanisms are a major force in the displacement of older conceptions of deity. Religion, traditionally dealing in psychic reassurance, promises of salvation, therapy and thaumaturgy is, even where these functions are maintained, less credible because these things cannot be brought into conformity with rational models. Since the ultimate commodities in which religion deals are nonrational this in itself imposes restrictions on the extent to which religion can use a rational structure as an appropriate form of organization.

Religion depends on face-to-face relationships, continuity of commitment to known persons and localities, diffuse role performances, the celebration of love and of community, enduring total and personal relationships. These implicit assumptions of religious concern stand in sharp, perhaps irreconcilable, contrast with the basic principles of organization and behavior in the dominant institutions of contemporary society. Even in its most routinized operations, in fundraising, publicity, missionary organization, there is a limit to the extent to which religious groups can adopt rational organizational structures and procedures.

The New Religions

Rational organization is a prominent feature in societies that have a culture of unbelief. The dominance of rationality in modern societies is but another indicator of the commonplace fact that traditional belief systems have lost centrality in the modern world. Together with all other social institutions that seek to mobilize affective dispositions, and that depend on diffuse role commitments, religion is set aside from the public sphere of operations, where power, wealth, and status are distributed—from work, government, law. Because it has lost its capacity to express the needs and concerns of the total society, which can no longer be expressed as a value-consensus, religion occupies the leisure sphere where private individuals may exercise their religious dispositions, gratify their interests in the supernatural and work out dependency relations that are unsustained in the rest of their social experience.

To be "authentic" in the way in which that word has come to be used in contemporary western society, religion virtually has to be private: certainly it cannot command respect if it is trammelled by the status systems of the world because men know that they are relative, while religion claims a certain absolute validity. Traditional belief systems continue, however, to use the idioms of dominance and social centrality—past circumstances that they no longer enjoy. The assumptions of their personnel, the claims of their creeds, the concessions claimed for their plant, economic operations and their expectations of social status, are ill adapted to their actual position of increasing social marginality. Without the fact of widespread allegiance, and without the means to command it or regain it, the postures of dominance assumed by old established religions serve only to irritate men, and to enhance their incredibility and irrelevance in the modern world.

All this notwithstanding, the ultimate concerns of men cannot be fully expressed, much less gratified, within wholly rational frameworks of utterance and action. Men still demand, if at different points and in different connections from those of the past, the psychic reassurances, fantasy outlets, affection and supernatural benefit, and special dispensations. Since, because of its postures, petrified in the social past, traditional religion is ill fitted to meet these needs, new religions may be expected to emerge to accommodate them. Sectarianism has frequently been associated with secularization. New religious movements are expression of man's need for religious gratifications and religious accommodation that arise in circumstances where old religions have ossified, where they have been overtaken by new knowledge, or have come into conflict with new cultures, new classes, new populations for whom the old styles, the old idioms, the old rituals, lack meaning.

The genesis and diffusion of new beliefs clearly demand the attention of those concerned with cultures of unbelief. But one cannot leap from the success of new religious movements to immediate conclusions about the dispositions of men in modern society. Both the availability and the acceptability of new patterns of belief and action demand attention. The organizational form of new movements—the means by which they recruit, the extrareligious functions that they fulfill, the ancillary goals that they consciously adopt, and the attitudes and activities toward both the secular society and traditional belief systems—are all of no less importance in assessing their cultural significance.

The pluralism of modern society facilitates the development of a range of religious responses that may, on the one hand, be said to offer specific gratifications for the various conditions of men, or, on the other, to address themselves to particular psycho-pathologies that, in societies in which the value-systems are falling apart, now find a new absence of restraint and new possibilities of expression. Traditional religions, in claiming societal universality, imposed particular patterns of social restraint: new ones, in appealing to limited constituencies, frequently offer help in dismantling the inhibiting mechanisms of socialization into the old and traditional social life styles.

The growth of movements like P. L. Kyodan, Soka Gakkai, Ittöen in Japan; of Kardecism, Umbanda, and Pentecostalism in Brazil; of Jehovah's Witnesses and Seventh Day Adventism in Africa and many other parts of the world; of Mormonism and Scientology in the western world; of the underground church in Catholic countries; and of the "charismatic movement" throughout western Christendom—all suggest that there is much to be learned from new religious movements taken as unconscious commentaries on the condition of traditional belief. The dissolution of old, and the formulation of new, ideologies point perhaps not so much to a culture of belief emerging from an earlier and similar culture, so much as to the development of many subcultures of belief, to be found in the interstices between the rationally coordinated frameworks which hold together the modern world.

14

BETWEEN RELIGION AND SOCIAL SCIENCE

.

ROBERT N. BELLAH

1

In this essay, let me talk about the religious implications of social science, a phrase that contains a certain amount of deliberate ambiguity. It suggests that social science not only has implications for religion, but that it has religious implications or aspects within itself. I start with the assumption that the relation between religion and social science is complex and in some ways organic. This is in conscious contrast to one view of secularization, the view that there is only a mechanical relation between science and religion—namely the more of the one, the less of the other—and that with the rise of science in the modern world religion has been steadily declining.

This notion of secularization is far from a simple empirical generalization. It is part of a theory of modern society, a theory that can almost be called a myth because it functions to create an emotionally coherent picture of reality. It is in this sense religious, not scientific at all. This theory or myth is that of the enlightenment which views science as the bringer of light relative to which religion and other dark things will vanish away. The story I want to tell is that of another theory, that also has its mythic dimensions, and that also has emerged out of social science itself, but that has a different conception of the human spirit, one in which religion has an integral place in a new conception of the unity of human consciousness.

The enlightenment theory of secularization and of the relation of religion and science is itself only understandable as a reaction to a particular religious tradition, one with a strong cognitive bias and a stress on orthodox belief. Had the enlightenment occurred first in a culture dominated by Zen Buddhism, for example, the outcome would have been very

Editor's note: This essay first appeared as chapter 15 in Robert N. Bellah, *Beyond Belief* (New York: Harper & Row, 1970) and is here reproduced with the permission of the author and the publishers.

different, for Zen never set a date for the creation of the world, argued for the literal inspiration of any scripture, or based any claim on the alleged occurrence of miracles. But the Christian faith in the eighteenth and nineteenth centuries contained a weighty baggage of cognitive assertions about nature and history that could be either disproved or rendered improbable by a critical science. There were many, of course, who argued for the "reasonableness of Christianity," even as early as the eighteenth century. But they tended to place inordinate hope in the gaps in existing scientific knowledge which it was believed only religious truths could fill. When these gaps were closed by science itself it was a terrible blow. No blow was greater than Darwin's theory of natural selection which provided the first scientific theory of the origin of species. Before that no one knew how species originated, so a theory of special creation by God was at least a defensible position.

Perhaps even more serious for the cognitive claims of religion than the challenge of the natural sciences was the criticism of the budding social sciences, which tended to explain religious beliefs in terms of ignorance and error or as deliberate falsehoods designed to keep the lower classes resigned to their miserable social conditions. Examples would be the anthropological theory that belief in spirits arose from primitive man's attribution of external reality to the figures who appear in dreams or the Marxian notion of religion as the opium of the people. By the late nineteenth century it seemed obvious to many that religion was on its way out and was soon to be replaced entirely by science. Theologians had never been so defensive. But at just this moment certain dramatic gaps in the enlightenment view of man began to develop in the social sciences themselves, gaps which, potentially at least, put the whole question of religion in a new light.

Perhaps the most dramatic example was Freud's discovery of the unconscious. With his great book, *The Interpretation of Dreams,* Freud for the first time put the unconscious and its modes of operation under scientific scrutiny. In one sense, of course, this was the culmination of the enlightenment. The unconscious itself was finally subject to conscious investigation. But in another sense Freud was the grave digger of the enlightenment, the man who disclosed that beneath the frail conscious ego are the enormous nonrational forces of the un- conscious. By the very nature of the case the unconscious proved refractory to rational analysis. Freud tried a number of formulations during the course of his productive life and never claimed to have fully plumbed those depths. Those who prefer to think of the world in neat conceptual packages re- sisted the concept of the unconscious from the beginning, and there are some who still hold out against it. But the discovery of the unconscious remains the single most important contri- bution of psychoanalysis to modern thought.

At about the same time that Freud was working out his theories of personality, Emile Durkheim was trying to under- stand the fundamental nature of society. In his later years he came to view society as a set of collective representations, common symbols, existing in the minds of its members. When, in his last major book, *The Elementary Forms of the Reli- gious Life,* he tried to face the problem of where the collective representations come from and how they get into people's heads, he developed the idea of collective effervescence. Col- lective effervescence was Durkheim's term for the kind of group frenzy that seemed to occur in some of the rituals of the Australian aborigines, but he also found it in such mass outbursts as the French Revolution. It was in these conditions of intense group activity, Durkheim thought, that collective representations are impressed on the minds of group mem- bers, and, as in the case of the French Revolution, new collec- tive representations are born. While the notion of collective effervescence was by no means as influential as Freud's idea of the unconscious, it was quite important to Durkheim, pro- viding a critical element in his theory of society. Perhaps it has been a mistake to overlook it. It is a concept much like that of the unconscious—it could almost be called a social unconscious—and it, too, serves to point to depths within human action that are not fully understood but do not fit into the convenient patterns of enlightenment thought, focus- ing around the twin ideas of interest maximization and cog- nitive accuracy.

The third term is very familiar, though in an increasingly debased form. That is Max Weber's notion of charisma, de- veloped contemporaneously with Freud's and Durkheim's ideas. Charisma is a concept central not only to Weber's sociology of religion but to his sociology of authority, for charismatic authority, along with rational-legal and traditional, is one of the three types of authority that lie at the basis of any social order. Unlike the present vulgarized usage of the term, where it has come close to being a mere synonym for popularity, charisma for Weber denoted some quality of the extraordinary, as its ancient religious usage in the sense of a divine gift or grace would imply. Charisma was especially important for Weber in that it was one of the most important ways in which something new could enter the historical process. The charismatic leader or prophet, on the sheer basis of his own extraordinary gift or divine calling, could introduce fundamentally new normative demands that would otherwise have small chance of acceptance. Of course, Weber was not using the term in its literal religious meaning. He left undetermined the exact mechanism by which charisma operates either in the prophet or on his followers. In this respect, as well as in others, charisma is a concept similar to those of Freud and Durkheim.

To some extent what I have said parallels the famous argument of Talcott Parsons in *The Structure of Social Action* that the great generation of social scientists at the turn of the century, in coming to deal with the phenomenon of religion, had to take into account nonrational factors that did not fit previous patterns of social explanation. Freud, Durkheim, and Weber were all preoccupied with religion— an interesting fact in itself—and all three developed theories of religion. Especially important is the presence in their explanatory conceptual apparatus of central terms that do not so much explain anything as point to dark recesses where powerful, but poorly understood, forces and processes seem to be affecting human action.

What I am suggesting is that the fact that these three great nonbelievers, the most seminal minds in modern social science, each in his own way ran up against nonrational, noncognitive factors of central importance to the understanding of human action (but which did not yield readily to any available conceptual resources) is in itself of great significance for religion in the twentieth century. Convinced of the invalidity of traditional religion, each rediscovered the power of the religious consciousness. What could perhaps be suggested on the basis of the work of these men is that when Western religion chose to make its stand purely on the ground of cognitive adequacy, it was forgetting the nature of the reality with which religion has to deal and the kind of symbols religion uses. Western religion in this context refers mainly to its theological defenders, not to the evangelists and preachers who addressed themselves to the anxieties, hopes, fears and emotions of their hearers. Even among the theologians there were men like Friedrich Schleiermacher who pointed out that religion is not primarily cognitive.

It is unfortunate, but not uncommon, that the insights of the masters are not readily appropriated by the followers. In this case the great breakthrough documented by Talcott Parsons in *The Structure of Social Action* has by no means entirely stuck. Much of social science has relapsed into the positivist utilitarian idiom in which only "hard and realistic" assumptions about human nature are allowed. In this idiom, human action is likened to a game where every player is trying to maximize his self-interest or is concerned only with the quid pro quo in an exchange network, and where there is no place for the murky concepts to which Freud, Durkheim, and Weber were driven. Religion for those of this persuasion could hardly be less important, or if its survival is recognized, it is explained away as a response to some sort of deprivation. It must be admitted that such views are widespread in social science today. They are convenient, for they fit the governing myth in which the world is seen as a highly complex machine entirely subject to rational calculation. Such a myth, alas, exists not only among social scientists but among those close to the buttons that could touch off nuclear war—men who deal with nuclear strategy simply as an extension of game theory.

A different view, both of social science and religion, has certainly not died out in social science. Some of the systems theorists such as Parsons and Karl Deutsch have conceived of human action as multilayered and open. Deutsch, for example, has spoken of the propensity for all highly complex systems to break down, and has borrowed the theological term "grace" to designate the indispensable, but unpredictable, situational conditions which seem to be necessary in order for any complex system to function at all.[1] Parsons, in his discussion of symbol systems, has argued that the ultimate nature of reality is not subject to empirical specification though any cultural system must have some way of symbolizing it.[2] What he calls "constitutive symbols" are not cognitive in the sense of scientific statements, though they provide the terms in which reality is coherent.

Parsons also speaks of expressive and moral symbol systems as partly autonomous. The point is not that these various types of symbol systems are entirely independent from each other, for there must certainly be some integration between them in any functioning culture, but that no one of them has a privileged position. Constitutive, expressive, and moral symbol systems for Parsons can never simply be deduced from cognitive symbol systems. This means that science can never wholly take over the job of making sense of the world. And Parsons has long insisted that part of the reality that man needs to make sense of is nonempirical, simply unavailable to any of the resources of science. In this way Parsons has kept alive the openness to the mystery of being, which the earlier great generation of social scientists had somewhat grudgingly come to recognize.

No one in that earlier generation of social scientists had a greater sense of the openness and multiplicity of reality than William James. Building partly on James, the Austrian-American social philosopher Alfred Schutz developed the idea of multiple realities,[3] which has been recently expounded by Peter Berger and Thomas Luckmann.[4] Basic to Schutz's idea is that reality is never simply given; it is constructed. The apprehension of reality is always an active process involving subject and object. Multiple realities arise because of the variety of modes of consciousness and schemas of interpreta-

1. Karl W. Deutsch, *The Nerves of Government* (Glencoe, Ill.: The Free Press, 1963), pp. 217, 236–240.

2. Talcott Parsons, Introduction to Part IV, "Culture and the Social System," in Talcott Parsons et al., eds., *Theories of Society* (Glencoe, Ill.: The Free Press, 1961).

3. Alfred Schutz, *Collected Papers, Volume I* (The Hague: Nijhoff, 1962), pp. 209–259.

4. Peter L. Berger and Thomas Luckmann, *The Social Construction of Reality* (New York: Doubleday, 1966).

tion that link the two. Schutz pointed out that besides the world of everyday life, which is the social world par excellence, there is the world of dreams, the world of art, the world of science, the world of religion. By showing that these worlds are partially autonomous and irreducible one to the other Schutz gave another powerful argument for the openness and multiplicity of the human spirit.

A similar point has been made by those who have criticized the correspondence theory of language. For certain purposes it may be convenient to imagine language as a passive reflection of some alleged objective reality. Strict correspondence between words and things may be highly desirable. But such strict correspondence, relative at best, can be maintained only under the operation of certain rigorous standards that are highly unlike the normal use of language. As Wittgenstein said, "Uttering a word is like striking a note on the keyboard of the imagination." [5] Language exists not simply to mirror passively some given world of objects. Imaginative language creates new meanings, defines new worlds.

Herbert Fingarette, a philosopher influenced by Wittgenstein and Freud argues that in psychoanalysis the unconscious is not simply uncovered, revealed in its previously hidden reality. Rather a new imaginative interpretation of the patient's life is worked out that opens possibilities previously closed. That which was unconscious is transformed, not simply revealed through being symbolized.[6] As Norman O. Brown has pointed out the symbol does not stand for the hidden reality but is the living link which joins the hidden and the revealed.[7] In general this understanding of language, which appreciates its imaginative function as not decorative but fundamental, is closer to that of the poets than of the physicists, though it must be added parenthetically that the physicists have often been more aware than their social scientific imitators that their language, too, is in large part imaginative. When William Butler Yeats said,

5. Ludwig Wittgenstein, *Philosophical Investigation* (New York: Macmillan, 1968), p. 4.

6. Herbert Fingarette, *The Self in Transformation* (New York: Harper & Row, Harper Torchbooks, 1965), part 1.

7. Norman O. Brown, *Love's Body* (New York: Random House, Vintage Books, 1968), pp. 216–217, 257–258, and elsewhere.

And I declare my faith:
I mock Plotinus' thought
And cry in Plato's teeth,
Death and life were not
Till man made up the whole,
Made lock, stock and barrel

Out of his bitter soul,
Aye, sun and moon and star,
    all,
And further add to that
That, being dead, we rise,
Dream and so create
Translunar paradise.[8]

we can understand it not as a flight of fancy but as a profound insight into human reality.

Let us return to the central issue of the relation between social science and religion. It was entirely necessary during the course of modern Western history for science in general and social science in particular to differentiate themselves from theology. The cognitive or pseudocognitive bias of Western religion made this process extremely painful, for some centuries close to warfare between science and religion. Partly because of the struggle some scientists and social scientists took on the characteristics of their most retrogressive opponents, hence we can speak of the rise of a literalist, fundamentalist religion. It was protagonists of this sort who saw the struggle as a battle to the death which only one side could win. In a few scattered examples, I have tried to show how the development of social science itself, especially since the turn of the century, has come to a new appreciation of the importance of precisely those aspects of human existence with which science cannot adequately deal, and that have classically been within the realm of religion.

We thus have the resources for carrying through a nonantagonistic differentiation, leaving behind the long and bitter controversy between religion and science. It is true that in recent decades the struggle has not been intense, but this has been mainly because of a tacit agreement between science and religion to ignore each other. Differentiation without any new integration, however, can be as destructive as open warfare; it can lead to the fragmentation and anomie that our universities presently exemplify. It is not enough simply to speak of the autonomy of various spheres when the meaningfulness of our entire intellectual endeavor is in question. It

8. William Butler Yeats, *The Variorum Edition of the Poems* (New York: Macmillan, 1968) pp. 414–415.

is my feeling that the resources for a new kind of integration actually exist and that such a new integration would contribute much to the reunification and reinvigoration of our culture by returning to the idea of truth not only rigor but vitality and comprehensiveness. In this way the desiccation of our culture, which is what secularization has often meant, might begin to be reversed.

When I speak of integration I do not mean some kind of fantastic syncretism of science and religion. They have different purposes, different limitations, different modes of action. But they are both part, and I would argue a necessary part, of every culture and every person. They need to exist in some vital and healthy whole in which each is integral. This means not simply a tacit agreement to ignore each other but open interchange between them with all the possibilities of mutual growth and transformation that that entails.

It seems to me that if religion could overcome its misplaced defensiveness and pull down the barricades it has erected on the wrong streets, it could make a major contribution to our present cultural crisis. For religion is not really a kind of pseudogeology or pseudohistory but an imaginative statement about the truth of the totality of human experience. So called postreligious man, the cool, self-confident secular man that even some theologians have recently celebrated, is trapped in a literal and circumscribed reality which is classically described in religious terms as the world of death and sin, the fallen world, the world of illusion. Postreligious man is trapped in hell. The world of everyday reality is a socially and personally constructed world. If one confuses that world with reality itself one then becomes trapped in one's own delusions, one projects one's wishes and fears onto others and one acts out one's own madness all the while believing one is a clear-headed realist. Christianity, Buddhism, and other religions have long known about such delusions. They are a kind of demonic possession, for the man who believes he is most in control of his world is just the one most in the power of demons.

In order to break through the literal univocal interpretation of reality that our pseudoscientific secular culture espouses, it is necessary for religion to communicate nonordinary reality that breaks into ordinary reality and exposes its pretensions. When ordinary reality turns into a nightmare, as it increasingly has in modern society, only some transcendental perspective offers any hope. It is of course impossible to prove Christianity or any religion, but it is impossible to prove cognitively or scientifically any ultimate perspective on human life including Marxism, rationalism, or any kind of scientism. The adequacy of any ultimate perspective is its ability to transform human experience so that it yields life instead of death. Our present fragmented and disorganized culture does not rank high on that criterion.

It it not my main purpose to deliver a jeremiad for I think there is much to be hopeful about. It is my feeling that there are greater resources now for healing the split between the imaginative and the cognitive, the intellectual and the emotional, and the scientific and the religious aspects of our culture and our consciousness than there have been for centuries. Social science is beginning, faintly and crudely, to be able to cope with the richness of reality as religion has seen it. Religious thinkers like Paul Tillich and Martin Buber have seen the importance of these gropings and have helped to relate the theological enterprise to them.

From my own knowledge of the major American divinity schools I would say there has never been a more open interest in the social sciences, not merely as tools for pastoral counseling or the organization of inner city parishes, but for suggestions about the theological enterprise itself. This situation has become possible only because both sides have seen that we can translate, painfully and tentatively, between different realms of reality without reducing the language of one to the language of the other. In particular some social sicentists have come to feel that there are profound depths in the religious symbols that we have scarcely begun to fathom, and that we have much to learn from any exchange. While remaining committed to enlightenment rationalism as the foundation of scientific work and accepting its canons with respect to our research, we nevertheless know that this is only one road to reality. It stands in tension with and under the judgment of other modes of consciousness. And finally we know that the great symbols that justify science itself rest on unprovable assumptions sustained at the deepest levels of our consciousness.

My conclusion, then, runs about as contrary to so-called secularization theory as is humanly possible. It is my feeling that religion, instead of becoming increasingly peripheral and vestigial, is again moving into the center of our cultural preoccupations. This is happening both for purely intellectual reasons having to do with the reemergence of the religious issue in the sciences of man, and for practical historical reasons having to do with the increasing disillusionment with a world built on utilitarianism and science alone. Religion was the traditional mode by which men interpreted their world to themselves. Increasingly modern man has turned to social science for this interpretation. As social science has attempted more and more to grasp the totality of man it has recognized many of the preoccupations of traditional religion. As traditional religion has sought to relate to the contemporary world it has leaned more and more on social scientific contributions to the understanding of man.

It seems to me that in the fruitful interchange between social science and religion we may be seeing the beginnings of the reintegration of our culture, a new possibility of the unity of consciousness. If so, it will not be on the basis of any new orthodoxy, either religious or scientific. Such a new integration will be based on the rejection of all univocal understandings of reality, of all identifications of one conception of reality with reality itself. It will recognize the multiplicity of the human spirit, and the necessity to translate constantly between different scientific and imaginative vocabularies. It will recognize the human proclivity to fall comfortably into some single literal interpretation of the world and therefore the necessity to be continuously open to rebirth in a new heaven and a new earth. It will recognize that in both scientific and religious culture all we have finally are symbols, but that there is an enormous difference between the dead letter and the living word.

2

There is probably nothing more important than intellectual history to help us understand how our culture has become so fragmented and dissociated that we find it almost impossible to communicate the integrated meaning our young people so passionately require of us. Aware of my lack of competence in intellectual history, I must nonetheless venture into it in order to deal with one central aspect of this fragmentation, namely, the split between theological and scientific (and here I mean mainly social scientific) language about Christianity or, more generally, the split between religious man and scientific man in the West.

Without going back before the seventeenth century, one can perhaps say that from that time almost to the present the dominant theological defense of Christianity has been what may be called "historical realism." The roots of this historical realism can be traced back to biblical historicism, Greek rationalism, and the new awareness of scientific method emerging in the seventeenth century. The figural and symbolic interpretation of Scripture that was characteristic of medieval thought was almost eliminated by Reformation and counter-Reformation theology. Modern consciousness required clear and distinct ideas, definite unambiguous relationships, and a conception of the past "as it actually was." The proponents of "reasonable Christianity" worked out a theology that seemed to fit these requirements. It is true that some of the most significant theological minds—such as Blaise Pascal, Jonathan Edwards, Friedrich Schleiermacher, and Kierkegaard—don't quite fit this formulation. Nevertheless for broad strata of educated laymen, and above all for the secular intellectuals, it was this understanding of Christianity that was decisive. Lest anyone think this kind of Christian thought is dead, let him pause for a moment to consider the recent popularity of apologists who have argued that "Christ must have been who he said he was or he was the greatest fraud in history."

There have always been those willing to pick up the gauntlet with that kind of argument. Particularly in the eighteenth century many secular intellectuals argued that Christ, or if not Christ certainly the priests, were indeed frauds. Meeting Christianity on the ground of historical realism they rejected it. When faced with the inevitable question of how something clearly fraudulent and indeed absurd could have been so powerful in human history, they answered that religion was propagated for the sake of political despotism, maintained by an unholy alliance of priestcraft and political despotism. This argument was a species of "consequential reductionism," the explanation of religion in terms of its functional conse-quences, which in cruder or subtler form has been a standard piece of intellectual equipment in the modern secular intel-lectuals' understanding of religion ever since.

The nineteenth century began with a partial reaction against the abstract rationalism of the Enlightenment and saw a growing awareness of the complex role of religion in the development of human consciousness. Yet at the same time the certainty grew among the secular intellectuals that Christianity, still defended largely by the old arguments and the old formulas, and with it religion generally, could not be taken seriously in its own terms. There grew up alongside the continuing use of consequential reductionism several va-rieties of what I would call "symbolic reductionism." From this point of view religion is not entirely fraudulent. It con-tains a certain truth. But it is necessary for the modern intel-lectual to discover what that truth is that is hidden in the fantastic myths and rituals of religion. Much of nineteenth-century social science developed out of the search for the kernel of truth hidden in the falsity of religion.

One of the great intellectual strategies of the symbolic re-ductionists was to treat religion as a phase in the history of science. Primitive man, unable to understand the great nat-ural phenomena of night and day, summer and winter, storm and drought, developed the fantastic hypotheses of religion to account for them. This kind of evolutionary rationalism has been enormously pervasive and has influenced religious thought as well as secular. How convenient for the Sunday-school teacher to be able to explain the strange dietary rules of the ancient Hebrews in terms of hygiene—an intuitive awareness that shellfish and pork easily spoil under the warm climatic conditions of the Middle East! Another version of evolutionary rationalism that the nineteenth century devel-oped with vast persuasiveness was the conception of religion as a stage in the development of human morality. The hidden truth of religion was the gradually growing perception of man's ethical responsibilities. The monotheistic God of the Bible could then be considered as the expression of a high ideal of man's ethical action.

For those perplexed that religion should continue to sur

vive even in scientifically and ethically enlightened times, more immediate, more existential forms of symbolic reductionism were developed. Following Ludwig Feuerbach's treatment of religion as the projection of human nature, Marx developed his famous conception of religion as the opium of the people. This is usually treated as a form of consequential reductionism, which it perhaps is, but if we look at the *locus classicus* we can see that it is even more an existential version of symbolic reductionism. In his introduction to the "Critique of Hegel's Philosophy of Right," Marx wrote: *"Religious* suffering is at the same time an *expression* of real suffering and a *protest* against real suffering. Religion is the sigh of the oppressed creature, the heart of a heartless world, and the soul of soulless conditions. It is the *opium* of the people." [9]

From the early decades of the twentieth century symbolic reductionist theories of religion gained new subtlety and new complexity. Freud and Durkheim developed comprehensive formulas for the translation of religious symbols into their real meanings. Freud, first in *Totem and Taboo,* and then more starkly in *The Future of an Illusion,* disclosed that the real meaning of religion is to be found in the Oedipus complex that it symbolically expresses. The biblical God stands for the primordial father toward whom the sons feel both rebellious and guilty. Christ sums up a whole set of conflicting Oedipal wishes: the wish to kill the father, the wish to be killed for one's guilty wishes, and the wish to be raised to the right hand of the father. Finally, for Freud, the psychologically courageous man will discard the religious symbols that cloak his neurosis and face his inner problems directly.

For Durkheim the reality behind the symbol was not the Oedipus complex but society, and the morality that expresses it. In one of his most important essays, "Individualism and the Intellectuals," [10] he attempts to describe the religion and morality appropriate to his own society. He finds this in a religion of humanity and a morality of ethical individualism. How does he treat Christianity? "It is a singular error," he says, "to present individualist morality as the antagonist of

9. Karl Marx, *Early Writings* (New York: McGraw-Hill, 1964), pp. 43–44.

10. Emile Durkheim, "L'individual et les intellectuels," *Revue Bleue,* 4ᵉ sér. 10 (1898): 7–13.

Christian morality; on the contrary it is derived from it." In contrast to the religion of the ancient city-state, he says, Christianity moved to the center of the moral life from outside to within the individual, who becomes the sovereign judge of his conduct without having to render account to anyone but himself and God. But, he says, today this morality does not need to be disguised under symbols or dissimulated with the aid of metaphors. A developed individualism, the appropriate morality of modern society, does not need the symbolic clothing of Christianity." [11]

Unlike Marx, Freud, and Durkheim, Max Weber made no claim to have the key to the reality that lies behind the façade of religious symbolization. He treated religions as systems of meaning to be understood in their own terms from the point of view of those who believe in them, even though in the observer they strike no personal response. In this attitude he was at one with a whole tradition of German cultural historians and phenomenologists. For all the sensitivity with which he treats Calvinism, for example, it is the consequences for the actions of the believers that interest him, not the beliefs themselves. Without ever quite taking the position of consequential reductionism, Weber still manages to convey the feeling that the scientific observer cannot finally take seriously the beliefs he is studying even though he must take seriously the fact that beliefs have profound social consequences.

For the moment I am not trying to refute any of these theories of religion. They all have a great deal of truth in them as far as they go. But it is notable that the best minds in social science by the third decade of the twentieth century were deeply alienated from the Western religious tradition. None of them were believers in the ordinary sense of that word. All of them believed themselves to be in possession of a truth superior to that of religion. But since none of them, except very hesitantly and partially, wanted to fill the role that religion had previously played, they contributed to the deep split in our culture between religion and science, a break just at that highest level of meaning where integration is of the greatest importance.

Meanwhile, back at the seminary, things went on much as

11. Ibid., p. 11.

usual. The same old books were picked up, thumbed through, and put down again. The contemporary proponents of the historical realist position cut and trimmed what no longer seemed tenable and hoped for the best. A Karl Barth had the courage to give vivid expression to the grand themes of biblical and Reformation theology as though nothing had happened intellectually in the nineteenth and twentieth centuries, at least nothing that could not be refuted with the magnificent rhetoric of divine initiative and revelation. A few—one thinks of Martin Buber and Paul Tillich—saw the problem and tried to heal the split. In their more ecstatic moments it is even possible to say that they did heal the split. But neither was quite able to come up with a theoretical formulation that would spell out their ecstatic insights.

It is my contention that implicit in the work of the great symbolic reductionists was another possible position with entirely different implications for the place of religion in our culture, a position I will call "symbolic realism" and will spend the rest of this essay trying to describe. Not only the great social scientists but many philosophical, literary, linguistic, and religious thinkers have contributed to this position, which has been gestating for a long time and has become increasingly explicit in the last twenty years.

Both consequential reductionism and symbolic reductionism are expressions of an objective cognitive bias that has dominated Western thought ever since the discovery of scientific method in the seventeenth century. This position has held that the only valid knowledge is in the form of falsifiable scientific hypotheses. The task then with respect to religion has been to discover the falsifiable propositions hidden within it, to discard the unverifiable assertions and those clearly false, and, even with respect to the ones that seem valid, to abandon the symbolic and metaphorical disguise in which they are cloaked. Both Durkheim and Freud, who are worth considering for a moment in this connection, ardently held to this conception of knowledge. Yet the work of both contains deep inner contradictions precisely with respect to this point.

Durkheim came to see that the most fundamental cultural forms, the collective representations, are not the product of the isolated reflective intelligence but are born out of the intense atmosphere of collective effervescence. Collective representations are based first of all on the sentiment of respect that they exact from individuals, and it is only through their discipline that rational thought becomes possible. Rational inquiry, then, rests on a necessary substratum of sentiments and representations that have neither the form nor the function of scientific hypotheses. Nor did Durkheim believe that the element of the sacred, which is what he called the symbolic expression of the collective vitality at the basis of society and culture, could ever be outgrown. It would always be an essential feature of social life, and the great terms which moved him and which he felt were so essential to modern society—individuality, reason, truth, morality, and society itself—were, as he knew, symbols, collective representations. In fact, he came to see that society itself is a symbolic reality. In his own terms, finally, symbolic reductionism comes to be self-contradictory and self-destructive. It is the reality of symbols that his life work goes to prove.

Freud's greatest discovery was the existence and nature of the unconscious. In his first and in many ways most fundamental major work, *The Interpretation of Dreams,* he showed that dreams are the royal road to the unconscious. Only through dreamlike symbolism can the primary process of the unconscious express itself. Although the rational understanding that he called secondary process can gradually increase its effective control, Freud never thought it could replace the unconscious. Indeed, he emphasized the relative weakness and fragility of rational processes. And in his own work he again and again abandoned the form of scientific hypothesis for the language of myth, image, and symbol, much to the dismay of subsequent academic psychologists. He named his most important psychological complex after a Greek myth. In his late years he constructed his own myth, the myth of the struggle of Eros and the death-instinct, in order to express his deepest intuitions. The unmasker of all symbols finally if implicitly admitted the necessity and reality of symbols themselves.

In recent years the knowledge that noncognitive and nonscientific symbols are constitutive of human personality and society—are real in the fullest sense of the word—has deepened and consolidated. Rather than the norm of scientific objectivity invading all spheres of human experience, the role of noncognitive factors in science itself have become increasingly recognized. As the philosopher of science Michael Polanyi says, "into every act of knowing there enters a passionate contribution of the person knowing. . . . This coefficient is no mere imperfection but a vital component of his knowledge." [12] What this signals is a shift away from the mechanical model of early natural science, in which reality was seen as residing in the object, the function of the observer was simply to find out the laws in accordance with which the object behaves, and "subjective" was synonymous with "unreal," "untrue," and "fallacious." For this mechanical model there has increasingly been substituted the interactionist model of social science, or what Talcott Parsons calls "action theory." Here reality is seen to reside not just in the object but in the subject, and particularly in the relation between subject and object. The canons of empirical science apply primarily to symbols that attempt to express the nature of objects, but there are nonobjective symbols that express the feelings, values, and hopes of subjects, or that organize and regulate the flow of interaction between subjects and objects, or that attempt to sum up the whole subject-object complex or even point to the context or ground of that whole. These symbols, too, express reality and are not reducible to empirical propositions. This is the position of symbolic realism.

If we define religion as that symbol system that serves to evoke what Herbert Richardson calls the "felt-whole," [13] that is, the totality that includes subject and object and provides the context in which life and action finally have meaning, then I am prepared to claim that as Durkheim said of society, religion is a reality *sui generis*. To put it bluntly, religion is true. This is not to say that every religious symbol is equally valid any more than every scientific theory is equally valid. But it does mean that since religious symbolization and religious experience are inherent in the structure of human existence, all reductionism must be abandoned. Symbolic realism is the only adequate basis for the social scientific study of religion. When I say religion is a reality *sui generis*

12. Michael Polanyi, *Personal Knowledge* (New York: Harper & Row, Harper Torchbooks, 1964), p. xiv.
13. Herbert W. Richardson, *Toward an American Theology* (New York: Harper & Row, 1967), ch. 3, esp. p. 64.

I am certainly not supporting the claims of the historical realist theologians, who are still working with a cognitive conception of religious belief that makes it parallel to objectivist scientific description. But if the theologian comes to his subject with the assumptions of symbolic realism, as many seem to be doing, then we are in a situation where for the first time in centuries theologian and secular intellectual can speak the same language. Their tasks are different but their conceptual framework is shared. What this can mean for the reintegration of our fragmented culture is almost beyond calculation.

But if a new integration is incipient, fragmentation still describes the present reality. Concentrating so heavily on the mastery of objects, we have too long neglected what Anais Nin calls the "Cities of the Interior," [14] and everywhere these neglected cities are in revolt. We have concentrated too much on what Polanyi calls explicit knowledge and too little on what he calls implicit knowing, and we have forgotten that the implicit knowing is the more fundamental, for all explicit knowledge depends on its unconscious assumptions.[15] As Yeats says,

> Whatever flames upon the night
> Man's own resinous heart has fed.[16]

We see the flames but we have forgotten the heart and its reasons that reason knows not of. The price of this neglect of the interior life (and I use interior not only to refer to the individual; there is a collective interior that contains vast forces) is the reification of the superficial, an entrapment in the world of existing objects and structures.

But the life of the interior, though blocked, is never destroyed. When thwarted and repressed the interior life takes its revenge in the form of demonic possession. Just those who feel they are most completely rational and pragmatic, and most fully objective in their assessment of reality, are most in the power of deep unconscious fantasies. Whole nations in this century have blindly acted out dark myths of destruction all the while imagining their actions dictated by external

14. The title of her multivolume "continuous novel."
15. Polyanyi, *Personal Knowledge*, p. x.
16. Yeats; *The Variorum Edition*, p. 438.

necessity. In our own country both the National Security Council and the Students for a Democratic Society (SDS) claim to be acting in accordance with the iron laws of politics at the same time that they seem trapped dreamlike in their own unconscious scenarios. All of this is the price we have paid for relegating art to the periphery of life, denying the central integrating role of myth and ritual, and letting our morality be dictated by our politics. For these reasons the issues of concern here are not academic, are not, to use a word that I have come to loathe in recent months, irrelevant. The future of our society, perhaps of life on this planet, depends on how we face them.

Perhaps the first fruit of symbolic realism, of taking seriously noncognitive symbols and the realms of experience they express, is to introduce a note of skepticism about all talk of reality. "Reality is never as real as we think." [17] Since for human beings reality is never simply "out there," but always also involves an "in here" and some way in which the two are related, it is almost certain that anything "out there" will have many meanings. Even a natural scientist selects those aspects of the external world for study that have an inner meaning to him, that reflect some often hidden inner conflict. But this is true of all of us. We must develop multiple schemas of interpretation with respect not only to others but ourselves. We must learn to keep the channels of communication open between the various levels of consciousness. We must realize with Alfred Schutz that there are multiple realities,[18] and that human growth requires the ability to move easily between them and will be blocked by setting up one as a despot to tyrannize over the others. Perhaps this is partly what is meant by what today is called "multimedia communication," but it is even more important to remember that any one medium or any one symbol has many meanings and many contexts of interpretation.

Let me conclude by applying these general remarks to the field of religion and to the problems that face those of us who think about religion today. If art and literature primarily express the realm of inner meaning and are free to ex-

17. Daniel Stern, in Anais Nin, *The Novel of the Future* (New York: Macmillan Co., 1968), p. 200.
18. Schutz, *Collected Papers*.

plore even the most aberrant and idiosyncratic wishes, hopes, and anxieties, religion is always concerned with the link between subject and object, with the whole that contains them and forms their ground. Though religion is not primarily subjective, it is not objective either. It symbolizes unities in which we participate, which we know, in Polanyi's words, not by observing but by dwelling in them.[19] While neither the churches nor our secular culture seem to be doing a terribly good job of providing the symbols that evoke the wholeness of life and give meaning to our participation in it, we must nonetheless look to whatever in our own culture or in any culture has played this role.

If we think especially of contemporary Christianity there are a number of theologians whose work seems relevant; such names as Wilfred Smith, Richard Niebuhr, Gordon Kaufmann, and Herbert Richardson come to mind. But for me Paul Tillich is still the great theologian of the century, perhaps because it was through his work that Christian symbols first began to live again for me after my adolescent loss of faith. Certainly no one had a clearer sense of the fatal consequences of objectivism in religion. When Tillich objected to such phrases as "God exists" or "God is a Being" or "the Supreme Being," it was because he felt they made God into an object, something finite, a being alongside other beings. His own conception of God was far more transcendent than the neofundamentalists ever realized. And yet even Tillich succumbed perhaps too much to the mania for interpretation, for discovering the rational core beneath the symbol, and the metaphysical structure in which he restated the fundamental Christian truths is after all not very persuasive. As one more schema of interpretation alongside others it certainly has its uses, but when he says that the statement "God is being-itself" is not symbolic he seems to be engaging in a kind of metaphysical reductionism.[20] Perhaps his greatest contribution and the line of work that is still worth pursuing today was his restless quest for the "dimension of depth" in all human social and cultural forms. This was his great contribution to breaking out of the institutional ghetto and see-

19. Polanyi, *Personal Knowledge*.
20. Paul Tillich, *Systematic Theology*, vol. 1 (Chicago: University of Chicago Press, 1951), p. 238.

ing once more, as Augustine did, the figure of Christ in the whole world.

Two secular intellectuals have made major contributions in recent years to the position I am trying to set forth: Herbert Fingarette in *The Self in Transformation* [21] and Norman O. Brown in *Love's Body*.[22] Both of them oppose any kind of symbolic reductionism; both of them know that reality is inner as well as outer and that the symbol is not decoration but our only way of apprehending the real. They both have much to teach us about the multiplicity of vision—poetic, Buddhist, primitive as well as Christian—which has become a possibility and, indeed, a necessity in the modern world. The work of these men is the most vivid illustration I know of the rapprochement between the language of religion and the language of the scientific analysis of religion.

As a sociologist I am by no means prepared to abandon the work of the great consequential and symbolic reductionists. They have pointed out valid implications of religious life that were not previously understood. But I am prepared to reject their assumption that they spoke from a higher level of truth than the religious systems they studied. I would point out instead their own implicit religious positions. Most of all I am not prepared to accept the implication that the religious issue is dead and that religious symbols have nothing directly to say to us.

Superficially the phenomenological school seems preferable on this score since it insists on describing religious systems as closely as possible in the term of those who hold them. But here there is the temptation to treat religious systems as embalmed specimens that could not possibly speak directly to those outside the charmed circle of believers.

I believe that those of us who study religion must have a kind of double vision; at the same time that we try to study religious systems as objects we need also to apprehend them as ourselves religious subjects. Neither evolutionist nor historical relativists nor theological triumphalist positions should allow us to deny that religion is one. I don't mean to say that all religions are saying the same thing in doctrinal or ethical terms; obviously they are not. But religion is one for

21. Fingarette, *The Self in Transformation*.
22. Brown, *Love's Body*.

the same reason that science is one—though in different ways
—because man is one. No expression of man's attempt to
grasp the meaning and unity of his existence, not even a
myth of a primitive Australian, is without meaning and value
to me. Perhaps this assertion will seem less radical to many
young people today, for example to the young anthropologist
Carlos Casteñeda who apprenticed himself to a Yaqui shaman,
than it does to those trained in my generation.

I am not advocating the abandonment of the canons of scientific objectivity or value neutrality, those austere disciplines
that will always have their place in scientific work. But those
canons were never meant to be ends in themselves, certainly
not by Weber, who was passionately committed to ethical and
political concerns. They are methodological strictures. They
neither relieve us of the obligation to study our subject as
whole persons, which means in part as religious persons, nor
do they relieve us of the burden of communicating to our
students the meaning and value of religion along with its
analysis. If this seems to confuse the role of theologian and
scientist, of teaching religion and teaching about religion,
then so be it.[23] The radical split between knowledge and commitment that exists in our culture and in our universities is
not ultimately tenable. Differentiation has gone about as far
as it can go. It is time for a new integration.

23. Randall Huntsberry, of the Department of Religion, Wesleyan
University, has recently discussed the untenability of the distinction
between teaching religion and teaching about religion in an unpublished paper, "Secular Education and Its Religion."

APPENDICES

PROGRAM OF THE SYMPOSIUM ON
THE CULTURE OF UNBELIEF

1969

Saturday, March 22
Opening session at the Gregorian University. Chairman: Peter L. Berger. Round table discussion. Position paper by Antonio Grumelli on: "Secularization: Between Belief and Unbelief." Discussants: Harvey Cox, Jean Danielou, Milan Machovec.

Monday, March 24
9:30 A.M. Plenary session. Position paper by Thomas Luckmann on: "Belief, Unbelief, and Religion." Response by Oleg Mandic. Discussion. 2:30 P.M. Group discussion. 4:30 P.M. Plenary session.

Tuesday, March 25
9:30 A.M. Plenary session. Position paper by Robert Bellah on: "The Historical Background of Unbelief." Response by Martin Marty. Discussion. 2:30 P.M. Group discussion. 4:30 P.M. Plenary session.

Wednesday, March 26
9:30 A.M. Plenary session. Position paper by Charles Glock on: "The Study of Unbelief: Perspectives on Research." Response by Bryan Wilson. Discussion. 2:30 P.M. Group discussion. 4:30 P.M. Plenary session.

Thursday, March 27
9:30 A.M. Conclusive Plenary session. Question-and-answer period for observers and participants. 12:00 noon. Private audience with Pope Paul VI at the Vatican. Closing of the symposium.

APPENDIX 2

BIOGRAPHICAL DESCRIPTIONS OF PARTICIPANTS IN THE SYMPOSIUM

SABINO S. ACQUAVIVA Professor of Sociology at the University of Padova. Lecturer in Political Sociology at the Institut Européen des Hautes Études Internationales, University of Nice. Editor of *Sociologia Religiosa*. Associate editor of *Cultura e Politica*. Major publications: *Automazione e nuova classe; L'ecclissi del sacro nella società industriale; La scelta illusoria*.

ROBERT N. BELLAH Ford Professor of Sociology and Comparative Studies at the University of California, Berkeley. Taught at McGill University and at Harvard University. Fulbright scholar in Japan and resident scholar at the Center for Advanced Studies in the Behavioral Sciences at Stanford. Chairman of the Center for Japanese and Korean Studies at the University of California, Berkeley. Major publications: *Religion and Progress in Modern Asia; Tokugawa Religion; Civil Religion in America; Beyond Belief*. Collaborator: International Encyclopedia of the Social Sciences.

PETER L. BERGER Professor of Sociology at Rutgers, The State University of New Jersey. Taught at the New School for Social Research; the City University of New York; Hartford Seminary; and at the University of North Carolina. Editor of *Social Research*. Major publications: *Invitation to Sociology; The Social Construction of Reality; A Treatise in the Sociology of Knowledge; The Sacred Canopy; Elements of a Sociological Theory of Religion; A Rumor of Angels*.

ROCCO CAPORALE Director of Research and Associate Professor, Pitzer College, Claremont, California. Taught at Manhattanville College, New York; the University of California, Berkeley; Loyola University, Chicago; Columbia University, New York; and St. John's University, New York. Major publications: *Vatican II: Last of the Councils; The Roman Catholic Laity in France, Chile and the USA*.

HERVÉ CARRIER, S.J. Rector of the Gregorian University, Rome; Lecturer at the Institute of Social Sciences of the same University. Taught at several Canadian, Italian, French, and Brazilian universities. Major publications: *Sociology of Religious Belonging; La vocazione: dinamismi psico-sociologici; Saggi di sociologia religiosa*.

HARVEY G. COX Professor of Theology at Harvard University, and William Belden Noble Lecturer. Taught at Oberlin College, at the American Baptist Home Mission Society, and at Andover Newton Theological School. Major publications: *The Secular City; The Situation Ethics Debate; The Church Amid Revolution; The Feast of Fools*.

JEAN DANIELOU A cardinal of the Roman Curia. Former editor of *Études*. Former Professor and Dean of the Faculty of Theology in Paris. Major publications: *Platonisme et Theologie mystique; Essai sur le mystère de l'Histoire; Dieu et nous; Scandaleuse verité; L'Oraison, probleme politique*.

HENRY DE LUBAC, S.J. Honorary professor at the University of Lyon. "Peritus" of the Vatican Council's Theological Commission. Member of the Institut de France. Consultant to the Vatican Secretariat for Non-Believers and for Non-Christians. Major publications: *Catholicisme; Aspects du Bouddhisme; Paradoxes et nouveaux paradoxes; La prière du P. Teilhard de Chardin; Atheisme et sens de l'homme*.

CHARLES Y. GLOCK Professor of Sociology, Chairman of the Department of Sociology, and former Director of the Survey Research Center at the University of California, Berkeley. Former Director of the Bureau of Applied Social Research, New York. Taught at Columbia University, New York; Luther Weigle Lecturer at Yale University. President of the Society for the Scientific Study of Religion. Major publications: *Christian Beliefs and Antisemitism; Religion and Society in Tension; Survey Research in the Social Sciences; To Comfort and to Challenge*.

ANTONIO GRUMELLI Professor of Sociology at the Universitá dell'Abbruzzo. Undersecretary to the Vatican Secretariat for Non-Believers. Major publications: *Sociologia del cattolicesmo; Il mondo in trasformazione; Amicizia e socialita; L'uomo oggi*.

FRANÇOIS HOUTART Professor of Sociology at the University of Louvain, Belgium, and Director of the Centre de Recherches Socio-Religieuses (FERES), Belgium. Major publications: *The Challenge to Change; The Church Confronts the Future; El Cambio Social en America Latina*.

FRANÇOIS ISAMBERT Professor of Sociology and Chairman of the Department of Sociology at the University of Lille. Cofounder of *Archives de Sociologie des Religions* and of *La Revue Françoise de Sociologie*. Major publications: *Christianisme et classe ouvrière; De la charbonnerie au Saint-Simonisme; Buchez ou l'age théologique de la Sociologie*.

GUY BENTON JOHNSON, JR. Professor of Sociology at the University of Oregon. Taught at the University of Georgia, North Carolina, Texas, and Wisconsin. Secretary to the Society for the Scientific Study of Religion. Major publications: *Religion and Occupational Behavior; The Negro and His Songs; Religion, Culture, and Society* (collaborator); *The Sociological Perspectives* (collaborator).

SAMUEL Z. KLAUSNER Professor of Psychology, University of Pennsylvania. Taught at the City College of New York; the Hebrew University, Jerusalem; Columbia University, N.Y.; the Union Theological, N.Y. Director of the Center for Research on the Acts of Man, and Editor, *Journal for the Scientific Study of Religion.* Major publications: *Psychiatry and Religion; The Study of Total Societies; The Quest for Self-Control; On Man in His Environment: Social Scientific Foundations for Research and Policy.*

SIEGFRIED VON KORTZFLEISCH Director of the Evangelischen Zentralstelle für Weltanschauungsfragen, Stuttgart. Former Director of Evangelischen Akademie Bad Boll. Major publications: *Mitten in Herzen der Massen Evangelischen Orden; Die Antiklerikalen und die Christen; Religion im Säkularismus; Kirche und Synagoge.*

THOMAS LUCKMANN Professor of Sociology at the University of Frankfurt. Taught at Hobart College, New York, and at the New School of Social Research, New York. Major publications: *The Social Construction of Reality; The Invisible Religion; The Problem of Religion in Modern Society.*

MILAN MACHOVEC Professor of Philosophy at the University of Prague. Lecturer at the Philosophical Institute of the University of Vienna. Major publication: *A Study on the Doctrine of John Huss.* Has contributed various articles to *Tijdschrift voor Filosofie.*

OLEG MANDIC Professor of Sociology and Law at the University of Zagreb. Former member of the People's Assembly of Istria. Former Chief of Protocol of the Yugoslavian Chief of State. Major publications: *Dal culto dei teschi alla Christianitá; Le caste nella storia delle societá; Dizionario del Giudaismo e della Cristianitá; Sociologia generale.*

RENÉ MARLÉ, S.J. Professor of Theology at the Catholic Institute of Paris. Taught Theology at the Catholic University of Angers. Editor of *Études* and of *Recherches de Science Religieuse.* Editor of the series *Christianisme foi chretienne; Bultmann et l'interpretation du Nouveau Testament; Le probleme theologique de l'hermeneutique; Dietrich Bonhoffer, temoin de Jesus-Christ parmi ses freres.*

DAVID MARTIN Professor of Sociology at the University of London. Associate Director of Socio-Religious Research Services. Editor of *A Sociological Yearbook of Religion in Britain* and *Anarchy and Culture: the Crisis in the Contemporary University.* Major publications: *Pacifism; A Sociology of English Religion; The Religious and the Secular.*

MARTIN E. MARTY Professor of Modern Church History at the University of Chicago. Associate editor of *Christian Century* and of *Church History;* Editor of *Harper Forum Books.* Major publications: *The New Shape of American Religion; Second Chance for American Protestants; Church Unity and Church Mission; Varieties of Unbelief.*

THOMAS F. O'DEA Professor of Sociology and Religious Studies and former Director of the Institute of Religious Studies, at the University of California, Santa Barbara. Taught at Stanford, M.I.T., Fordham University, the University of Utah, and Columbia University. Major publications: *The Mormons; American Catholic Dilemma; Sociology of Religion; The Catholic Crisis; Sociology and the Study of Religion;* collaborator to the International Encyclopedia of the Social Sciences.

TALCOTT PARSONS Professor of Sociology at Harvard since 1927. Fellow of the Ford Center for Advanced Study in the Behavioral Sciences. Former Chairman of the Department of Social Relations, and Member of the School for Overseas Administration at Harvard. Major publications: *Structure of Social Action; Toward a General Theory of Action; The Social System; Essays in Sociological Theory; Structure and Process in Modern Societies; Social Structure and Personality; American Sociology.*

EMIL PIN, S.J. Professor of Sociology at the Institut Catholique of Paris and the Gregorian University of Rome. Director of CIRIS (International Center of Social Research) in Rome. Taught Social Science in Chantilly; was visiting professor at the Catholic University of Ottawa and at the University of Detroit. Major publications: *La pratica religiosa e le classi sociali; Elementi per una sociologia del Cattolicesimo Latino-Americano; Saggi di sociologia religiosa; Sociologia del cristianesimo.*

THEODORE M. STEEMAN, O.F.M. Lecturer in Theology, Boston College, Massachusetts. Former member of the Institute for Socio-Ecclesiastical Research, The Hague. Member of the Editorial Committee of *Concilium.* Major publications: *The Sacred and the Secular; The Study of Atheism.* Contributed various articles to *Social Compass, Sociological Analysis, Journal for the Scientific Study of Religion, Concilium, The Religious Situation 1969.*

IVAN VARGA Professor of Sociology at the University College of Dar es-Salaam, Tanzania.

ANTOINE VERGOTE Professor of Psychology and Director of the Center for the Study of Psychology of Religion at the Catholic University of Louvain, Belgium. Major publications: *Psychanalyse et Phenomenologie* in *Problems de Psychanalise; The Symbol in Philosophy Today; Demythisation et morale; Psychologie religieuse.*

BRYAN WILSON Reader in Sociology at the University of Oxford. Taught at the University of Leeds; was fellow at All Souls College, Oxford, and visiting scholar at the University of California, Berkeley. Major publications: *Sects and Society; Religion in Secular Society; Patterns of Sectarianism.*

ADDRESS BY PAUL VI TO THE
PARTICIPANTS IN THE SYMPOSIUM

It is with respectful regard that We greet Our visitors, participants in the symposium on "The Culture of Unbelief." We thank them for this visit, which takes on for Us the character of a highly significant encounter. This is not the usual meeting of friendly persons; it is rather the encounter of diverse cultures and differing thoughts. We say this with humility; We know that here before us are men of high intellect and deep study; but We say this also with joy and with hope; for it is always Our desire to listen to those voices which express the thinking of our times, as it is ever Our desire that Our own voice should be heard—a voice which, only because of the debility and lack of skill of Our lips, may seem to be uncertain and out of tune; yet, We must add, holds within itself the sureness of the truth, and the yearning to communicate its message of hope and of life.

This moment, therefore, seems to Us to be as it were dramatic and symbolic.

The Secretariat which is called that for Non-Believers was instituted, first of all, for the purpose of promoting the study of those attitudes of negation which modern man assumes—whether in cultural expressions, in sociological and political terms, or in practical and unthinking ways—with regard to that religion which believes in a transcendental, personal God, the beginning and end of the entire universe, including man, and with regard to that religion which finds in Christ the solution of the great problem of the true and living God, the loving God of our salvation.

Thus it comes about that we must recognize many aspects and many motives of nonbelief; that we must receive the many objections which nonbelief proposes to us; that we must respect the scientific contribution which it makes to the study of the religious problem, with arguments drawn from unquestionable sciences such as psychology and sociology; that we must admit the difficulties raised today by the pedagogico-social context, particularly in young minds engaged in scientific studies, and in the employment of sensitive knowledge, when dealing with the traditional religious mentality. We wish also to acknowledge that frequently a religious form which defines itself as secularization, and is so widely spread today, is not in itself antireligious; rather, it tends to claim for the autonomous forces of human reason the knowledge and exploitation of the world as proposed to man's direct experience. In a word, then, we are fair, and in part assenting in regard to "nonbelievers."

At a certain time, however, we must say that we, too, are "nonbelievers." For example, we do not believe that the development of modern thought, provided it is consistent with its intrinsic exigencies, leads of necessity to the denial of God. Moreover, although we admit that the knowledge of God requires an assistance which only God can give (cf. Ps. XXXV.10; Denz.-Sch., n. 2732), we do not believe that the certitude of God's existence is inaccessible to the human mind (cf. Rom. I. 20; Denz.-Sch., n. 3004); that is to say, we do not believe that science and belief in God are antithetical terms, mutually exclusive of each other; we do not believe that the theoretical and practical forms of the modern denial of God are beneficial to the progress of culture and of human happiness; we do not believe that the economic, social and civil liberation of man requires the necessity of banishing religion as being a deviation from the struggle to establish truly human dimensions and to build up the earthly city (cf. Gaudium et spes, n. 21); and finally we do not believe that the ineffable, mysterious, transcendental and unknown God is inaccessible and distant (cf. Acts. XVII, 22–28; De Dubac: Sur les chemins de Dieu, p. 112). In this, we too are "protesters"!

We are protesters because we wish to raise up again the idea of God, from the degradation into which it has fallen with many men of our time, and from the fantastic, superstitious or idolatrous counterfeit which we often encounter, even in modern life, as well as from the despair, the anguish, the void, which its absence produces in the heart of man.

Therefore We greet with pleasure the initiative taken by the Secretariat for Non-Believers, and by its Eminent President, Cardinal König, with the valid and disinterested contribution of the Giovanni Agnelli Foundation of Turin, and the scientific collaboration of the Department of Sociology of the University of California, by convoking in Rome during these days a group of illustrious scholars from various parts of the world, who have, under the chairmanship of Professor Peter Berger and in the company of several theologians, analyzed the theme: "The Culture of Unbelief."

Together with Our congratulations for the good work done, We express the hope that these studies will continue, and develop, by means of collaboration with personalities and institutions of the scientific world. The Church will, to the extent of her possibilities, favor this type of undertaking which, besides the contribution which it can offer to her own specific mission, will also, We fervently hope, share in securing peaceful and orderly living together of all peoples.